and hope to achieve enlightenment?

Bracketology—the practice of parsing people, places, and things into discrete one-on-one matchups to determine which of the two is superior or preferable—works because it is simple. What could be simpler then breaking down a choice into either/or, black or white, this one or that one?

For example, not long ago I was discussing favorite foods with a friend of mine. She happens to be a successful dancer and choreographer, a woman of extraordinary physical discipline, intellectual rigor, and moral certitude. Being an athlete in perpetual training, she has always been careful about what she eats. So I asked her to name her last bite on earth—the one item of food she craves regardless of its impact on her waistline or cardiovascular health. It's one of those desert island questions that I find intriguing and revealing. Her answer:

a hard-boiled egg.

I was surprised—and I wasn't. It wouldn't be my first choice. But given her life of monklike asceticism, it was *the* perfect food. Simple, elegant, practically colorless, and loaded with protein. No excess. No spare parts (not even the yolk).

A few months later, when the subject came up again, she surprised me by changing her mind. Her last bite on earth, she insisted, would be a bowl of popcorn. This change of heart was very uncharacteristic. I've always known her to be a woman who knows her mind. And yet here she was, on a matter involving the most basic issue of taste, flip-flopping.

It wouldn't have happened if she knew Bracketology.

Ask me the same question and I wouldn't hesitate to choose a Hebrew National salami. I know this because I've pitted this marvel of encased beef, salt, hydrolyzed soy protein, garlic, paprika, and other mysterious flavorings against every other food I love. And it always comes out on top. I've done it using Bracketology, in a competition that looks like this:

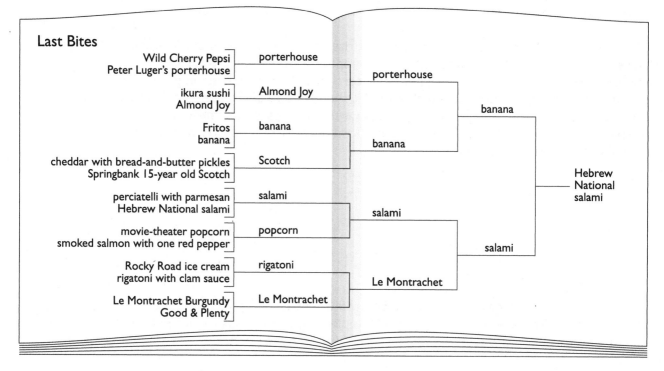

Last Bites

Wild Cherry Pepsi
Peter Luger's porterhouse — porterhouse
ikura sushi
Almond Joy — Almond Joy
— porterhouse
Fritos
banana — banana
cheddar with bread-and-butter pickles
Springbank 15-year old Scotch — Scotch
— banana
perciatelli with parmesan
Hebrew National salami — salami
movie-theater popcorn
smoked salmon with one red pepper — popcorn
— salami
Rocky Road ice cream
rigatoni with clam sauce — rigatoni
Le Montrachet Burgundy
Good & Plenty — Le Montrachet
— Le Montrachet
— banana
— salami
— Hebrew National salami

You could argue that these foods, from the candy to the junk food to the fine wine to the robust meals, represent not only one individual's palate but also a lifetime of associated memories, like Proust's madeleine. What you were celebrating with that great Burgundy. Or what sorrow you were drowning with the Springbank whisky. What great movie you were watching when you roared through the value-sized bag of popcorn. Or what stress you were relieving with that quart of Rocky Road. Who you were with when you first visited Peter Luger's Steak House. Or what deliriously happy segment of childhood you mentally call up every time you open a box of Good & Plenty.

In that sense, choosing your last bite is not necessarily just about food. It's quite possibly about your entire life. In opting for one last bite over another you may also be revealing to yourself—perhaps for the first time—the who, what, when, and where in your personal narrative that lifts your spirit and puts a smile on your face. Can you think of a better path to enlightenment?

When I consider all that is good and life-affirming and happy in this world—not to mention indelibly tasteful—I choose a Hebrew National salami. Go figure.

In this book, we have.

So can you.

March Madness Moments

by GARY PARRISH

Contrary to popular belief, not to mention that melodramatic, end-of-the-final song, there is no single shining moment in the NCAA men's basketball tournament. There are actually lots of shining moments—three weeks of them every March, some of them very good (Bryce Drew's shot against Ole Miss) and some of them very bad (Mr. Webber, you are flat out of time-outs). Shining moments linger in memory or have a lasting impact, and don't need a song, or Dick Vitale, to validate them.

Editors' note: Our obligatory homage. Without these moments, there are no brackets in your sports section, no NCAA pool at your office, and no book in your hand.

GARY PARRISH is the national college basketball columnist at CBS SportsLine.com. His most memorable—and devastating—March Madness Moment is losing $900 at a blackjack table in New Orleans about 15 hours before Carmelo Anthony led Syracuse to a win over Kansas in the title game right down the street. That night, Roy Williams cursed at Bonnie Bernstein. Gary's wife cursed, too.

Matchups	Winner
Al McGuire crying in victory in 1977 / Al McGuire dancing with Syracuse players in 1996	McGuire crying
Chris Webber's terrible time-out in 1993 / Fred Brown's terrible pass in 1982	Webber's TO
Lorenzo Charles's tip-in to give NC State the 1983 title / Jim Valvano's frantic jog after Lorenzo Charles's tip-in	Valvano's jog
War in Iraq starts on day 1 of the 2003 tournament / Indiana wins 1981 title on day President Reagan is shot	War in Iraq
Sean May wins 2005 title on his birthday / Elvin Hayes omitted from 1968 all-tournament team	Sean May
Mississippi State, all white, loses to Loyola in 1963 / Texas Western, all black, beats Kentucky in 1966	Texas Western
Eduardo Najera–Mateen Cleaves collision in 1999 / IU wins 1976 title despite Bob Wilkerson's concussion	Najera–Cleaves
Danny Ainge's coast-to-coast winner in 1981 / Tyus Edney's coast-to-coast winner in 1995	Edney's winner
Villanova shoots 78.6 percent against G'town in 1985 / George Mason beats UConn, goes to 2006 Final Four	Villanova
Bill Walton makes 21 of 22, beats Memphis in 1973 / Keith Smart's shot to beat Syracuse for 1987 title	Walton's 21-of-22
Michael Jordan's shot to beat G'town for 1982 title / Scotty Thurman's shot to beat Duke for 1994 title	Jordan's shot
Michigan's Rumeal Robinson makes two FT's in 1989 / Louisville's Terry Howard misses FT in 1975	Robinson's FT's
No. 1 DePaul loses opener in 1980 to UCLA / No. 1 DePaul loses opener in 1981 to Saint Joseph's	DePaul loses to SJU
Magic beats Bird to win 1979 title / Carmelo beats nation, as a freshman, to win 2003 title	Magic beats Bird
Arkansas's U.S. Reed's buzzer beater shot from halfcourt against Louisville in 1981 / Valparaiso's Bryce Drew's shot to beat Ole Miss in 1998	Reed
Danny Manning leads KU to 1988 title in Kansas City / Christian Laettner's shot to beat Kentucky in 1992	Laettner

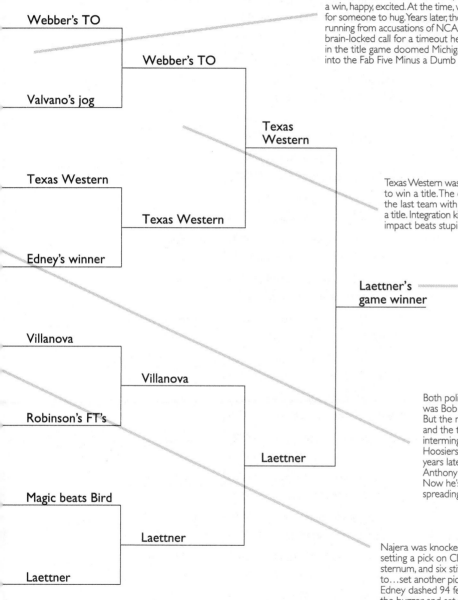

Webber's TO

Valvano's jog

Webber's TO

Texas Western

Edney's winner

Texas Western

Texas Western

Villanova

Robinson's FT's

Villanova

Magic beats Bird

Laettner

Laettner

Laettner

Laettner's game winner

It seemed like a sweet moment, a coach jogging erratically after a win, happy, excited. At the time, we thought Valvano was looking for someone to hug. Years later, though, we learned he was simply running from accusations of NCAA rules violations. But Webber's brain-locked call for a timeout he didn't have with 11 ticks left in the title game doomed Michigan and turned the Wolverines into the Fab Five Minus a Dumb One.

Texas Western was the first team with five black starters to win a title. The other side of that is Kentucky was the last team with five white starters to compete for a title. Integration killed all-white basketball. And historical impact beats stupidity any day.

Texas Western's triumph was wonderful for race relations in this country. It demonstrated tolerance, and broke down multiple barriers for coaches, players and fans. That's strong and indisputable. But Laettner's shot on Grant Hill's improbable pass was a singular moment in sports history that also taught us a valuable lesson: always guard the inbounds passer.

Both political events were significant, but heck, so was Bob Knight winning his second NCAA title. But the nearly simultaneous tip-offs of the war and the tournament take precedence over the intermingling of Reagan's shooting and the Hoosiers' victory because the war continues four years later and Reagan recovered. Carmelo Anthony was a freshman when the war started. Now he's a four-year pro. Time flies when you're spreading democracy.

Najera was knocked out cold following the hit he took while setting a pick on Cleaves. He had a concussion, a bruised sternum, and six stitches in his lip, but re-entered the game to...set another pick! Some say that's tough. I say that's stupid. Edney dashed 94 feet in 4.8 seconds to bank in a lay-up at the buzzer and set the stage for UCLA to win yet another title, sans concussion.

Where Were You When Moments

(Boomer Edition)

by MARK REITER

"Where Were You When" moments tend to involve death—via natural disasters, hostile acts, the unexpected passing of very famous people, or bad things happening at NASA. Seldom happy events, such as the first time you heard the Beatles (for me: at age 11, in an orphanage in Hershey, PA, it was a reel-to-reel tape recording my brother made from a shortwave radio broadcast of "I Want to Hold Your Hand," still the most thrilling sound I've ever heard), they tend to be memorable because you witnessed or heard about them on television. Our criterion is simple: How deeply has the event singed itself on your memory? For an older generation, the death of FDR, VE Day, Hiroshima, and "Have you no sense of decency" are surely indelible. So we established a cutoff date at 1957, using a rough rule based on whether Tom Brokaw (born in 1940) would remember where he was when.

MARK REITER, the coeditor of this book, was in Mr. Kleinfelter's health class in Hershey when he heard JFK was shot. On the morning of 9/11, after landing at 5:45 a.m. at Newark International on a red-eye flight from Los Angeles, he was standing on Manhattan's Sixth Avenue, looking south with thousands of New Yorkers, as the second tower came down.

Matchup	Winner
Berlin Wall comes tumbling down (1989) / Apollo I disaster: Grissom, White, Chaffee die (1967)	Berlin Wall
first time you heard the Beatles (1963) / Nixon resigns over Watergate (1974)	Beatles
Mount St. Helens erupts (1980) / Katrina hits New Orleans (2005)	Katrina
O. J. verdict (1995) / first Clay–Liston fight (1964)	O. J.
Miracle on Ice (1980) / Oklahoma City bombing (1995)	Oklahoma City
JFK assassinated (1963) / John Glenn orbits Earth (1962)	JFK
John Lennon shot (1980) / Elvis Presley dies at 42 (1977)	Lennon
RFK assassinated (1968) / Kent State shootings (1970)	RFK
Woodstock festival (1969) / San Francisco World Series earthquake (1989)	Woodstock
Buddy Holly dies (1959) / first man on the moon (1969)	man on the moon
Princess Diana dies (1997) / Three Mile Island nuclear accident (1979)	Princess Diana
Munich Olympics terrorist attack (1972) / Reagan shot (1981)	Reagan
Shuttle *Challenger* explodes (1986) / Martin Luther King assassinated (1968)	*Challenger*
JFK Jr. dies in plane crash (1999) / Shuttle *Columbia* disintegrates on re-entry (2003)	JFK Jr.
9/11 attacks (2001) / Asian tsunami (2004)	9/11 attacks
Dale Earnhardt dies at Daytona (2001) / Russians launch Sputnik (1957)	Earnhardt

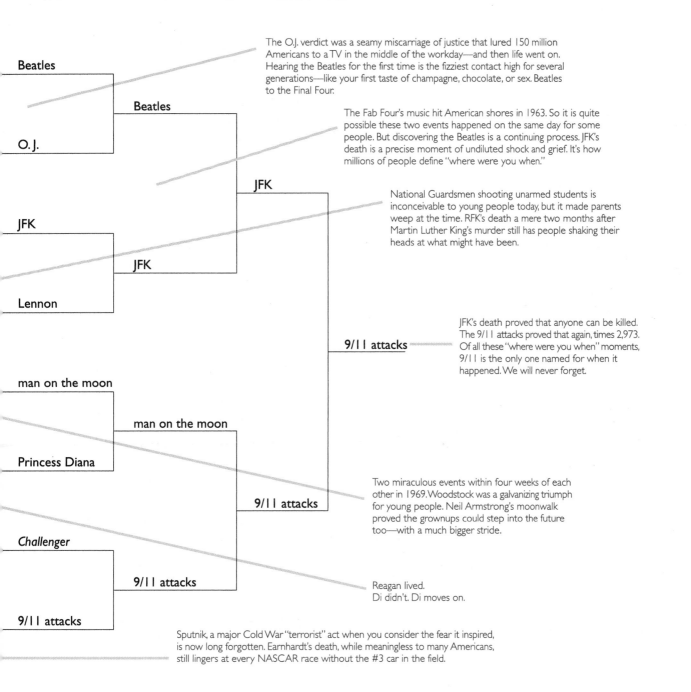

Beatles

O.J.

Beatles

The O.J. verdict was a seamy miscarriage of justice that lured 150 million Americans to a TV in the middle of the workday—and then life went on. Hearing the Beatles for the first time is the fizziest contact high for several generations—like your first taste of champagne, chocolate, or sex. Beatles to the Final Four.

JFK

The Fab Four's music hit American shores in 1963. So it is quite possible these two events happened on the same day for some people. But discovering the Beatles is a continuing process. JFK's death is a precise moment of undiluted shock and grief. It's how millions of people define "where were you when."

JFK

JFK

Lennon

National Guardsmen shooting unarmed students is inconceivable to young people today, but it made parents weep at the time. RFK's death a mere two months after Martin Luther King's murder still has people shaking their heads at what might have been.

9/11 attacks

JFK's death proved that anyone can be killed. The 9/11 attacks proved that again, times 2,973. Of all these "where were you when" moments, 9/11 is the only one named for when it happened. We will never forget.

man on the moon

Princess Diana

man on the moon

9/11 attacks

Two miraculous events within four weeks of each other in 1969. Woodstock was a galvanizing triumph for young people. Neil Armstrong's moonwalk proved the grownups could step into the future too—with a much bigger stride.

Challenger

9/11 attacks

Reagan lived.
Di didn't. Di moves on.

9/11 attacks

Sputnik, a major Cold War "terrorist" act when you consider the fear it inspired, is now long forgotten. Earnhardt's death, while meaningless to many Americans, still lingers at every NASCAR race without the #3 car in the field.

Animation Characters

by ROZ CHAST

As a kid, I loved watching the antics of snappy, funny, anti-authoritarian, never-give-a-sucker-an-even-break characters more than the sweet, nice ones. My childhood viewing provided me with the basic formula for a great animated character: it must have an engaging personality, which could be obnoxious or asinine, but never boring or stupid—and it must seem real. I can't stand feeling like I'm watching a puppet speaking the lines of a bunch of sitcom writers. I have to believe that this is a real, sentient being.

SpongeBob is loving, generous, and spontaneous, a sea creature who wants everyone, even his sourpuss friend, Squidward, to enjoy life as much as he does. Ren is a psychotic, apoplectic Chihuahua, yet very, very deep down, he loves his simple-minded pal Stimpy. You sense that if they met, SpongeBob's complete package of sweetness would turn Ren into a friend.

ROZ CHAST's cartoons appear regularly in the *New Yorker*. Her cartoons from 1978 to 2006 have been "selected, collected, and health-inspected" in *Theories of Everything* (Bloomsbury, 2006). She was born in Brooklyn, New York, and currently resides in Connecticut.

Snoopy	Droopy Dog
Droopy Dog	
Donald Duck	Daffy Duck
Daffy Duck	
Bugs Bunny	Bugs Bunny
Mickey Mouse	
Rocky the Flying Squirrel	Rocky the Flying Squirrel
Astro Boy	
Daria	Daria
Beavis	
Lucy Van Pelt	Lisa Simpson
Lisa Simpson	
Goofy	Bullwinkle
Bullwinkle	
Bobby Hill	Bobby Hill
Charlie Brown	
Eric Cartman	Eric Cartman
Marge Simpson	
Betty Boop	Betty Boop
Olive Oyl	
Elmer Fudd	Popeye
Popeye	
Principal Skinner	Dr. Katz
Dr. Katz	
Ren Hoek	SpongeBob SquarePants
SpongeBob SquarePants	
Stewie Griffin	Stewie Griffin
Porky Pig	
Homer Simpson	Homer Simpson
Fred Flintstone	
Bart Simpson	Bart Simpson
Ned Flanders	

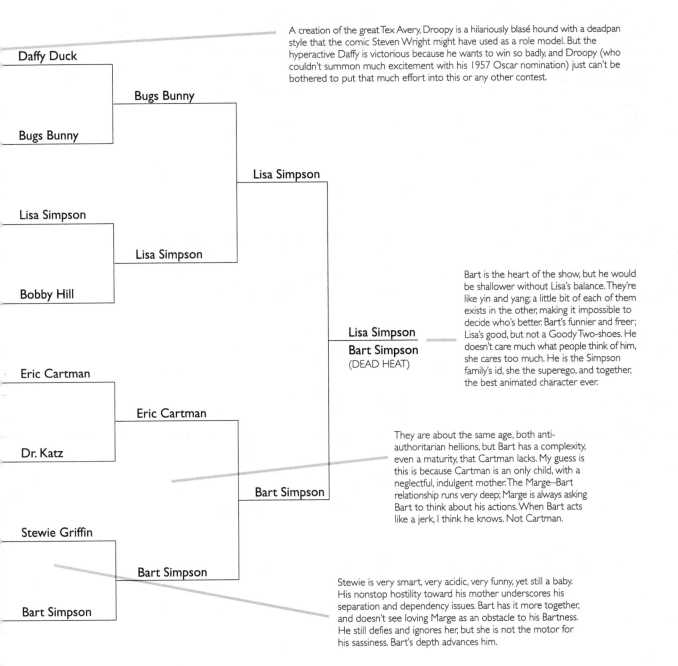

Daffy Duck

Bugs Bunny

Bugs Bunny

A creation of the great Tex Avery, Droopy is a hilariously blasé hound with a deadpan style that the comic Steven Wright might have used as a role model. But the hyperactive Daffy is victorious because he wants to win so badly, and Droopy (who couldn't summon much excitement with his 1957 Oscar nomination) just can't be bothered to put that much effort into this or any other contest.

Lisa Simpson

Lisa Simpson

Lisa Simpson

Bobby Hill

Lisa Simpson
Bart Simpson
(DEAD HEAT)

Bart is the heart of the show, but he would be shallower without Lisa's balance. They're like yin and yang; a little bit of each of them exists in the other, making it impossible to decide who's better. Bart's funnier and freer; Lisa's good, but not a Goody Two-shoes. He doesn't care much what people think of him, she cares too much. He is the Simpson family's id, she the superego, and together, the best animated character ever.

Eric Cartman

Eric Cartman

Dr. Katz

Bart Simpson

They are about the same age, both anti-authoritarian hellions, but Bart has a complexity, even a maturity, that Cartman lacks. My guess is this is because Cartman is an only child, with a neglectful, indulgent mother. The Marge–Bart relationship runs very deep; Marge is always asking Bart to think about his actions. When Bart acts like a jerk, I think he knows. Not Cartman.

Stewie Griffin

Bart Simpson

Bart Simpson

Stewie is very smart, very acidic, very funny, yet still a baby. His nonstop hostility toward his mother underscores his separation and dependency issues. Bart has it more together, and doesn't see loving Marge as an obstacle to his Bartness. He still defies and ignores her, but she is not the motor for his sassiness. Bart's depth advances him.

Ad Slogans

by PHIL DUSENBERRY

A great ad slogan reveals the disproportionate power of a few carefully chosen and arranged words. It can send a product soaring, save a business, launch a career. A great slogan must, first, be memorable. It has to go in one ear and stay there, forcing consumers to recall the brand name again and again. It has to differentiate you from the other guy. It has to be strategic and promise something the others don't. And it must be enduring. "Come to Marlboro Country" ran for decades and "We bring good things to life" was GE's calling card for 24 years. I go for slogans that trigger the emotions rather than challenge the intellect. For me, softer works harder. And I'm a sucker for sly wit. Oh yes, keep it simple. The best slogans do.

PHIL DUSENBERRY, former chairman of BBDO North America, was inducted into the Advertising Hall of Fame in 2004. He is the author of the practical memoir *One Great Insight Is Worth a Thousand Good Ideas* (Portfolio, 2005) and, with Roger Towne, wrote the screenplay for *The Natural*.

Slogans	Match
Where's the beef? (Wendy's)	Where's the beef?
Finger-lickin' good (KFC)	
You've come a long way, baby (Virginia Slims)	You've come a long way
I'd walk a mile for a Camel	
Just wait'll we get our Hanes on you	Just do it
Just do it (Nike)	
Have it your way (Burger King)	You deserve a break
You deserve a break today (McDonald's)	
The pause that refreshes (Coke)	The Pepsi Generation
The Pepsi Generation	
It takes a tough man to make a tender chicken (Perdue)	M'm! M'm! Good
M'm! M'm! Good (Campbell's)	
Does she or doesn't she? Only her hairdresser knows for sure (Clairol)	Does she or doesn't she?
If I have only one life to live, let me live it as a blonde (Clairol)	
Fair and Balanced (Fox News)	All the news that's fit
All the news that's fit to print (*New York Times*)	
The family that prays together stays together (Family Theater)	A mind is a terrible thing
A mind is a terrible thing to waste (United Negro College Fund)	
Got milk? (California Milk Board)	Plop, plop, fizz, fizz
Plop, plop, fizz, fizz—oh what a relief it is (Alka-Seltzer)	
Reach out and touch someone (AT&T)	Reach out and touch
Be all that you can be (U.S. Army)	
When it absolutely positively has to be there overnight (FedEx)	absolutely positively
You're in good hands with Allstate	
Betcha can't eat just one (Lay's Potato Chips)	Betcha can't
With a name like Smucker's, it has to be good	
M&M's melt in your mouth, not in your hands	Schaefer is the one beer
Schaefer is the one beer to have when you're having more than one	
A diamond is forever (De Beers)	A diamond is forever
It takes a lickin' and keeps on tickin' (Timex)	
We try harder (Avis)	We try harder
We love to fly and it shows (Delta)	

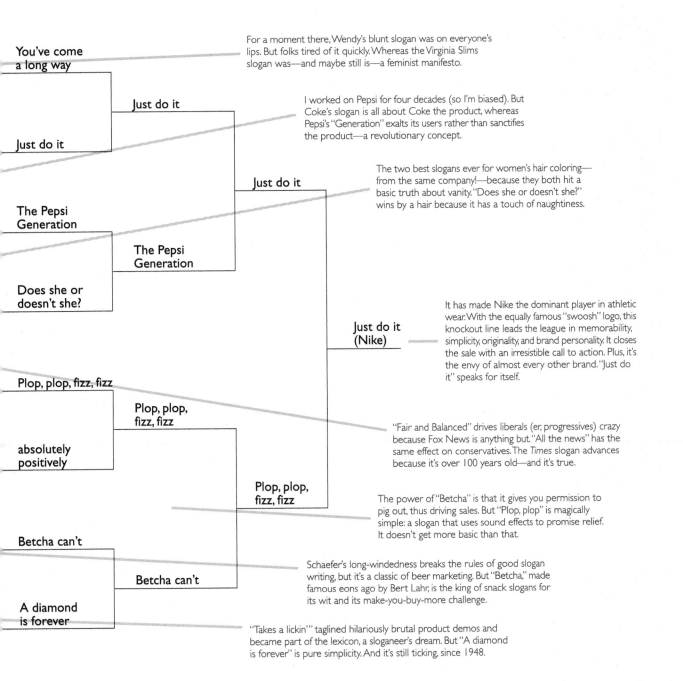

You've come
a long way

For a moment there, Wendy's blunt slogan was on everyone's lips. But folks tired of it quickly. Whereas the Virginia Slims slogan was—and maybe still is—a feminist manifesto.

Just do it

Just do it

I worked on Pepsi for four decades (so I'm biased). But Coke's slogan is all about Coke the product, whereas Pepsi's "Generation" exalts its users rather than sanctifies the product—a revolutionary concept.

The Pepsi
Generation

Just do it

The two best slogans ever for women's hair coloring—from the same company!—because they both hit a basic truth about vanity. "Does she or doesn't she?" wins by a hair because it has a touch of naughtiness.

The Pepsi
Generation

Does she or
doesn't she?

Just do it
(Nike)

It has made Nike the dominant player in athletic wear. With the equally famous "swoosh" logo, this knockout line leads the league in memorability, simplicity, originality, and brand personality. It closes the sale with an irresistible call to action. Plus, it's the envy of almost every other brand. "Just do it" speaks for itself.

Plop, plop, fizz, fizz

Plop, plop,
fizz, fizz

"Fair and Balanced" drives liberals (er, progressives) crazy because Fox News is anything but. "All the news" has the same effect on conservatives. The Times slogan advances because it's over 100 years old—and it's true.

absolutely
positively

Plop, plop,
fizz, fizz

The power of "Betcha" is that it gives you permission to pig out, thus driving sales. But "Plop, plop" is magically simple: a slogan that uses sound effects to promise relief. It doesn't get more basic than that.

Betcha can't

Betcha can't

Schaefer's long-windedness breaks the rules of good slogan writing, but it's a classic of beer marketing. But "Betcha," made famous eons ago by Bert Lahr, is the king of snack slogans for its wit and its make-you-buy-more challenge.

A diamond
is forever

"Takes a lickin'" taglined hilariously brutal product demos and became part of the lexicon, a sloganeer's dream. But "A diamond is forever" is pure simplicity. And it's still ticking, since 1948.

Alt-Country Songs

by PETER BLACKSTOCK and GRANT ALDEN

Music lovers of a certain stripe still debate the existence of alternative country—whether it ever did exist, or if it still does today. Certainly at alt-country's mid-'90s zenith people knew it when they heard it, which explains why a big chunk of our tourney entries come from that period. But we've also included proto-alt-country (the Byrds, the Blasters) and present-day representatives (the Duhks, Old Crow Medicine Show) to give all generations their due and underline the historical arc of the form. Whatever it is, we're still listening, debating, and writing about it.

GRANT ALDEN and PETER BLACKSTOCK are the coeditors and cofounders of *No Depression*, a bimonthly magazine that was launched in the fall of 1995 and quickly became known as the authority on all things alt-country, and now covers the broad variety of American roots music.

Son Volt, "Windfall" — "Windfall"
Old 97's, "Big Brown Eyes"

Steve Earle, "Ellis Unit One" — "Ellis Unit One"
Bobby Bare Jr., "I'll Be Around"

Jimmie Dale Gilmore, "Dallas" — "Dallas"
Gram Parsons, "$1000 Wedding"

Doug Sahm, "Texas Tornado" — "Kerosene"
The Bottle Rockets, "Kerosene"

Shaver, "Blood Is Thicker Than Water" — "Blood Is Thicker"
Blood Oranges, "Hell's Half Acre"

Jon Dee Graham, "Big Sweet Life" — "The Living Bubba"
Drive-By Truckers, "The Living Bubba"

Mike Ireland & Holler, "House of Secrets" — "Angels Are Messengers"
Whiskeytown, "Angels Are Messengers from God"

Dave Alvin, "Fourth of July" — "Hickory Wind"
The Byrds, "Hickory Wind"

Johnny Cash, "Time of the Preacher" — "Marie Marie"
The Blasters, "Marie Marie"

The Jayhawks, "Settled Down Like Rain" — "Settled Down Like Rain"
BR5-49, "Even If It's Wrong"

Lucinda Williams, "Changed the Locks" — "Changed the Locks"
Alejandro Escovedo, "Five Hearts Breaking"

Richard Buckner, "Lil Wallet Picture" — "Wagon Wheel"
Old Crow Medicine Show, "Wagon Wheel"

Gillian Welch, "I Dream a Highway" — "I Dream a Highway"
Mary Gauthier, "Mercy Now"

Uncle Tupelo, "Whiskey Bottle" — "Whiskey Bottle"
The Duhks, "Heaven's My Home"

Robbie Fulks, "She Took a Lot Of Pills (and Died)" — "Rex's Blues"
Townes Van Zandt, "Rex's Blues"

Buddy Miller, "With God on Our Side" — "With God on Our Side"
Kasey Chambers, "The Captain"

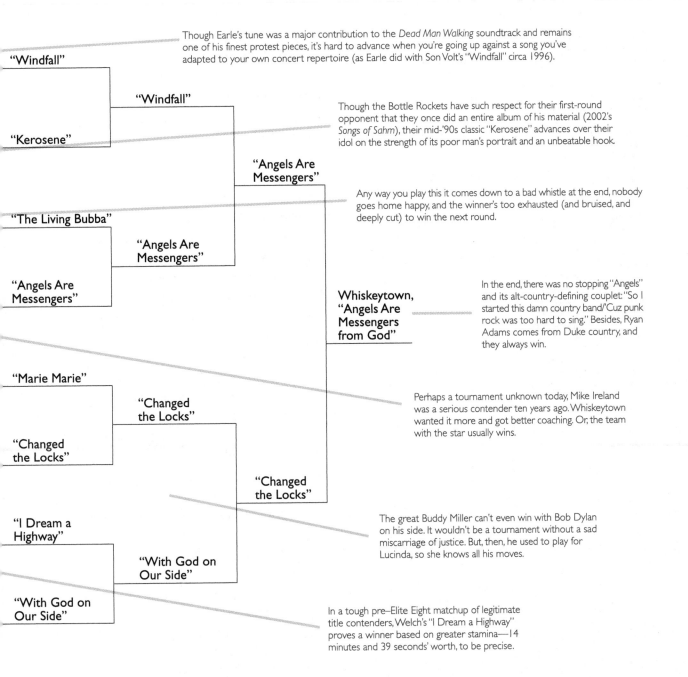

"Windfall"

"Windfall"

Though Earle's tune was a major contribution to the *Dead Man Walking* soundtrack and remains one of his finest protest pieces, it's hard to advance when you're going up against a song you've adapted to your own concert repertoire (as Earle did with Son Volt's "Windfall" circa 1996).

"Kerosene"

Though the Bottle Rockets have such respect for their first-round opponent that they once did an entire album of his material (2002's *Songs of Sahm*), their mid-'90s classic "Kerosene" advances over their idol on the strength of its poor man's portrait and an unbeatable hook.

"Angels Are Messengers"

"The Living Bubba"

Any way you play this it comes down to a bad whistle at the end, nobody goes home happy, and the winner's too exhausted (and bruised, and deeply cut) to win the next round.

"Angels Are Messengers"

"Angels Are Messengers"

Whiskeytown, "Angels Are Messengers from God"

In the end, there was no stopping "Angels" and its alt-country-defining couplet: "So I started this damn country band/'Cuz punk rock was too hard to sing." Besides, Ryan Adams comes from Duke country, and they always win.

"Marie Marie"

"Changed the Locks"

Perhaps a tournament unknown today, Mike Ireland was a serious contender ten years ago. Whiskeytown wanted it more and got better coaching. Or, the team with the star usually wins.

"Changed the Locks"

"Changed the Locks"

"I Dream a Highway"

The great Buddy Miller can't even win with Bob Dylan on his side. It wouldn't be a tournament without a sad miscarriage of justice. But, then, he used to play for Lucinda, so she knows all his moves.

"With God on Our Side"

"With God on Our Side"

In a tough pre–Elite Eight matchup of legitimate title contenders, Welch's "I Dream a Highway" proves a winner based on greater stamina—14 minutes and 39 seconds' worth, to be precise.

American Beers
by MAUREEN OGLE

The beers had to be brewed in the USA (adios, Corona). They had to be available in Ames, Iowa, where I live and where my neighborhood distributors stock 602 different beers (but alas, no Yuengling). They had to be available year-round—no Oktoberfests, Cranberry Lambics, or other seasonals. I resisted cutesy labels and names, although Turbodog survived after I realized that the elegant design of both label and bottle reflected the concept of "turbo." Nor did I play sentimental favorites with plucky microbrews at the expense of the omnipresent macros; Pabst, Bud, and Miller all got invites to the show. Bouquet and color mattered, but far behind the governing criterion of *how the beer tasted*. Rather than rely on taste memory, I ran it like a strict tournament over three days. By late afternoon on day 2, nearing successful aversion therapy for lager and ale, I opted to wait 48 hours before diving into the Final Two.

MAUREEN OGLE is a writer and historian, and the author of *Ambitious Brew: The Story of American Beer* (Harcourt, 2006). She's not sure if beer equals life or life equals beer, but she's convinced that neither means much without the other.

A tough matchup. Beautiful colors, both. Complex flavors. Turbo wins by a nose: literally. Its bouquet seduced me.

Two of the original microbreweries duke it out. A quarter century on, both are national powerhouses, but Red Hook long ago "partnered" with the 800-pound gorilla, Anheuser-Busch. Sierra Nevada's Ken Grossman still goes it alone—and he's still got the goods.

I last experienced these two during dime-beer hour at the Vine in Iowa City in the 1970s. How far would nostalgia and Proustian aromatics carry this pair? (Answer: Not far.)

Bracket:

- Samuel Adams Cream Stout / Abita Turbodog → **Abita Turbodog**
- Samuel Adams Brown Ale / Sierra Nevada Brown Ale → **Sierra Nevada Brown Ale**
- Dogfish Head 60 Minute IPA / Anchor Liberty Ale → **Anchor Liberty Ale**
- Summit Extra Pale Ale / Samuel Adams Boston Ale → **Summit Extra Pale Ale**
- Redhook Blonde Ale / Sierra Nevada Pale Ale → **Sierra Nevada Pale Ale**
- Summit Grand Pilsener / Michelob Amber Bock → **Summit Grand Pilsener**
- Shiner 97 / Leinenkugel's Creamy Dark → **Leinenkugel's Creamy Dark**
- Stevens Point Amber / Capital Wisconsin Amber → **Stevens Point Amber**
- Schell FireBrick / Anchor Steam → **Schell FireBrick**
- Capital 1900 / Samuel Adams Boston Lager → **Capital 1900**
- Boulevard Pale Ale / Elmwood Lawnmower Ale → **Elmwood Lawnmower**
- Anheuser-Busch Budweiser / Leinenkugel's Original → **Leinenkugel's Original**
- Stevens Point Special Lager / Millstream German Pilsner → **Millstream German Pilsner**
- Pabst Blue Ribbon / Miller High Life → **Pabst Blue Ribbon**
- Leinenkugel's Northwoods Lager / Saranac Adirondack Lager → **Saranac Adirondack Lager**
- Heileman's Old Style / Grain Belt → **Grain Belt**

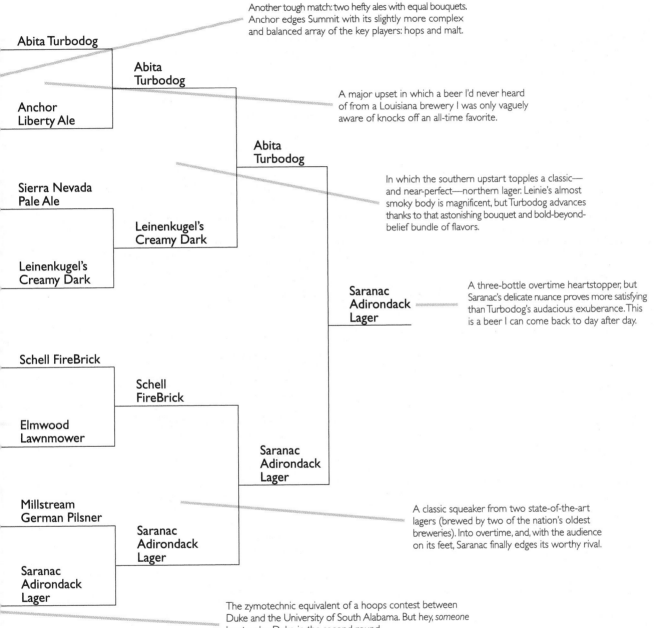

Abita Turbodog

Anchor Liberty Ale

Another tough match: two hefty ales with equal bouquets. Anchor edges Summit with its slightly more complex and balanced array of the key players: hops and malt.

Abita Turbodog

A major upset in which a beer I'd never heard of from a Louisiana brewery I was only vaguely aware of knocks off an all-time favorite.

Sierra Nevada Pale Ale

Leinenkugel's Creamy Dark

Abita Turbodog

In which the southern upstart topples a classic—and near-perfect—northern lager. Leinie's almost smoky body is magnificent, but Turbodog advances thanks to that astonishing bouquet and bold-beyond-belief bundle of flavors.

Leinenkugel's Creamy Dark

Saranac Adirondack Lager

A three-bottle overtime heartstopper, but Saranac's delicate nuance proves more satisfying than Turbodog's audacious exuberance. This is a beer I can come back to day after day.

Schell FireBrick

Elmwood Lawnmower

Schell FireBrick

Saranac Adirondack Lager

Millstream German Pilsner

Saranac Adirondack Lager

A classic squeaker from two state-of-the-art lagers (brewed by two of the nation's oldest breweries). Into overtime, and, with the audience on its feet, Saranac finally edges its worthy rival.

Saranac Adirondack Lager

The zymotechnic equivalent of a hoops contest between Duke and the University of South Alabama. But hey, *someone* has to play Duke in the second round.

Great American Plays
by PETER MARKS

Some plays, by dint of indelible characters or extraordinary language, are built to last. These are plays you could see again and again; it's hard to tire of them. Some propel the dramatic form forward. Others express a profound truth about America, whether the subject is salesmanship or slavery or family dynamics. Some are just funny. Eight playwrights with a minimum of four great works play through in this bracket, which eliminated those entrants without the required quartet: Lillian Hellman (*The Little Foxes*), Thornton Wilder (*Our Town*), Tony Kushner (*Angels in America*), and Charles MacArthur and Ben Hecht (*The Front Page*).

PETER MARKS's love of the theater began at age 5, when he saw *The Sound of Music*, with Mary Martin, on Broadway, and it continues today in his job as the chief theater critic of the *Washington Post*. Since graduating from Yale, he has worked at six newspapers, including the *New York Times*, which first gave him the chance to be a drama critic, and where he was in the no. 2 slot until his move to the *Post*.

ARTHUR MILLER REGIONAL
- The Crucible — Crucible
- A View from the Bridge
- Death of a Salesman — Salesman
- All My Sons

AUGUST WILSON REGIONAL
- Ma Rainey's Black Bottom — Ma Rainey
- Joe Turner's Come and Gone
- The Piano Lesson — Fences
- Fences

SAM SHEPARD REGIONAL
- Buried Child — Buried Child
- True West
- Curse of the Starving Class — Tooth of Crime
- The Tooth of Crime

EDWARD ALBEE REGIONAL
- Who's Afraid of Virginia Woolf — Virginia Woolf
- Three Tall Women
- A Delicate Balance — Delicate Balance
- The Zoo Story

EUGENE O'NEILL REGIONAL
- Long Day's Journey into Night — Long Day's
- Mourning Becomes Electra
- The Iceman Cometh — Iceman
- A Moon for the Misbegotten

DAVID MAMET REGIONAL
- American Buffalo — American Buffalo
- Speed-the-Plow
- Glengarry Glen Ross — Glengarry
- The Cryptogram

CLIFFORD ODETS REGIONAL
- Awake and Sing! — Awake and Sing!
- Golden Boy
- Waiting for Lefty — Waiting for Lefty
- The Country Girl

TENNESSEE WILLIAMS REGIONAL
- A Streetcar Named Desire — Streetcar
- Cat on a Hot Tin Roof
- Sweet Bird of Youth — The Glass Menagerie
- The Glass Menagerie

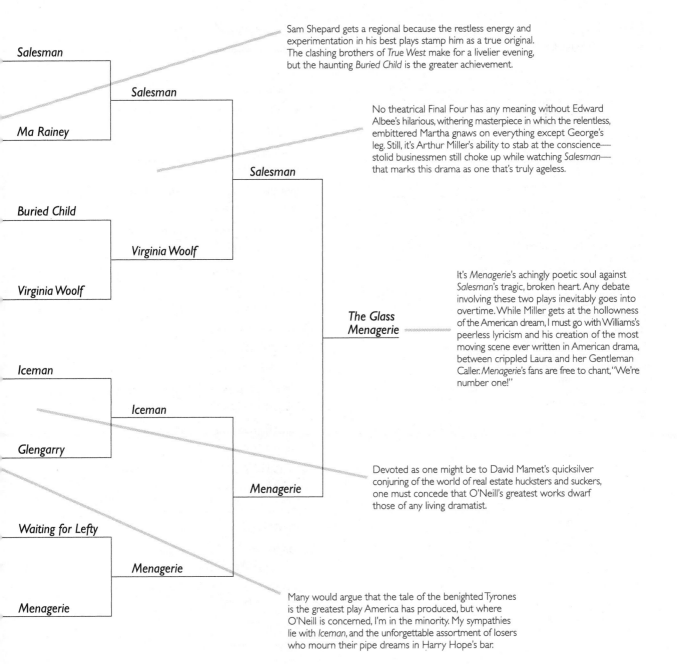

Salesman

Salesman

Ma Rainey

Sam Shepard gets a regional because the restless energy and experimentation in his best plays stamp him as a true original. The clashing brothers of *True West* make for a livelier evening, but the haunting *Buried Child* is the greater achievement.

Salesman

No theatrical Final Four has any meaning without Edward Albee's hilarious, withering masterpiece in which the relentless, embittered Martha gnaws on everything except George's leg. Still, it's Arthur Miller's ability to stab at the conscience—stolid businessmen still choke up while watching *Salesman*—that marks this drama as one that's truly ageless.

Buried Child

Virginia Woolf

Virginia Woolf

The Glass Menagerie

It's *Menagerie*'s achingly poetic soul against *Salesman*'s tragic, broken heart. Any debate involving these two plays inevitably goes into overtime. While Miller gets at the hollowness of the American dream, I must go with Williams's peerless lyricism and his creation of the most moving scene ever written in American drama, between crippled Laura and her Gentleman Caller. *Menagerie*'s fans are free to chant, "We're number one!"

Iceman

Iceman

Glengarry

Menagerie

Devoted as one might be to David Mamet's quicksilver conjuring of the world of real estate hucksters and suckers, one must concede that O'Neill's greatest works dwarf those of any living dramatist.

Waiting for Lefty

Menagerie

Menagerie

Many would argue that the tale of the benighted Tyrones is the greatest play America has produced, but where O'Neill is concerned, I'm in the minority. My sympathies lie with *Iceman*, and the unforgettable assortment of losers who mourn their pipe dreams in Harry Hope's bar.

Bald Guys
by RICHARD SANDOMIR

Some men are born to baldness, some embrace it. Hence, this 32-man "Follicle Challenge" divides cleanly into fringe-hair and shaved-headed regionals. Some in the shaved-headed regional doubtlessly viewed incipient male-pattern baldness as an opportunity to go smooth, but historically, they are in the minority, which gives the shaved-headers a particularly large challenge against befringed superstars like Churchill, Eisenhower, Lenin, Picasso, Caesar, Darwin, and a darn good pope. Nonetheless, to those not obsessed with hair, there is beauty in the natural fringe and in those who take the plunge into total baldness, vide Brynner, Savalas, and Jordan. In the end, the main criterion was each man's impact on our mental imagery: when you thought of the individual, did their follicular condition come first to mind—or did you think of something else?

RICHARD SANDOMIR, co-editor of this book and author of the memoir *Bald Like Me*, was genetically disposed to baldness and sported a fringe for many years until advised by Charles Barkley that what he had—a Larry Fine hairdo, which was fine for Larry, a Stooge—was no longer working for him. Sandomir now shaves his head with a Gillette Mach 3 Turbo razor and Gillette Sensitive Skin gel every other day.

FRINGED REGIONAL

There is a delightful pumpkin quality to Churchill's baldness, a head that perfectly supported a bowler, upon a body nourished happily with a steady stream of wine, whisky, and cigars. Giuliani came late to the proper look, hair combed back on a bullet-head, after a lifetime combover that had its last gasp after 9/11. Rudy, alas, departs because Churchill would never have gone out in public with a combover.

SHAVED-HEADED REGIONAL

These are the shaved-head godfathers, the smooth-skinned pioneers of bald society. How unfair that they must meet in the first round. On closer inspection, these hairless deities are different. Brynner's head was perfectly designed to play the role of archetypal baldie. Savalas's lumpy dome, often covered by a hat in his Kojak years, was more of a prop that provided him with the insouciance to say "Who loves ya, baby?"

First Round	Second Round
Homer Simpson / Charlie Brown	Homer Simpson
John Glenn / Sean Connery	John Glenn
Pope John Paul II / Julius Caesar	Pope JP II
Larry David / Nikita Khrushchev	Larry David
Dwight Eisenhower / Adlai Stevenson	Adlai Stevenson
Rudy Giuliani / Winston Churchill	Winston Churchill
V. I. Lenin / Charles Darwin	Charles Darwin
Pablo Picasso / Mikhail Gorbachev	Pablo Picasso
Telly Savalas / Yul Brynner	Yul Brynner
Michael Jordan / Shaquille O'Neal	Michael Jordan
Mahatma Gandhi / Barry Bonds	Mahatma Gandhi
Tupac Shakur / Curly Howard	Curly Howard
Patrick Stewart / Samuel L. Jackson	Samuel L. Jackson
Benito Mussolini / Andre Agassi	Andre Agassi
George Foreman / Dr. Evil	George Foreman
Charles Barkley / Marvelous Marvin Hagler	Charles Barkley

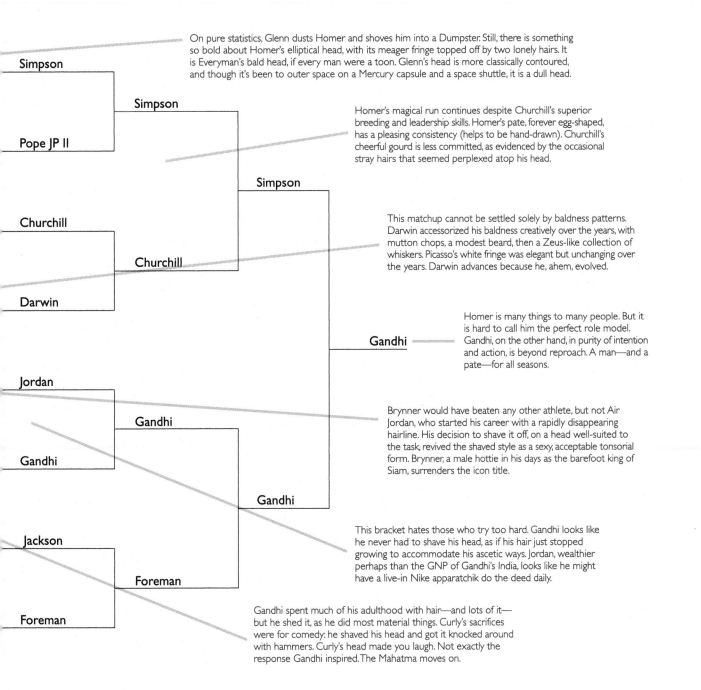

Simpson

Pope JP II

Simpson

Churchill

Darwin

Churchill

Simpson

Gandhi

Jordan

Gandhi

Gandhi

Gandhi

Jackson

Foreman

Foreman

On pure statistics, Glenn dusts Homer and shoves him into a Dumpster. Still, there is something so bold about Homer's elliptical head, with its meager fringe topped off by two lonely hairs. It is Everyman's bald head, if every man were a toon. Glenn's head is more classically contoured, and though it's been to outer space on a Mercury capsule and a space shuttle, it is a dull head.

Homer's magical run continues despite Churchill's superior breeding and leadership skills. Homer's pate, forever egg-shaped, has a pleasing consistency (helps to be hand-drawn). Churchill's cheerful gourd is less committed, as evidenced by the occasional stray hairs that seemed perplexed atop his head.

This matchup cannot be settled solely by baldness patterns. Darwin accessorized his baldness creatively over the years, with mutton chops, a modest beard, then a Zeus-like collection of whiskers. Picasso's white fringe was elegant but unchanging over the years. Darwin advances because he, ahem, evolved.

Homer is many things to many people. But it is hard to call him the perfect role model. Gandhi, on the other hand, in purity of intention and action, is beyond reproach. A man—and a pate—for all seasons.

Brynner would have beaten any other athlete, but not Air Jordan, who started his career with a rapidly disappearing hairline. His decision to shave it off, on a head well-suited to the task, revived the shaved style as a sexy, acceptable tonsorial form. Brynner, a male hottie in his days as the barefoot king of Siam, surrenders the icon title.

This bracket hates those who try too hard. Gandhi looks like he never had to shave his head, as if his hair just stopped growing to accommodate his ascetic ways. Jordan, wealthier perhaps than the GNP of Gandhi's India, looks like he might have a live-in Nike apparatchik do the deed daily.

Gandhi spent much of his adulthood with hair—and lots of it— but he shed it, as he did most material things. Curly's sacrifices were for comedy: he shaved his head and got it knocked around with hammers. Curly's head made you laugh. Not exactly the response Gandhi inspired. The Mahatma moves on.

Baseball Myths
by RICHARD LALLY

From the time Abner Doubleday didn't invent baseball in Cooperstown, New York, the national pastime has been rife with clichés, empty adages, half-truths, and downright falsehoods that pros who play the sport, writers who cover it, and fans who follow it tout as holy writ. Fortunately, baseball statistics are the thinking man's oxygen, so we have ways to affirm or dispute conventional wisdom. The criterion here is as blunt as a bunt: which truism is not only false but also treacherous? Which lie, if you believe it and follow it, will doom you to lose? Let's play hardball as the game's biggest whoppers toss beanballs at each other, with the survivor ascending to the throne as the King of Diamond Canards.

RICHARD LALLY is the author or coauthor of 19 books, including the baseball classic *The Wrong Stuff* (with former Boston Red Sox ace Bill "Spaceman" Lee) and *Baseball for Dummies* (with Hall of Famer Joe Morgan). He lives in New York City, where he roots for both the Yankees and the Mets.

chemistry creates winning teams
top draft picks usually become stars — **chemistry**

Mark McGwire cheated
revenue sharing equals parity — **Mark McGwire**

always play the hot hand
the DH curtails strategy — **hot hand**

closers are hard to find
walks are as good as hits — **closers**

a gold glove equals a silver bat
Curt Flood fathered free agency — **gold glove**

the DH was an American League creation
power pitchers throw rising fastballs — **power pitchers**

modern pitchers eat quiche
intentionally walking Bonds makes sense — **modern pitchers**

winning teams make productive outs
free agency killed team loyalty — **productive outs**

Bruce Sutter popularized the splitter
base thieves make the best lead-off men — **base thieves**

strikeouts don't matter
wild cards hold the aces in October — **wild cards**

contented role players form great benches
some pitchers just know how to win — **pitchers know**

home runs are overrated
superstars add 20 wins — **home runs**

hustle trumps talent
hitting is contagious — **hustle**

expansion dilutes the talent pool
pitching isn't 75% of the game — **pitching isn't 75%**

baseball's golden age: the 1950s
every bullpen needs a lefty — **1950s**

bunts boost offenses
control pitchers outlast fastballers — **bunts**

chemistry

chemistry

closers

chemistry

gold glove

modern pitchers

modern pitchers

wild cards

home runs

home runs

pitching isn't 75%

pitching isn't 75%

pitching isn't 75%

bunts

chemistry creates winning teams

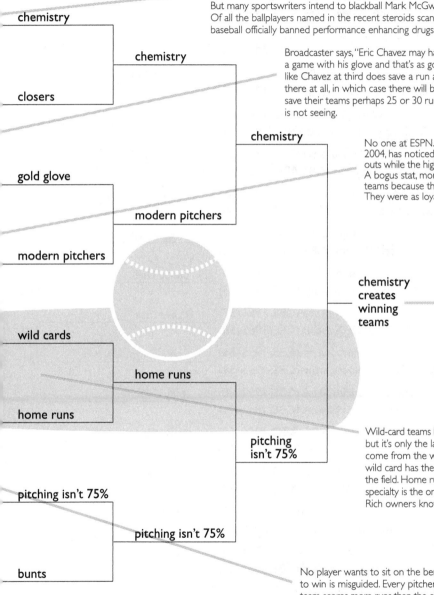

Revenue sharing has created enough parity to give us seven different World Series champions in this millennium. But many sportswriters intend to blackball Mark McGwire in their Hall of Fame voting because he "cheated." Of all the ballplayers named in the recent steroids scandal, McGwire was one of the few who retired before baseball officially banned performance enhancing drugs. Is it cheating if it ain't illegal?

Broadcaster says, "Eric Chavez may have slumped with the bat this year, but he saved a run a game with his glove and that's as good as driving one in." Is it? Having a great defender like Chavez at third does save a run a game, but only if the alternative is playing no one there at all, in which case there will be a lot of doubles hit down the line. The best fielders save their teams perhaps 25 or 30 runs per season, no more. As for rising fastballs, believing is not seeing.

No one at ESPN.com, which introduced Productive Outs as a stat in 2004, has noticed that teams with poor offenses have many productive outs while the high-octane offenses such as the New York Yankees don't. A bogus stat, more dubious than team loyalty. Players stayed with their teams because the reserve clause bound them to their clubs for life. They were as loyal as indentured servants.

The modern emphasis on run scoring has led many analysts to downgrade the role pitching plays in a team's success. However, an above-average pitching staff is three times more likely to lift a below-average offense than vice versa. But the contribution of team chemistry to winning is easily the biggest hype in sports. Players don't have to get along to succeed. When the 2002 San Francisco Giants won a National League pennant despite fisticuffs between team stars Barry Bonds and Jeff Kent, Kent said, "Chemistry only exists when you win." Amen.

Wild-card teams like the Angels and Marlins have won the World Series, but it's only the law of averages at play. Two of the eight playoff teams come from the wild card. Since any team can win a short series, the wild card has the same chance—one out of four—as anyone else in the field. Home run hitters are disparaged as one-dimensional, but their specialty is the only hit guaranteed to score a run. And runs win games. Rich owners know this, which is why they overpay power hitters.

No player wants to sit on the bench. But the adage that some pitchers just know how to win is misguided. Every pitcher knows how to win. Just work on the day when your team scores more runs than the opposition. Nothing exerts a greater impact on whether a hurler notches a W than the run support he receives. Pitchers can't control that.

Black-and-White TV Programs

by ROBERT THOMPSON

Ten years after the first U.S. color TV sets were introduced in 1954, 97 percent of homes still didn't have one. This made sense, since the dramaturgy of the first two decades of American TV was itself pretty black and white. Though network standards were usually hostile to complexity, controversy, and anything unfit for an eight-year-old, some masterpieces in monochrome made it through nevertheless. Only prime-time entertainment series are considered here; some of them—*The Ed Sullivan Show, The Andy Griffith Show, The Beverly Hillbillies, Gunsmoke, Combat*—evolved into color.

ROBERT THOMPSON is a professor at Syracuse University, where he directs the Bleier Center for Television and Popular Culture. He has written or edited six books about American TV.

Your Show of Shows (NBC, 1950–54) — Your Show of Shows
The Ed Sullivan Show (CBS, 1948–71)

The Dick Van Dyke Show (CBS, 1961–66) — Dick Van Dyke
The George Burns and Gracie Allen Show (CBS, 1950–58)

Leave It to Beaver (CBS/ABC, 1957–63) — Leave It to Beaver
The Many Loves of Dobie Gillis (CBS, 1959–63)

Car 54, Where Are You? (NBC, 1961–63) — Ernie Kovacs
The Ernie Kovacs Specials (ABC, 1961–62)

Playhouse 90 (CBS, 1956–61) — Playhouse 90
Omnibus (CBS/ABC, 1952–61)

The Goodyear TV Playhouse (NBC, 1951–60) — Goodyear TV Playhouse
The United States Steel Hour (ABC/CBS, 1953–63)

The Twilight Zone (CBS, 1959–65) — Twilight Zone
Alfred Hitchcock Presents (CBS/NBC, 1955–62)

Studio One (CBS, 1948–58) — Studio One
The Philco Television Playhouse (NBC, 1948–55)

I Love Lucy (CBS, 1951–57) — I Love Lucy
The $64,000 Question (CBS, 1955–58)

The Honeymooners (CBS, 1955–56) — The Honeymooners
The Phil Silvers Show (CBS, 1955–59)

The Andy Griffith Show (CBS, 1960–68) — Andy Griffith
The Beverly Hillbillies (CBS, 1962–71)

The Steve Allen Show (NBC/ABC, 1956–61) — Steve Allen
The Nat "King" Cole Show (NBC, 1956–57)

Gunsmoke (CBS, 1955–75) — Maverick
Maverick (ABC, 1957–62)

Dragnet (NBC, 1951–59) — Untouchables
The Untouchables (ABC, 1959–63)

Ben Casey (ABC, 1961–66) — Defenders
The Defenders (CBS, 1961–65)

The Fugitive (ABC, 1963–67) — Fugitive
Combat! (ABC, 1962–67)

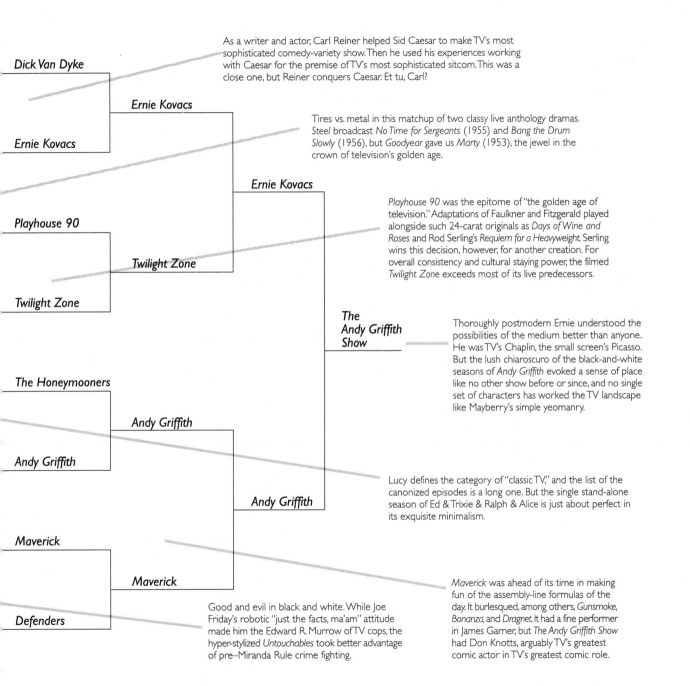

Dick Van Dyke

Ernie Kovacs

Ernie Kovacs

Ernie Kovacs

As a writer and actor, Carl Reiner helped Sid Caesar to make TV's most sophisticated comedy-variety show. Then he used his experiences working with Caesar for the premise of TV's most sophisticated sitcom. This was a close one, but Reiner conquers Caesar. Et tu, Carl?

Tires vs. metal in this matchup of two classy live anthology dramas. *Steel* broadcast *No Time for Sergeants* (1955) and *Bang the Drum Slowly* (1956), but *Goodyear* gave us *Marty* (1953), the jewel in the crown of television's golden age.

Playhouse 90

Twilight Zone

Twilight Zone

Playhouse 90 was the epitome of "the golden age of television." Adaptations of Faulkner and Fitzgerald played alongside such 24-carat originals as *Days of Wine and Roses* and Rod Serling's *Requiem for a Heavyweight*. Serling wins this decision, however, for another creation. For overall consistency and cultural staying power, the filmed *Twilight Zone* exceeds most of its live predecessors.

The Andy Griffith Show

Thoroughly postmodern Ernie understood the possibilities of the medium better than anyone. He was TV's Chaplin, the small screen's Picasso. But the lush chiaroscuro of the black-and-white seasons of *Andy Griffith* evoked a sense of place like no other show before or since, and no single set of characters has worked the TV landscape like Mayberry's simple yeomanry.

The Honeymooners

Andy Griffith

Andy Griffith

Andy Griffith

Lucy defines the category of "classic TV," and the list of the canonized episodes is a long one. But the single stand-alone season of Ed & Trixie & Ralph & Alice is just about perfect in its exquisite minimalism.

Maverick

Maverick

Defenders

Good and evil in black and white. While Joe Friday's robotic "just the facts, ma'am" attitude made him the Edward R. Murrow of TV cops, the hyper-stylized *Untouchables* took better advantage of pre–Miranda Rule crime fighting.

Maverick was ahead of its time in making fun of the assembly-line formulas of the day. It burlesqued, among others, *Gunsmoke*, *Bonanza*, and *Dragnet*. It had a fine performer in James Garner, but *The Andy Griffith Show* had Don Knotts, arguably TV's greatest comic actor in TV's greatest comic role.

James Bond Gadgets

by LOIS H. GRESH and ROBERT WEINBERG

James Bond is defined by girls, martinis, guns, cars, and toys that are outlandish and, therefore, Bondish. Some are more Bondish than others, meaning they are more clever, high-tech, outrageous, yet still realistic. In making our choices, coolness was a factor too. Of course, if coolness was the sole criterion and we didn't have to concern ourselves with gadgets not being people and people not being gadgets, then Sean Connery would be the ultimate Bond gadget of all.

LOIS H. GRESH is the author of 17 books and serves as technical communications director of science, technology, engineering, and math at the University of Rochester. ROBERT WEINBERG is the author of 34 books and a two-time winner of the World Fantasy Award. Together, they are coauthors of *The Science of James Bond* (Wiley, 2006), which explains everything from dirty bombs to space lasers to the medicinal merits of the martini.

Walther PPK 7.65 mm firearm (*Dr. No*, 1962) — Walther PPK 7.65 mm
dirty bomb (*Goldfinger*, 1964)

nuclear weapon (*Thunderball*, 1965) — Solex agitator
Solex agitator (*The Man with the Golden Gun*, 1974)

artificial fingerprints (*Diamonds are Forever*, 1971) — Lektor message decoder
Lektor message decoder (*From Russia with Love*, 1963)

voice duplicator (*Diamonds Are Forever*, 1971) — U.S. Clipper Chip
U.S. Clipper Chip (*GoldenEye*, 1995)

video camera ring (*A View to a Kill*, 1985) — video camera ring
camera rocket launcher (*The Man with the Golden Gun*, 1974)

1961 Sunbeam Alpine light blue convertible (*Dr. No*, 1962) — martini
martini (nearly all Bond movies)

BMW Z8 car (*The World Is Not Enough*, 1999) — Aston Martin DB5
Aston Martin DB5 car (*Goldfinger*, 1964)

Bentley Mark IV convertible (*From Russia with Love*, 1963) — Aston Martin V12
invisible Aston Martin V12 Vanquish (*Die Another Day*, 2002)

AMC Matador flying car (*The Man with the Golden Gun*, 1974) — Lotus car-sub
Lotus Esprit car-submarine (*The Spy Who Loved Me*, 1977)

Geiger counter wristwatch (*Thunderball*, 1965) — Geiger counter watch
Omega wristwatch bomb detonator (*Tomorrow Never Dies*, 1997)

Omega bomb-arming wristwatch with laser cutter (*GoldenEye*, 1995) — bomb-arming watch
circular saw wristwatch (*Live and Let Die*, 1973)

hydrofoil boat (*Thunderball*, 1965) — hydrofoil boat
gondola hovercraft (*Moonraker*, 1979)

invisible stealth ship (*Tomorrow Never Dies*, 1997) — gobbling spaceship
gobbling spaceship (*You Only Live Twice*, 1967)

Moonraker space station (*Moonraker*, 1979) — Moonraker space station
autogyro (*You Only Live Twice*, 1967)

Gustav Graves DNA plastic surgery (*Die Another Day*, 2002) — Jaws
Jaws (*The Spy Who Loved Me*, 1977, and *Moonraker*, 1979)

Max Zorin Nazi genetics research (*A View to a Kill*, 1985) — Jill Masterson golden girl
Jill Masterson golden girl (*Goldfinger*, 1964)

Solex agitator

U.S. Clipper Chip

U.S. Clipper Chip

Both encryption methods are based on real techniques, the Lektor probably on the Enigma cipher device, in which agents fed data in one end and decoded messages came out the other end on a paper roll. The U.S. Clipper Chip is still very cutting edge for a Bond film. Never mind that Bond's villain instantly cracks the Clipper Code, most likely untangling the Skipjack algorithm. In 1998, the NIST needed 22 pages of math to describe Skipjack.

Aston Martin DB5

A choice between Bond's first car and first drink. Bond's cars were always important. But the light blue convertible appeared only in *Dr. No*, whereas the martini stayed forever. Debate over "shaken, not stirred" will never be settled. But James would never bruise the gin.

martini

Aston Martin DB5

Aston Martin DB5

Aston Martin DB5 car
(*Goldfinger*, 1964)

Played by actor Richard Kiel, Jaws is a 7-foot assassin possessing incredible physical strength and titanium-steel teeth, capable of ripping out human throats and biting through the cable supporting a cable car above Rio de Janeiro. But in Bond, cars rule. Q updates Bond's DB5 with machine guns hidden behind the parking lights, smoke canisters fired from the exhaust, a sliding steel plate in the rear to repel bullets, and tire cutters extending from the hubcaps. It also has GPS, and reappeared in *Thunderball* and, much later, *GoldenEye*. The DB5 was the first truly over-the-top Bond car that did it all.

Lotus car-sub

Lotus car-sub

hydrofoil boat

The hydrofoil boat in *Thunderball* actually is nothing new, simply blending aero- and hydrodyamics. The Lotus Esprit car-submarine dives beneath the ocean, with four rear sprayers behind the license that fire cement at pursuers. In the water, it can discharge floating mines, underwater color smoke screens, torpedoes, even surface-to-air missiles. Very cool.

Jaws

The cool car-submarine versus Jaws. Dare we send two cars to the finals? Tough choice, but it's hard to turn thumbs down on a biting machine that treats industrial cable as dental floss. It has to be Jaws.

gobbling spaceship

Jaws

Jaws

A matchup in outer space. The space station is "radar invisible" until Bond turns off the radar-jamming system, at which point a battle ensues between marines and the bad guy, Drax, and the station catches fire. The gobbling spaceship is equally outrageous, but watching it "eat" the Jupiter 16 ship capsule is unforgettable.

Dodosaurs
by RICK MEYEROWITZ

The dinosaurs we know about were pretty strange. The ones we don't know about were even weirder. These creatures were called the Dodosaurs, and they were the first examples of Intelligent Design. Believe that and you can draw a line from the heyday of the Dodosaurs 70 million years ago during the Moronic Period, straight through the front door of the 700 Club. But that's a line for you to draw. My task is to choose Dodosaurs to "bracketize" here. I had to leave out some of the more interesting ones, such as the horribly unlucky Alleyoopteryx and the zonked-out Oblividont, but the list presented here gives you a pretty good idea of what Mother Nature was doing when she should've been working.

RICK MEYEROWITZ was the most prolific contributor of illustrated articles for *National Lampoon* magazine. He painted the poster for *Animal House* and was the creator of the magazine's trademark visual, the Mona Gorilla, which has been called "one of the enduring icons of American humor." Way back in the '80s Rick and Henry Beard published *Dodosaurs: The Dinosaurs That Didn't Make It*. After 9/11 Rick and Maira Kalman created the most loved *New Yorker* cover in recent memory, "New Yorkistan," about which the *New York Times* wrote, "when their cover came out, a dark cloud seemed to lift."

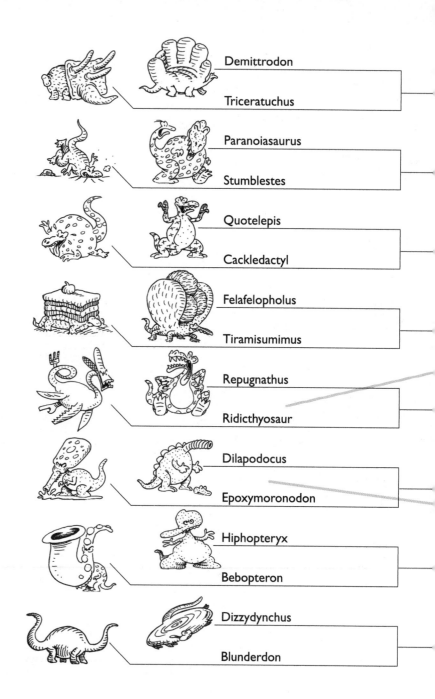

Demittrodon

Triceratuchus

Paranoiasaurus

Stumblestes

Quotelepis

Cackledactyl

Felafelopholus

Tiramisumimus

Repugnathus

Ridicthyosaur

Dilapodocus

Epoxymoronodon

Hiphopteryx

Bebopteron

Dizzydynchus

Blunderdon

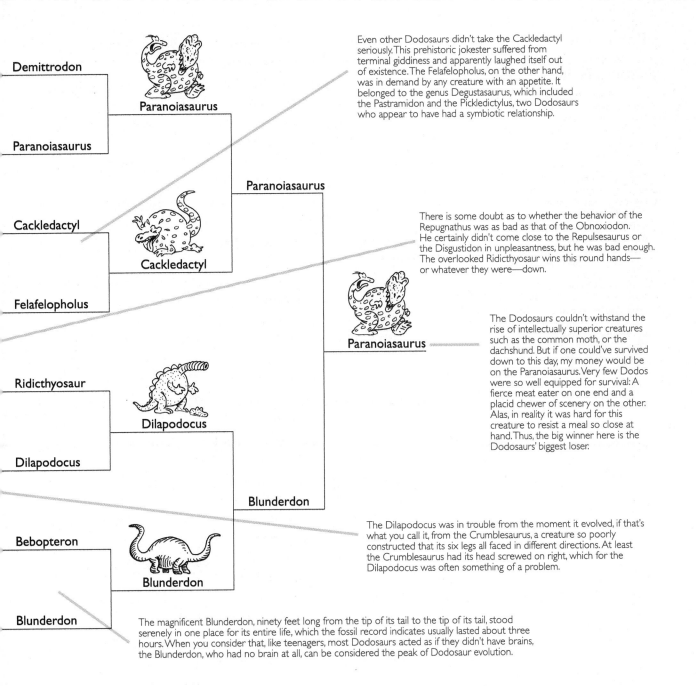

Demittrodon

Paranoiasaurus

Paranoiasaurus

Paranoiasaurus

Cackledactyl

Cackledactyl

Felafelopholus

Ridicthyosaur

Dilapodocus

Dilapodocus

Bebopteron

Blunderdon

Blunderdon

Paranoiasaurus

Blunderdon

Even other Dodosaurs didn't take the Cackledactyl seriously. This prehistoric jokester suffered from terminal giddiness and apparently laughed itself out of existence. The Felafelopholus, on the other hand, was in demand by any creature with an appetite. It belonged to the genus Degustasaurus, which included the Pastramidon and the Pickledictylus, two Dodosaurs who appear to have had a symbiotic relationship.

There is some doubt as to whether the behavior of the Repugnathus was as bad as that of the Obnoxiodon. He certainly didn't come close to the Repulsesaurus or the Disgustidon in unpleasantness, but he was bad enough. The overlooked Ridicthyosaur wins this round hands— or whatever they were—down.

The Dodosaurs couldn't withstand the rise of intellectually superior creatures such as the common moth, or the dachshund. But if one could've survived down to this day, my money would be on the Paranoiasaurus. Very few Dodos were so well equipped for survival: A fierce meat eater on one end and a placid chewer of scenery on the other. Alas, in reality it was hard for this creature to resist a meal so close at hand. Thus, the big winner here is the Dodosaurs' biggest loser.

The Dilapodocus was in trouble from the moment it evolved, if that's what you call it, from the Crumblesaurus, a creature so poorly constructed that its six legs all faced in different directions. At least the Crumblesaurus had its head screwed on right, which for the Dilapodocus was often something of a problem.

The magnificent Blunderdon, ninety feet long from the tip of its tail to the tip of its tail, stood serenely in one place for its entire life, which the fossil record indicates usually lasted about three hours. When you consider that, like teenagers, most Dodosaurs acted as if they didn't have brains, the Blunderdon, who had no brain at all, can be considered the peak of Dodosaur evolution.

Bob Dylan Cover Songs

by DALTON DELAN

There are approximately 6,000 commercially issued "covers" of Bob Dylan songs. The Internet has added about 10,000 more, though most are "live-in-concert" versions on song-sharing sites. Only the Beatles are covered more. Dylan tunes invite interpretation. Jimi Hendrix's transformative "All Along the Watchtower" proved in 1968 that Bob's rough-diamond style leaves plenty of room for cover artists to remake and even improve upon Dylan's songs. Dylan's most covered song by far is "Blowin' in the Wind," with almost 400 recordings, most of them ruinously saccharine. With such a huge catalog, some songs remain under the covers. My criteria were threefold: The cover had to (a) reimagine the song, (b) improve on the original, but (c) not distort it.

DALTON DELAN, an award-winning public television executive, is chief programming officer at WETA in Washington, D.C., producing music performances from the White House and many other popular programs. He can warble most Bob Dylan songs off-key, indisputable proof of a misspent youth.

Elvis Costello, "I Threw It All Away" — **Elvis Costello**
Elvis Presley, "Tomorrow Is a Long Time"

Janis Joplin, "Dear Landlord" — **Bonnie Raitt**
Bonnie Raitt, "Let's Keep It Between Us"

George Harrison, "If Not for You" — **George Harrison**
Richie Havens, "Just Like a Woman"

Neil Young, "Just Like Tom Thumb's Blues" — **Neil Young**
Joan Osborne, "Make You Feel My Love"

Jimi Hendrix, "All Along the Watchtower" — **Jimi Hendrix**
Eric Clapton, "Sign Language"

Bruce Springsteen, "Chimes of Freedom" — **Tom Petty**
Tom Petty & the Heartbreakers, "License to Kill"

The Waterboys, "Nobody 'Cept You" — **The Waterboys**
Ronnie Wood, "Seven Days"

The Everly Brothers, "Abandoned Love" — **Fairport Convention**
Fairport Convention, "Si Tu Dois Partir"

Patti Smith, "Wicked Messenger" — **Patti Smith**
Dixie Chicks, "Mississippi"

Joan Baez, "Love Is Just a Four-Letter Word" — **Nico**
Nico, "I'll Keep It with Mine"

The Band, "I Shall Be Released" — **The Band**
The Byrds, "Mr. Tambourine Man"

Thunderclap Newman, "Open the Door, Homer" — **Warren Zevon**
Warren Zevon, "Knockin' on Heaven's Door"

Roger McGuinn, "Up to Me" — **Roger McGuinn**
Rod Stewart, "The Groom's Still Waiting at the Altar"

Manfred Mann, "Quinn the Eskimo (The Mighty Quinn)" — **Pearl Jam**
Pearl Jam, "Masters of War"

Arlo Guthrie, "When the Ship Comes In" — **Arlo Guthrie**
Nanci Griffith, "Boots of Spanish Leather"

Coulson, Dean, McGuiness, Flint, "Sign on the Cross" — **The Searchers**
The Searchers, "Coming from the Heart (The Road Is Long)"

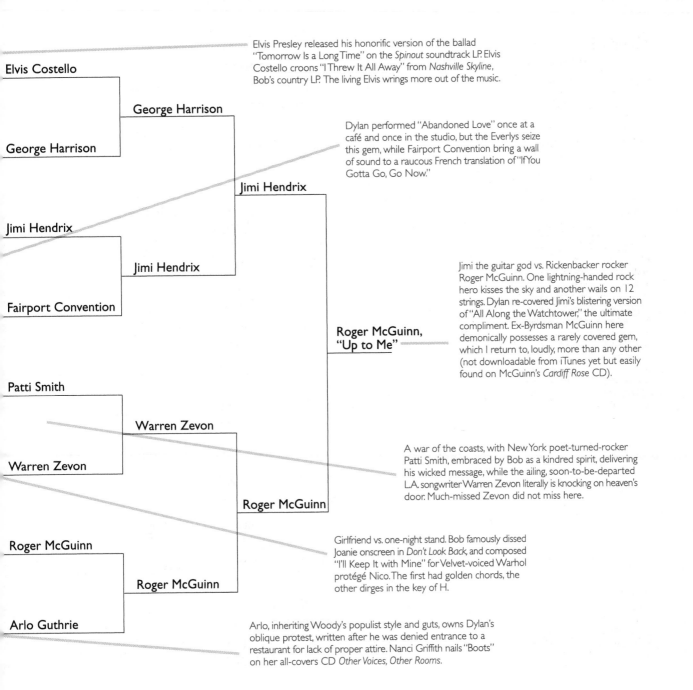

Elvis Costello

George Harrison

George Harrison

Jimi Hendrix

Jimi Hendrix

Jimi Hendrix

Fairport Convention

Roger McGuinn,
"Up to Me"

Patti Smith

Warren Zevon

Warren Zevon

Roger McGuinn

Roger McGuinn

Roger McGuinn

Arlo Guthrie

Elvis Presley released his honorific version of the ballad "Tomorrow Is a Long Time" on the *Spinout* soundtrack LP. Elvis Costello croons "I Threw It All Away" from *Nashville Skyline*, Bob's country LP. The living Elvis wrings more out of the music.

Dylan performed "Abandoned Love" once at a café and once in the studio, but the Everlys seize this gem, while Fairport Convention bring a wall of sound to a raucous French translation of "If You Gotta Go, Go Now."

Jimi the guitar god vs. Rickenbacker rocker Roger McGuinn. One lightning-handed rock hero kisses the sky and another wails on 12 strings. Dylan re-covered Jimi's blistering version of "All Along the Watchtower," the ultimate compliment. Ex-Byrdsman McGuinn here demonically possesses a rarely covered gem, which I return to, loudly, more than any other (not downloadable from iTunes yet but easily found on McGuinn's *Cardiff Rose* CD).

A war of the coasts, with New York poet-turned-rocker Patti Smith, embraced by Bob as a kindred spirit, delivering his wicked message, while the ailing, soon-to-be-departed L.A. songwriter Warren Zevon literally is knocking on heaven's door. Much-missed Zevon did not miss here.

Girlfriend vs. one-night stand. Bob famously dissed Joanie onscreen in *Don't Look Back*, and composed "I'll Keep It with Mine" for Velvet-voiced Warhol protégé Nico. The first had golden chords, the other dirges in the key of H.

Arlo, inheriting Woody's populist style and guts, owns Dylan's oblique protest, written after he was denied entrance to a restaurant for lack of proper attire. Nanci Griffith nails "Boots" on her all-covers CD *Other Voices, Other Rooms*.

Candy Bars
by SCOTT MOWBRAY

A great candy bar is pitch-perfect food. It's hard to innovate, though: chocolate, caramel, nuts, nougat, brittle, and/or peanut butter are unavoidable staples. Brand extensions such as extra-crispy Kit Kats and white-chocolate Reese's cups didn't make the cut. Nor did overpriced single-cocoa-plantation bars—I'm not interested in paying $7 for a munch. American entries had stiff competition, not least from the Brits, who put their candy bars in chilled vending machines in the London Underground, and the Canadians, who produce bars as good as Eugene Levy is funny. Not every entrant is a bar. Raisinets and Milk Duds are movie candy, included for their *bijou* functionality and nostalgia. The immortal and highly snackable Japanese Pocky is here but not the Cadbury Finger, clear antecedent of Twix. Taste is all. My taste.

SCOTT MOWBRAY is executive editor of Time Inc. He has eaten candy bars in North America, Europe, Africa, India, Afghanistan, Southeast Asia, Japan, and South America.

Pocky, the Japanese chocolate-covered pretzel rod, beats Hershey's Take 5; a pity, since Take 5 is one of the few recent innovations, featuring a convincing pretzel crunch.

What's this? The holy Butterfinger dropped by a Canadian import? Yes, CC's flaky-brittle peanut center is better than Butterfinger's.

Coffee Crisp, a recent import to the U.S. (2006), in a huge upset over classic Kit Kat. This Nestlé bar highlights how rare an ingredient coffee is in candy bars, presumably because kids don't drink a lot of coffee. It wins because of its superb wafer crunch and a distinct creamy-coffee note.

Dove bar — Dove bar
Hershey bar
Neilson Jersey Milk (Canada) — Jersey Milk
Toblerone (Swiss)
Nutrageous — 5th Avenue
5th Avenue
Reese's Peanut Butter Cup — Reese's PBC
Mr. Goodbar
Pocky (Japan) — Pocky
Take 5
Cadbury Burnt Almond (UK) — Eat-More
Eat-More (Canada)
Twix — Twix
PayDay
Neilson Crispy Crunch (Canada) — Crispy Crunch
Butterfinger
Cadbury Flake (UK) — Aero
Aero (UK)
Skor — Skor
Heath
Almond Joy — Mounds
Mounds
Kit Kat — Coffee Crisp
Coffee Crisp (Canada)
Snickers — Snickers
Baby Ruth
Mars — Mars
Milky Way
Hershey's Cookies 'n' Mint — H C&M
York Peppermint Pattie
Raisinets — Raisinets
Milk Duds

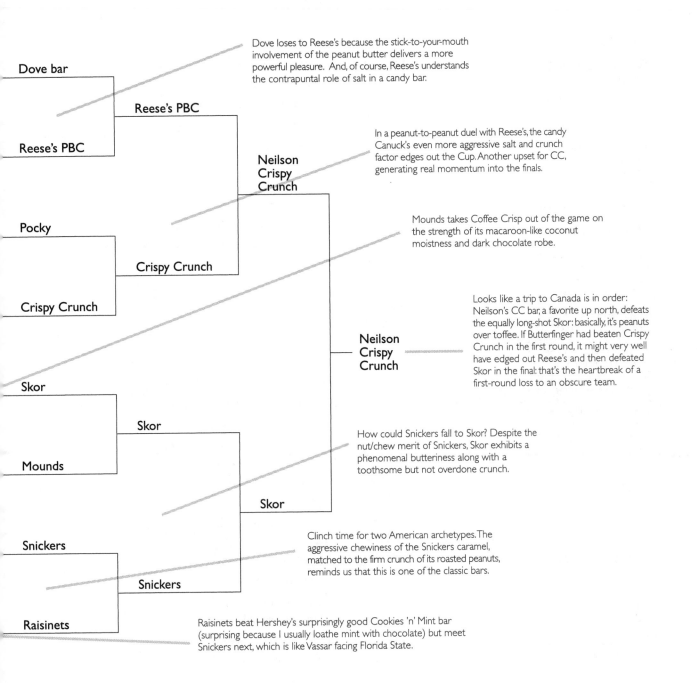

Dove bar

Reese's PBC

Reese's PBC

Dove loses to Reese's because the stick-to-your-mouth involvement of the peanut butter delivers a more powerful pleasure. And, of course, Reese's understands the contrapuntal role of salt in a candy bar.

In a peanut-to-peanut duel with Reese's, the candy Canuck's even more aggressive salt and crunch factor edges out the Cup. Another upset for CC, generating real momentum into the finals.

Neilson Crispy Crunch

Pocky

Crispy Crunch

Crispy Crunch

Mounds takes Coffee Crisp out of the game on the strength of its macaroon-like coconut moistness and dark chocolate robe.

Looks like a trip to Canada is in order: Neilson's CC bar, a favorite up north, defeats the equally long-shot Skor: basically, it's peanuts over toffee. If Butterfinger had beaten Crispy Crunch in the first round, it might very well have edged out Reese's and then defeated Skor in the final: that's the heartbreak of a first-round loss to an obscure team.

Neilson Crispy Crunch

Skor

Skor

Mounds

How could Snickers fall to Skor? Despite the nut/chew merit of Snickers, Skor exhibits a phenomenal butteriness along with a toothsome but not overdone crunch.

Skor

Snickers

Snickers

Clinch time for two American archetypes. The aggressive chewiness of the Snickers caramel, matched to the firm crunch of its roasted peanuts, reminds us that this is one of the classic bars.

Raisinets

Raisinets beat Hershey's surprisingly good Cookies 'n' Mint bar (surprising because I usually loathe mint with chocolate) but meet Snickers next, which is like Vassar facing Florida State.

Mondegreens, or Misheard Lyrics

by MIKKI HALPIN

A mondegreen is more than just a misheard lyric. It's a line that has been both misheard and rewritten in the bizarre recesses of the hearer's mind, creating new meaning. The term *mondegreen* was coined by Sylvia Wright in the November 1954 *Harper's Magazine*. Wright's mother often read to her from Percy's *Reliques*, including a poem which begins:

Ye Highlands and ye Lowlands
Oh, where hae ye been?
They hae slain the Earl o' Murray,
And laid him on the green.

Wright heard the last line as "And Lady Mondegreen," and declared that all such misheard lines would henceforth be known as mondegreens. Contenders who do well here combine musical fidelity to the original with the most ridiculous reinterpretation. The only thing funnier than a mondegreen is catching a friend singing one at top volume.

MIKKI HALPIN is a writer living in Brooklyn. She never got over misunderstanding the words to a Weirdos song in high school.

Lyric	Answer
Filling me softly with Islam	Islam
Oh, I wish I was an octopus's weiner	
Dirty jeans in a jungle jeep	pee
Let's pee in the corner	
Last night I dreamt of salt bagels	bagels
Go, go, Jason…water calls	
Where the sheeps have lo mein	Rita
No one wants to eat it, Rita	
Take yo ass and smash the elf	elf
Rikki don't lose that rubber	
Ten-inch waistband	bathroom
There's a bathroom on the right	
Had my first real sex dream	sex dream
'Scuse me while I kiss this guy	
Slow motion Walter, the fire engine guy	Jesus
All we are saying, is give Jesus pants	
The girl with colitis goes by	colitis
Bingo Jed had a light on	
I stood back in my pickup	pizza
I'll never leave your pizza burnin'	
A piece of Mama Daddy never had	Mama
Thought my mom sat on you	
Deck the halls with Buddy Holly	boobs
She's got electric boobs, her mom does too	
I've got two chickens to paralyze	chickens
Wrapped up like a douche, he had a boner in the night	
Waving your bladder all over the place	bacon
I wanna piece of bacon	
Hold me closer, Tony Danza	Danza
Edith was troubled by her horrible ass	
You made the rice; I made the gravy	gravy
Well, I work all day and I piddle in a can	

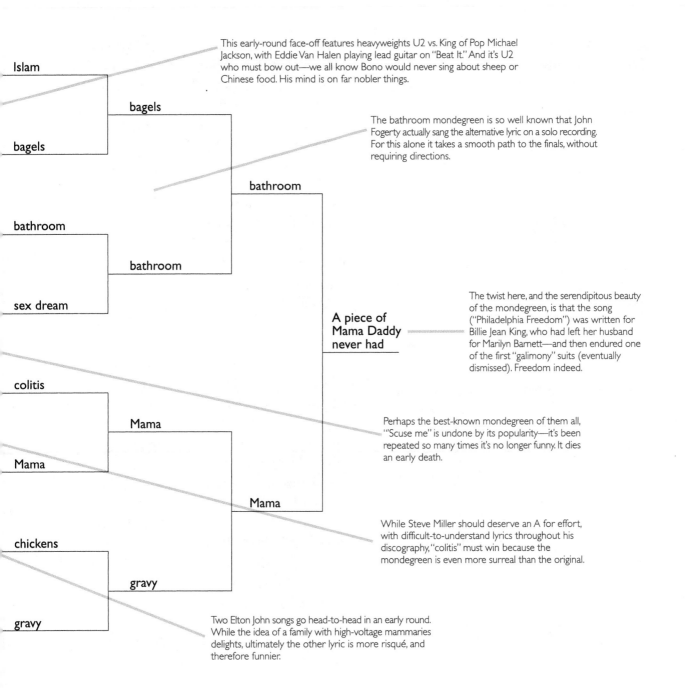

Islam

bagels

bagels

bathroom

bathroom

bathroom

bathroom

sex dream

A piece of
Mama Daddy
never had

colitis

Mama

Mama

Mama

Mama

chickens

gravy

gravy

This early-round face-off features heavyweights U2 vs. King of Pop Michael Jackson, with Eddie Van Halen playing lead guitar on "Beat It." And it's U2 who must bow out—we all know Bono would never sing about sheep or Chinese food. His mind is on far nobler things.

The bathroom mondegreen is so well known that John Fogerty actually sang the alternative lyric on a solo recording. For this alone it takes a smooth path to the finals, without requiring directions.

The twist here, and the serendipitous beauty of the mondegreen, is that the song ("Philadelphia Freedom") was written for Billie Jean King, who had left her husband for Marilyn Barnett—and then endured one of the first "galimony" suits (eventually dismissed). Freedom indeed.

Perhaps the best-known mondegreen of them all, "'Scuse me" is undone by its popularity—it's been repeated so many times it's no longer funny. It dies an early death.

While Steve Miller should deserve an A for effort, with difficult-to-understand lyrics throughout his discography, "colitis" must win because the mondegreen is even more surreal than the original.

Two Elton John songs go head-to-head in an early round. While the idea of a family with high-voltage mammaries delights, ultimately the other lyric is more risqué, and therefore funnier.

Celebrity Sports Couples

by SELENA ROBERTS

Power couples in sports—whether jocks hooking up with jocks, or jocks with famous non-jocks—not only provide a peephole into the intimate lives of sports icons but also a glimpse into ourselves: Did you believe Agassi was a Zen fool for Barbra Streisand or better off with Brooke Shields? Are you warmed by the 50-year marriage between NBA star Ernie Vandeweghe and Miss America 1952, Colleen Kay Hutchins, or shattered by the breakup between Lance Armstrong and Sheryl Crow? Where were you when Claudine Longet, a French chanteuse of the '60s, killed boyfriend Spider Sabich, an American champion skier, to launch one of the most riveting court trials of the '70s? It's a process of intangibles, but the greatest celebrity sports couples make you believe that love endures long after the cheering stops. It doesn't happen that often.

SELENA ROBERTS is the first woman sports columnist at the New York Times and the author of A Necessary Spectacle: Billie Jean King, Bobby Riggs, and the Tennis Match That Leveled the Game.

Namath and DiMaggio are two of the grandest names in New York sports history. But while DiMaggio fell in love with Marilyn, Joplin was only a passing fancy for Broadway Joe. Namath is eliminated here, but his link to Joplin will live on. She included Namath's name in the lyrics of a song, "Ego Rock."

Couples	
Rick Fox–Vanessa Williams	Fox–Williams
Eva Longoria–Tony Parker	
Andre Agassi–Steffi Graf	Agassi–Graf
Mia Hamm–Nomar Garciaparra	
Andre Agassi–Brooke Shields	Agassi–Shields
Olivier Chandon de Briailles–Christie Brinkley	
Pete Sampras–Bridgette Wilson	Agassi–Streisand
Andre Agassi–Barbra Streisand	
Jane Russell–Bob Waterfield	Russell–Waterfield
Frank Gifford–Kathie Lee Gifford	
Martina Hingis–Sergio Garcia	King–Riggs
Billie Jean King–Bobby Riggs	
Ashley Judd–Dario Franchitti	Knight–Lopez
Ray Knight–Nancy Lopez	
Anna Kournikova–Enrique Iglesias	Vandeweghe–Hutchins
Ernie Vandeweghe–Colleen Kay Hutchins	
Terry Bradshaw–Jo Jo Starbuck	Bradshaw–Starbuck
Mark Gastineau–Brigitte Nielsen	
Joe DiMaggio–Marilyn Monroe	DiMaggio–Monroe
Joe Namath–Janis Joplin	
Lance Armstrong–Sheryl Crow	Armstrong–Crow
Chris Webber–Tyra Banks	
Wayne Gretzky–Janet Jones	Gretzky–Jones
Andy Roddick–Mandy Moore	
Ahmad Rashad–Phylicia Rashad	Rashad–Rashad
Brian Urlacher–Paris Hilton	
Chris Evert–Burt Reynolds	Evert–Connors
Chris Evert–Jimmy Connors	
Bart Connor–Nadia Comaneci	Connor–Comaneci
Martina Navratilova–Judy Nelson	
Claudine Longet–Spider Sabich	Beckham–Spice
David Beckham–Posh Spice	

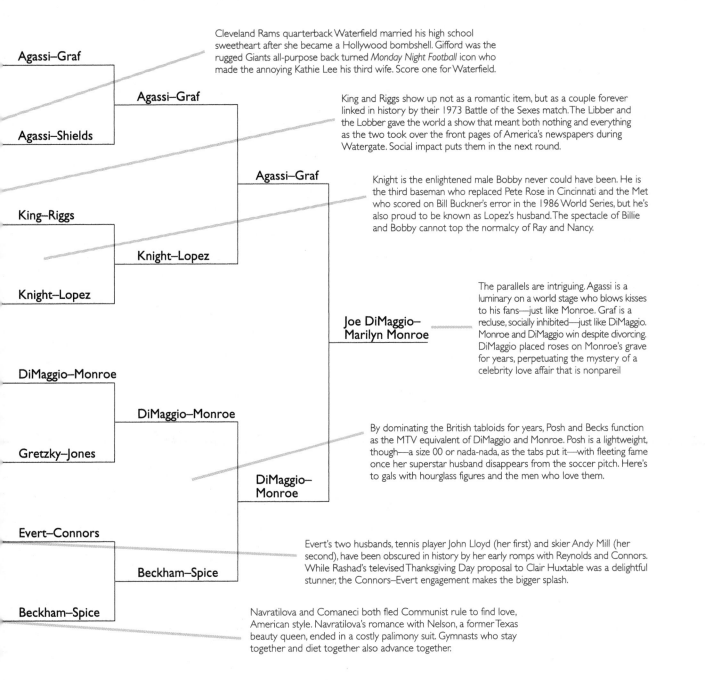

Agassi–Graf

Agassi–Graf

Agassi–Shields

Agassi–Graf

King–Riggs

Agassi–Graf

Knight–Lopez

Knight–Lopez

Joe DiMaggio–
Marilyn Monroe

DiMaggio–Monroe

DiMaggio–Monroe

Gretzky–Jones

DiMaggio–
Monroe

Evert–Connors

Beckham–Spice

Beckham–Spice

Cleveland Rams quarterback Waterfield married his high school sweetheart after she became a Hollywood bombshell. Gifford was the rugged Giants all-purpose back turned *Monday Night Football* icon who made the annoying Kathie Lee his third wife. Score one for Waterfield.

King and Riggs show up not as a romantic item, but as a couple forever linked in history by their 1973 Battle of the Sexes match. The Libber and the Lobber gave the world a show that meant both nothing and everything as the two took over the front pages of America's newspapers during Watergate. Social impact puts them in the next round.

Knight is the enlightened male Bobby never could have been. He is the third baseman who replaced Pete Rose in Cincinnati and the Met who scored on Bill Buckner's error in the 1986 World Series, but he's also proud to be known as Lopez's husband. The spectacle of Billie and Bobby cannot top the normalcy of Ray and Nancy.

The parallels are intriguing. Agassi is a luminary on a world stage who blows kisses to his fans—just like Monroe. Graf is a recluse, socially inhibited—just like DiMaggio. Monroe and DiMaggio win despite divorcing. DiMaggio placed roses on Monroe's grave for years, perpetuating the mystery of a celebrity love affair that is nonpareil

By dominating the British tabloids for years, Posh and Becks function as the MTV equivalent of DiMaggio and Monroe. Posh is a lightweight, though—a size 00 or nada-nada, as the tabs put it—with fleeting fame once her superstar husband disappears from the soccer pitch. Here's to gals with hourglass figures and the men who love them.

Evert's two husbands, tennis player John Lloyd (her first) and skier Andy Mill (her second), have been obscured in history by her early romps with Reynolds and Connors. While Rashad's televised Thanksgiving Day proposal to Clair Huxtable was a delightful stunner, the Connors–Evert engagement makes the bigger splash.

Navratilova and Comaneci both fled Communist rule to find love, American style. Navratilova's romance with Nelson, a former Texas beauty queen, ended in a costly palimony suit. Gymnasts who stay together and diet together also advance together.

CEOs
by JOHN A. BYRNE

Great CEOs are either Charismatics, who lead by force of personality; Entrepreneurs, who invent businesses that did not exist before; Statesmen, who operate on a vast geopolitical stage; or Operators, who keep the machine moving forward. There used to be a time when creating jobs and making America strong were serious benchmarks of a CEO's effectiveness. Now the yardsticks favor competing in a global economy, nurturing an unblemished public image, increasing productivity and cutting costs, creating shareholder wealth, and not backdating your stock options.

JOHN A. BYRNE is the executive editor of *Business Week*. He is the author or coauthor of seven business books, including *Jack*, his collaboration with former General Electric CEO Jack Welch, and *Odyssey*, his collaboration with former Apple Computer CEO John Sculley.

Marvin Bower (McKinsey) — **Bower**
Walter Wriston (Citibank)

Jack Welch (General Electric) — **Welch**
Alfred P. Sloan (General Motors)

Donald M. Kendall (Pepsi) — **Kendall**
Roberto Goizueta (Coca-Cola)

Lee Iacocca (Chrysler) — **Ford**
Henry Ford (Ford Motor)

Bill Gates (Microsoft) — **Dell**
Michael Dell (Dell Computer)

Bill Paley (CBS) — **Graham**
Katharine Graham (Washington Post)

Tom Watson, Jr. (IBM) — **Watson**
Andy Grove (Intel)

James E. Burke (J&J) — **Burke**
George Merck (Merck)

Steve Jobs (Apple) — **Jobs**
Howard Schultz (Starbucks)

Pete Rozelle (NFL) — **Rozelle**
Harold Geneen (ITT)

Warren Buffett (Berkshire Hathaway) — **Buffett**
Rupert Murdoch (News Corporation)

John H. Patterson (NCR) — **Smith**
Fred Smith (Federal Express)

David Packard (Hewlett-Packard) — **Packard**
Herb Kelleher (Southwest Airlines)

Walt Disney (Disney) — **Disney**
Amadeo Peter Giannini (Bank of America)

Ray Kroc (McDonald's) — **Kroc**
George Marshall (Marshall Plan)

Sam Walton (Wal-Mart) — **Walton**
J. Willard Marriott (Marriott Hotels)

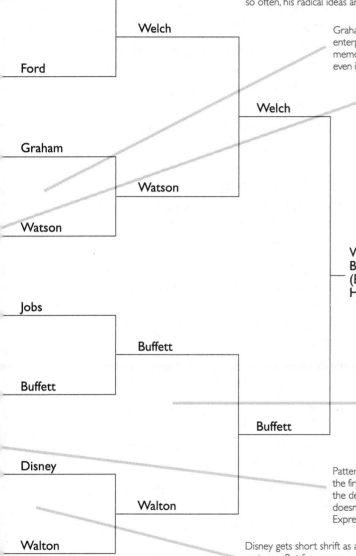

A battle of two oft-quoted management thinkers and doers. Sloan ran GM as a behemoth, smothering all in its path. Welch, at equally mammoth GE, was a more disruptive force. He taught managers that it's okay to "blow it up" if time has passed your business by. Quoted so often, his radical ideas are now conventional wisdom, sometimes clichés. Jack advances.

Graham is the only woman here, but her *Washington Post* is the only enterprise that brought down a president. And she's the only exec whose memoir won a Pulitzer. Watson, however, is the quintessential manager, even if his theories are what Welch, Jobs, Walton, and Buffett were fighting.

Rozelle marketed the NFL into America's biggest sport by launching the Super Bowl and somehow taming two dozen fractious super-wealthy team owners. Jobs, America's coolest entrepreneur, advances for teaching Apple to innovate and make a profit with less than 10 percent market share. Also, with iPod, iTunes, and Pixar, Jobs executed one of the all-time great second acts.

Warren Buffett (Berkshire Hathaway)

Creating more than $450 billion in market value, Welch made thousands of GE shareholders and managers very wealthy (but so did Gates, Dell, Walton, and, well, almost everyone here). Buffett created many Berkshire millionaires as well, but astonishingly in 2006 gave nearly all of his fortune back in the largest charitable bequest ever. Letting the Gates Foundation spend more than $30 billion of his money is a management stroke of Shakespearean brilliance. A CEO who gives it all back? What a concept. That's why Buffett wins. Besides, as coauthor of Welch's first book and editor of his weekly column for *Business Week*, I would stand accused of favoritism.

A toss-up, even though Walton is the ultimate hands-on builder, while Buffett is the ultimate macro-delegator, trusting like-minded managers at his mishmash of a conglomerate, Berkshire Hathaway, to do it their way. Which would be his way. Buffett's sleight of hand is more impressive. So is the folksy wisdom dispensed in his must-read annual reports.

Patterson ran NCR from 1884 to 1921 and might have been the first CEO as we now know the term. Even though he invented the designated sales territory and the paid suggestion system, he doesn't stand up well against Smith, who thought up Federal Express and made us rethink what "fast" really means.

Disney gets short shrift as a CEO because he built an empire on cartoons. But few names so clearly stand for something—still. Walton wins because he took a hoary idea—sell it cheaper—and executed it so well that Wal-Mart is literally its own economy.

Spokescharacters Who Will Shill for Food

by STUART ELLIOTT

Madison Avenue has long sought to personify its products in tangible form, the better to burn brand names into the minds of busy, distracted consumers. The colorful "critters" who peddle cereals, fast food, vegetables, fruit, candy, snacks, beer, and soft drinks enthusiastically beg to be consumed from endless supermarket shelves with the tools of their trade: distinctive, sharply drawn personalities and memorable catchphrases. The 32 entries were selected after a difficult culling of a century's worth of food spokescharacters, from the Morton Salt Girl and Uneeda Biscuit Boy—who for some unknown reason both walk around in raincoats—to the more visually sophisticated, yet still shill-happy, pitchfigures of the 21st century.

STUART ELLIOTT is the longtime advertising columnist at the New York Times and is making his foray into new media with e-mail newsletters and podcasts for New York Times Digital. He is not old enough to remember Mr. Peanut's birth but recalls the stores that the dapper legume presided over in Times Square and on the Atlantic City boardwalk.

Burger King	Burger King
Ronald McDonald	
Wendy (of Wendy's)	Jack
Jack (of Jack in the Box)	
Big Boy	Spongmonkeys
Quiznos Spongmonkeys	
Tony the Tiger	Tony
Cornelius (Kellogg's Corn Flakes rooster)	
Sonny the Cuckoo (Cocoa Puffs)	Trix rabbit
Trix rabbit	
Cap'n Crunch	Lucky
Lucky the Leprechaun (Lucky Charms)	
Snap, Crackle, and Pop (Rice Krispies)	Snap, Crackle, and Pop
Keebler elves	
Mr. Peanut	Mr. Peanut
Frito Bandito	
Choo Choo Charlie (Good & Plenty)	Bazooka Joe
Bazooka Joe (Bazooka gum)	
Chester Cheetah (Cheetos)	Jack and Bingo
Sailor Jack and Bingo (Cracker Jack)	
Poppin' Fresh, the Pillsbury Doughboy	Pillsbury Doughboy
Quaker Man	
Jolly Green Giant	Green Giant
Heinz Tomato Man	
Chiquita Banana	Chiquita
California Raisins	
Punchy (Hawaiian Punch)	Punchy
Tropic-Ana (Tropicana orange juice)	
Psyche (White Rock soft drinks)	Coca-Cola Sprite Boy
Coca-Cola Sprite Boy	
Hamm's bear	Hamm's bear
Bert and Harry Piel (Piel's beer)	

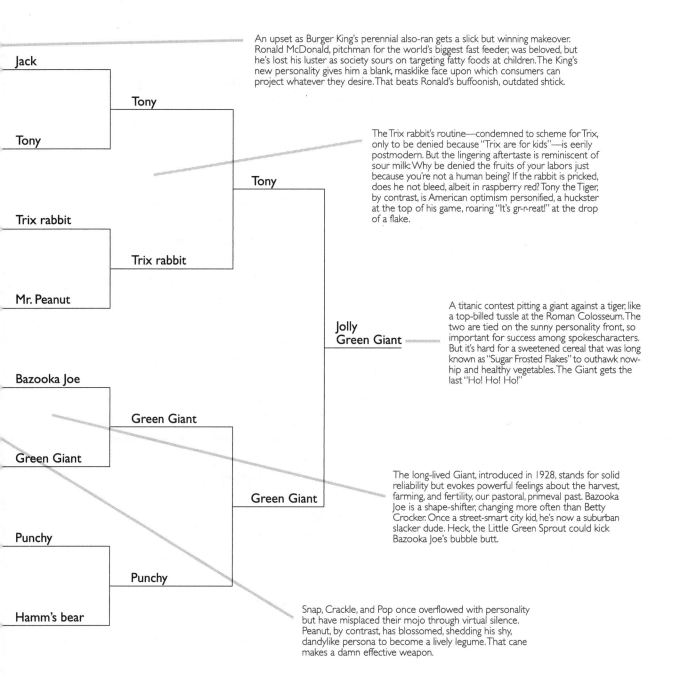

Jack

Tony

Tony

An upset as Burger King's perennial also-ran gets a slick but winning makeover. Ronald McDonald, pitchman for the world's biggest fast feeder, was beloved, but he's lost his luster as society sours on targeting fatty foods at children. The King's new personality gives him a blank, masklike face upon which consumers can project whatever they desire. That beats Ronald's buffoonish, outdated shtick.

Tony

The Trix rabbit's routine—condemned to scheme for Trix, only to be denied because "Trix are for kids"—is eerily postmodern. But the lingering aftertaste is reminiscent of sour milk: Why be denied the fruits of your labors just because you're not a human being? If the rabbit is pricked, does he not bleed, albeit in raspberry red? Tony the Tiger, by contrast, is American optimism personified, a huckster at the top of his game, roaring "It's gr-r-reat!" at the drop of a flake.

Trix rabbit

Trix rabbit

Mr. Peanut

Jolly
Green Giant

A titanic contest pitting a giant against a tiger, like a top-billed tussle at the Roman Colosseum. The two are tied on the sunny personality front, so important for success among spokescharacters. But it's hard for a sweetened cereal that was long known as "Sugar Frosted Flakes" to outhawk now-hip and healthy vegetables. The Giant gets the last "Ho! Ho! Ho!"

Bazooka Joe

Green Giant

Green Giant

Green Giant

The long-lived Giant, introduced in 1928, stands for solid reliability but evokes powerful feelings about the harvest, farming, and fertility, our pastoral, primeval past. Bazooka Joe is a shape-shifter, changing more often than Betty Crocker. Once a street-smart city kid, he's now a suburban slacker dude. Heck, the Little Green Sprout could kick Bazooka Joe's bubble butt.

Punchy

Punchy

Hamm's bear

Snap, Crackle, and Pop once overflowed with personality but have misplaced their mojo through virtual silence. Peanut, by contrast, has blossomed, shedding his shy, dandylike persona to become a lively legume. That cane makes a damn effective weapon.

Cheese

by MAX McCALMAN
and DAVID GIBBONS

Top-quality cheese is a miracle born of the many factors that comprise *terroir*—location, microclimate, animal breed, and seasonal fluctuations—coupled with the skills of artisans who manage and milk the herds and curdle and cure the milk. Among the world's 200 or so elite cheeses, many are fringe players that fade in and out of obscurity quickly. The 32 entries here, though reliable and accessible, are still moving targets. Humble achievers may peak just in time to eliminate more famous presumptive champions. Household names such as Cheddar, Parmesan, and Gouda are represented here only by the genuine, raw-milk artisanal versions—not by the industrial, commercialized brands found in most supermarket dairy cases.

Maître fromager MAX McCALMAN plies his trade as an exacting yet sympathetic professional cheese snob at Picholine and Artisanal restaurants in Manhattan, and at Artisanal Premium Cheeses, the ripening facility, wholesaler, and education center. With DAVID GIBBONS, he has coauthored *The Cheese Plate* and the 2006 James Beard Award–winning *Cheese: A Connoisseur's Guide to the World's Best.*

Round 1	Round 2
Sbrinz	Sbrinz
Brillat-Savarin	
Queso de la Serena	Queso de la Serena
Uplands Pleasant Ridge Reserve	
Vacherin Fribourgeois	Vacherin Fribourgeois
Époisses	
Rogue River Blue	Stilton
Stilton	
English Farmhouse Cheddar (Montgomery's)	Monty's Cheddar
Brie de Melun	
Azeitao	Azeitao
Le Moulis	
Saint-Félicien	Stanser Schafkäse
Stanser Schafkäse	
Harbourne Blue	Parmigiano-Reggiano
Parmigiano-Reggiano	
Roquefort	Roquefort
Camembert	
Lancashire	Lancashire
Pouligny-Saint-Pierre	
Monte Enebro	Monte Enebro
Zamorano	
Mimolette	Gruyère
Gruyère (genuine Swiss farmhouse)	
Aged Farmhouse Gouda	Gouda
Vacherin du Haut-Doubs	
Valençay	Stanser Rötelli
Stanser Rötelli	
Cabrales	Cabrales
Robiola (tre latti)	
Banon	Spenwood
Spenwood	

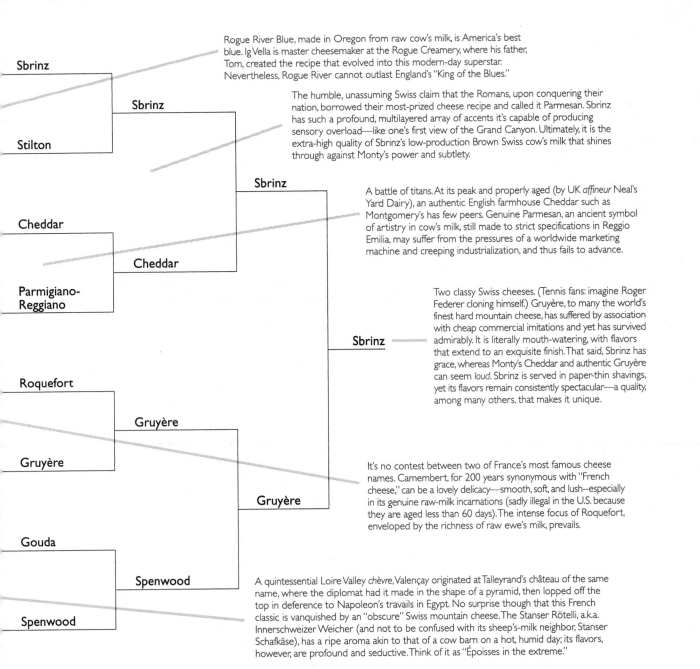

Sbrinz

Stilton

Cheddar

Parmigiano-Reggiano

Roquefort

Gruyère

Gouda

Spenwood

Sbrinz

Cheddar

Gruyère

Spenwood

Sbrinz

Sbrinz

Gruyère

Sbrinz

Rogue River Blue, made in Oregon from raw cow's milk, is America's best blue. Ig Vella is master cheesemaker at the Rogue Creamery, where his father, Tom, created the recipe that evolved into this modern-day superstar. Nevertheless, Rogue River cannot outlast England's "King of the Blues."

The humble, unassuming Swiss claim that the Romans, upon conquering their nation, borrowed their most-prized cheese recipe and called it Parmesan. Sbrinz has such a profound, multilayered array of accents it's capable of producing sensory overload—like one's first view of the Grand Canyon. Ultimately, it is the extra-high quality of Sbrinz's low-production Brown Swiss cow's milk that shines through against Monty's power and subtlety.

A battle of titans. At its peak and properly aged (by UK *affineur* Neal's Yard Dairy), an authentic English farmhouse Cheddar such as Montgomery's has few peers. Genuine Parmesan, an ancient symbol of artistry in cow's milk, still made to strict specifications in Reggio Emilia, may suffer from the pressures of a worldwide marketing machine and creeping industrialization, and thus fails to advance.

Two classy Swiss cheeses. (Tennis fans: imagine Roger Federer cloning himself.) Gruyère, to many the world's finest hard mountain cheese, has suffered by association with cheap commercial imitations and yet has survived admirably. It is literally mouth-watering, with flavors that extend to an exquisite finish. That said, Sbrinz has grace, whereas Monty's Cheddar and authentic Gruyère can seem *loud*. Sbrinz is served in paper-thin shavings, yet its flavors remain consistently spectacular—a quality, among many others, that makes it unique.

It's no contest between two of France's most famous cheese names. Camembert, for 200 years synonymous with "French cheese," can be a lovely delicacy—smooth, soft, and lush--especially in its genuine raw-milk incarnations (sadly illegal in the U.S. because they are aged less than 60 days). The intense focus of Roquefort, enveloped by the richness of raw ewe's milk, prevails.

A quintessential Loire Valley *chèvre*, Valençay originated at Talleyrand's château of the same name, where the diplomat had it made in the shape of a pyramid, then lopped off the top in deference to Napoleon's travails in Egypt. No surprise though that this French classic is vanquished by an "obscure" Swiss mountain cheese. The Stanser Rötelli, a.k.a. Innerschweizer Weicher (and not to be confused with its sheep's-milk neighbor, Stanser Schafkäse), has a ripe aroma akin to that of a cow barn on a hot, humid day; its flavors, however, are profound and seductive. Think of it as "Époisses in the extreme."

Chick Flicks
by CARRIE GERLACH CECIL

Any chick-flick checklist includes: (1) an empowered female lead overcoming insurmountable relationship obstacles, (2) a real woman in search of a fantasy man who changes or comes back, (3) female friendship and bonding, (4) women kicking ass metaphorically and physically, (5) copious tears, (6) belly laughter, and (7) quotable lines that make it to the water cooler or into a wedding speech. In addition, you see your BFF (best friend forever), your ex, or yourself in it. It induces groans from guys when you rent it. There's a 30 percent chance that Tom Hanks, Julia Roberts, or Hugh Grant is in it. And your mom loves it.

With two chick-flick staples—Julia Roberts *and* Hugh Grant—you'd think the smartly written *Notting Hill* would get out of the early rounds. But even ultra-sappy lines like "Don't forget, I'm also just a girl, standing in front of a boy, asking him to love her" can't beat Babs and Bob.

Two black-and-white beauties with Cary Grant. *Philadelphia Story* has the sophisticated talk, but *Affair* goes straight to the cardiovascular system. It even gets a featured role in *Sleepless in Seattle*.

CARRIE GERLACH CECIL's first novel, *Emily's Reasons Why Not*, was adapted into a comedy for ABC, starring Heather Graham, of which she was a producer. She is married to Chuck Cecil, a former Pro Bowl safety and now a defensive coach for the Tennessee Titans. They have a daughter, Charli Alleene. *Sports Illustrated* once put Chuck on the cover, asking if he was "Too Vicious for the NFL?" Yet he quotes *Forrest Gump* lines and stops switching radio stations when "The Wind Beneath My Wings" is playing. Carrie is currently at work on her second novel and two television pilots.

So what if Anthony Minghella's *The English Patient* won the Oscar? Ralph Fiennes's war-scarred lover is not as cavity-causing as Tom Hanks's lovable widower in *Sleepless in Seattle*. The Golden Kleenex to Meg Ryan and Hanks for being the dominant chick-flick couple of the 1990s.

Bracket

- Beaches
- Bend It Like Beckham
  - → Beaches
- The Bodyguard
- Forrest Gump
  - → Forrest Gump
- Pretty Woman
- Sense and Sensibility
  - → Pretty Woman
- Charlie's Angels
- The Women
  - → The Women
- Titanic
- Bridget Jones's Diary
  - → Titanic
- Notting Hill
- The Way We Were
  - → The Way We Were
- Sophie's Choice
- An Officer and a Gentlemen
  - → Sophie's Choice
- Barefoot in the Park
- When Harry Met Sally
  - → When Harry Met Sally
- An Affair to Remember
- The Philadelphia Story
  - → An Affair to Remember
- Working Girl
- The First Wives Club
  - → The First Wives Club
- Love Story
- The Shop Around the Corner
  - → Love Story
- Erin Brockovich
- Terms of Endearment
  - → Terms of Endearment
- Steel Magnolias
- Ghost
  - → Steel Magnolias
- Four Weddings and a Funeral
- Something's Got to Give
  - → Something's Got to Give
- Sleepless in Seattle
- The English Patient
  - → Sleepless in Seattle
- The Notebook
- Bull Durham
  - → The Notebook

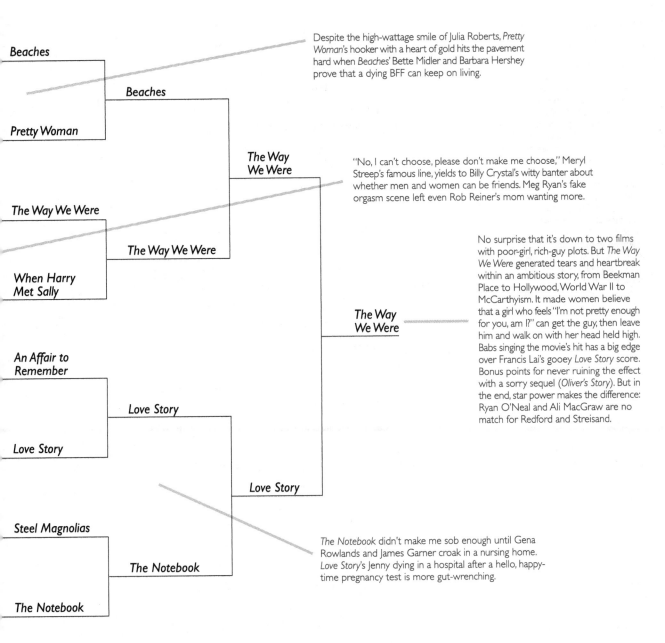

Beaches

Pretty Woman

Beaches

The Way
We Were

The Way We Were

When Harry
Met Sally

The Way We Were

An Affair to
Remember

Love Story

Love Story

The Way
We Were

Love Story

Steel Magnolias

The Notebook

The Notebook

Despite the high-wattage smile of Julia Roberts, *Pretty Woman*'s hooker with a heart of gold hits the pavement hard when *Beaches*' Bette Midler and Barbara Hershey prove that a dying BFF can keep on living.

"No, I can't choose, please don't make me choose," Meryl Streep's famous line, yields to Billy Crystal's witty banter about whether men and women can be friends. Meg Ryan's fake orgasm scene left even Rob Reiner's mom wanting more.

No surprise that it's down to two films with poor-girl, rich-guy plots. But *The Way We Were* generated tears and heartbreak within an ambitious story, from Beekman Place to Hollywood, World War II to McCarthyism. It made women believe that a girl who feels "I'm not pretty enough for you, am I?" can get the guy, then leave him and walk on with her head held high. Babs singing the movie's hit has a big edge over Francis Lai's gooey *Love Story* score. Bonus points for never ruining the effect with a sorry sequel (*Oliver's Story*). But in the end, star power makes the difference: Ryan O'Neal and Ali MacGraw are no match for Redford and Streisand.

The Notebook didn't make me sob enough until Gena Rowlands and James Garner croak in a nursing home. *Love Story*'s Jenny dying in a hospital after a hello, happy-time pregnancy test is more gut-wrenching.

Crosswordese
by TYLER HINMAN

Crossword puzzles have taken a decidedly modern leap in recent years, with greater emphasis on pop culture and modern words and phrases. However, the exigencies of crossword construction sometimes can only be eased by words with friendly letter patterns, and this ensures the eternal life of some words that would otherwise be doomed to obscurity. Thirty-two examples of crosswordese do battle here. Many more examples exist, but these make the cut for their frequent use and virtual unknowability to a puzzling novice.

TYLER HINMAN is an on-and-off crossword constructor. He is better known as the youngest champion in the history of the American Crossword Puzzle Tournament and one of the featured solvers in the 2005 documentary *Wordplay*. He received a degree in information technology from Rensselaer Polytechnic Institute (go Engineers!) in 2006. He is currently a bond trader in Chicago.

mine entrance = ADIT — **ADIT**
Greek portico = STOA

cube creator Rubik = ERNO — **ESNE**
feudal laborer = ESNE

mythical king of the Huns = ATLI — **MOA**
extinct bird of New Zealand = MOA

seed covering = ARIL — **ODA**
harem chamber = ODA

Asian nursemaid = AMAH — **AMAH**
Persian fairy = PERI

former name of Tokyo = EDO — **INEE**
arrow poison = INEE

architect Saarinen = EERO — **GOA**
former Portuguese colony in India = GOA

banned orchard spray = ALAR — **PROA**
Malay sailboat = PROA

currency transaction fee = AGIO — **SERE**
bone-dry = SERE

Bambi's aunt = ENA — **EVOE**
Greek reveler's cry = EVOE

early Icelandic literature = EDDA — **EDDA**
"Dies ____" (hymn) = IRAE

indigo dye source = ANIL — **ANIL**
Oklahoma Indian = OTOE

Celebes ox = ANOA — **ANOA**
S-shaped molding = OGEE

westernmost Aleutian island = ATTU — **ATTU**
ancient road to Rome = ITER

muse of love poems = ERATO — **ETUI**
small ornamental case = ETUI

petri dish gelatin = AGAR — **AGAR**
British WWII gun = STEN

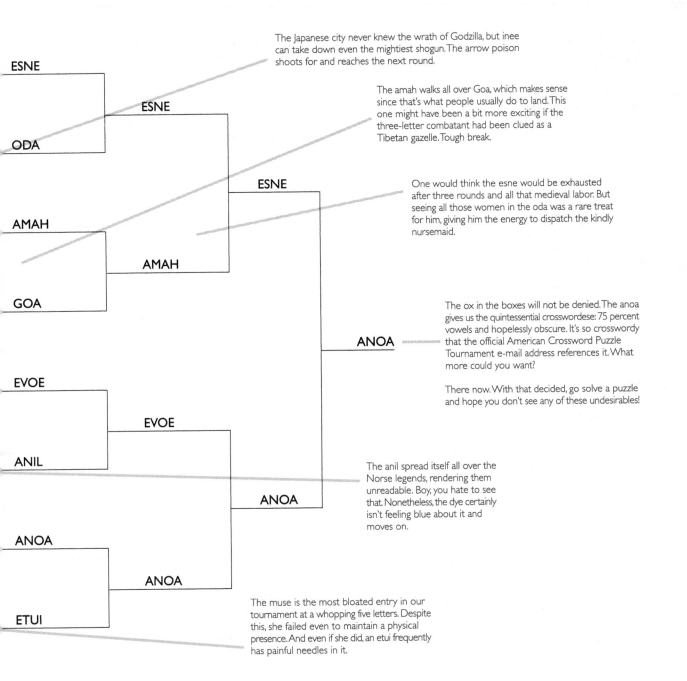

ESNE

ODA

ESNE

The Japanese city never knew the wrath of Godzilla, but inee can take down even the mightiest shogun. The arrow poison shoots for and reaches the next round.

ESNE

The amah walks all over Goa, which makes sense since that's what people usually do to land. This one might have been a bit more exciting if the three-letter combatant had been clued as a Tibetan gazelle. Tough break.

AMAH

GOA

AMAH

ESNE

One would think the esne would be exhausted after three rounds and all that medieval labor. But seeing all those women in the oda was a rare treat for him, giving him the energy to dispatch the kindly nursemaid.

ANOA

The ox in the boxes will not be denied. The anoa gives us the quintessential crosswordese: 75 percent vowels and hopelessly obscure. It's so crosswordy that the official American Crossword Puzzle Tournament e-mail address references it. What more could you want?

There now. With that decided, go solve a puzzle and hope you don't see any of these undesirables!

EVOE

ANIL

EVOE

ANOA

The anil spread itself all over the Norse legends, rendering them unreadable. Boy, you hate to see that. Nonetheless, the dye certainly isn't feeling blue about it and moves on.

ANOA

ETUI

ANOA

The muse is the most bloated entry in our tournament at a whopping five letters. Despite this, she failed even to maintain a physical presence. And even if she did, an etui frequently has painful needles in it.

Classic Movie Comedies

by ROBERT WUHL

In a crowded category where standards such as *Bringing Up Baby* and *The Philadelphia Story*, both with Katharine Hepburn and Cary Grant; the underrated *Lover Come Back*, starring Rock Hudson and Doris Day; *The Thrill of It All*, a funny/smart Doris Day–James Garner sendup of TV written by Carl Reiner; and Edward G. Robinson's hilarious *A Slight Case of Murder* did not merit invitations, the criterion is blunt but simple: If these two films were on at the same time, which one would I watch with someone special for the first time? To merit the term "classic," they must be at least 25 years old. (Sorry, *Wedding Crashers*.) My bias leans to romantic comedies, especially those that skillfully transition from broad comedy to satire to pathos. I do not discriminate among the subgenres of Slapstick, Gross-Out, Dialogue-Driven, or Urbane, but you won't find any Chaplin or Keaton (Buster, not Diane) here; those masters of the silent era were left behind because only films with dialogue made the initial cut.

ROBERT WUHL is a two-time Emmy Award–winning writer. He also appeared in the films *Bull Durham*, *Cobb*, *Batman*, and *Good Morning, Vietnam*. He was the creator and star of the television series *Arli$$* and *Assume the Position with Mr. Wuhl*.

The Thin Man is a seamless combination of screwball comedy and murder mystery by which all comedy/mysteries are measured. Plus, I'd rather hang out with Asta than Otter.

A neglected satire of small-time beauty pageants bests the 1932 Marx Brothers classic because of Jerry Belson's knockout script and Barbara Feldon as a has-been beauty queen.

Despite a sly performance by Victor Mature and being Neil Simon's first screenwriting credit, *After the Fox*, a Peter Sellers caper, yields to one of the few comedies to win a Best Director Oscar (for Leo McCarey).

An early Preston Sturges smackdown. *McGinty* is a snappy satire of big-city politics, but *July*, a workplace farce about a radio contest and the American dream, has a killer payoff that lets it advance.

A closer look at these two trenchant by-products of the Nixon years shows that Altman's *M*A*S*H* is almost as episodic as the *Police Academy* series, albeit much smarter. *Shampoo* is witty and very sexy. A winning combo.

Round 1	Round 2
The Odd Couple / The Apartment	The Apartment
Blazing Saddles / The Producers	The Producers
Young Frankenstein / Abbott and Costello Meet Frankenstein	Abbott and Costello
Animal House / The Thin Man	The Thin Man
Horse Feathers / Smile	Smile
The Awful Truth / After the Fox	The Awful Truth
The Graduate / Heaven Can Wait (1978)	The Graduate
Annie Hall / Bananas	Annie Hall
The Court Jester / Some Like It Hot	Some Like It Hot
The Great McGinty / Christmas in July	Christmas in July
Shampoo / M*A*S*H	Shampoo
To Be or Not to Be (1941) / The Loved One	To Be or Not to Be
It's a Mad, Mad, Mad, Mad World / Cat Ballou	Cat Ballou
It Happened One Night / The Pink Panther (1963)	It Happened One Night
His Girl Friday / Network	Network
The Ruling Class / Dr. Strangelove	Dr. Strangelove

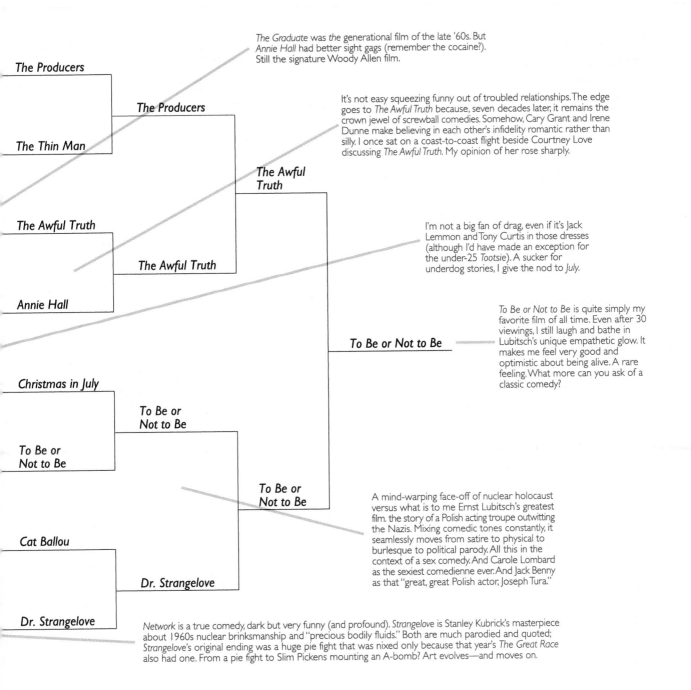

The Producers

The Producers

The Thin Man

The Graduate was *the* generational film of the late '60s. But *Annie Hall* had better sight gags (remember the cocaine?). Still the signature Woody Allen film.

The Awful Truth

The Awful Truth

It's not easy squeezing funny out of troubled relationships. The edge goes to *The Awful Truth* because, seven decades later, it remains the crown jewel of screwball comedies. Somehow, Cary Grant and Irene Dunne make believing in each other's infidelity romantic rather than silly. I once sat on a coast-to-coast flight beside Courtney Love discussing *The Awful Truth*. My opinion of her rose sharply.

The Awful Truth

Annie Hall

I'm not a big fan of drag, even if it's Jack Lemmon and Tony Curtis in those dresses (although I'd have made an exception for the under-25 *Tootsie*). A sucker for underdog stories, I give the nod to *July*.

To Be or Not to Be

To Be or Not to Be is quite simply my favorite film of all time. Even after 30 viewings, I still laugh and bathe in Lubitsch's unique empathetic glow. It makes me feel very good and optimistic about being alive. A rare feeling. What more can you ask of a classic comedy?

Christmas in July

To Be or Not to Be

To Be or Not to Be

To Be or Not to Be

A mind-warping face-off of nuclear holocaust versus what is to me Ernst Lubitsch's greatest film. the story of a Polish acting troupe outwitting the Nazis. Mixing comedic tones constantly, it seamlessly moves from satire to physical to burlesque to political parody. All this in the context of a sex comedy. And Carole Lombard as the sexiest comedienne ever. And Jack Benny as that "great, great Polish actor, Joseph Tura."

Cat Ballou

Dr. Strangelove

Dr. Strangelove

Network is a true comedy, dark but very funny (and profound). *Strangelove* is Stanley Kubrick's masterpiece about 1960s nuclear brinksmanship and "precious bodily fluids." Both are much parodied and quoted; *Strangelove*'s original ending was a huge pie fight that was nixed only because that year's *The Great Race* also had one. From a pie fight to Slim Pickens mounting an A-bomb? Art evolves—and moves on.

Conspiracy Theories

by KURT ANDERSEN

Real conspiracies exist, of course. The Mafia is a conspiracy. The late Philip Johnson's influence over architecture amounted to a conspiracy for half a century. There really is a de facto vast right-wing conspiracy that demonized the Clintons, just as there is a de facto vast left-wing conspiracy that controls the academy. Iran-contra and BCCI and Enron were pretty effective conspiracies while they lasted. And not every conspiracy is malign. None of the earnestly alleged conspiracy theories here, however, has been proved. Indeed, they range from the almost certainly untrue to the preposterous to the insane—which doesn't mean that millions of people don't believe them. The outcomes are democratically decided: in each round, the theory with the greatest number of devotees who display the greatest passion wins.

KURT ANDERSEN is the author of the novels *Turn of the Century* and *Heyday*, host of the public radio show *Studio 360*, and a columnist for *New York* magazine. He cofounded *Spy* and Inside.com, was editor in chief of *New York*, and has been a columnist and critic for the *New Yorker* and *Time*.

The Bilderberg Group (like the Trilateral Commission and the Council on Foreign Relations) actually is a group of powerful VIPs scheming to influence international politics and economics—and they're very secretive. Of the first-round theories, among the least implausible.

Reptilian humanoids are descendants of dinosaurs from Antarctica who now live in various remote areas; they may shape-shift; and both presidents Bush are quite possibly Reptoids—which gives the first-round battle against GOP-loving Diebold a certain intramural frisson.

Tournament bracket:

- lunar landings faked / Kennedys killed Marilyn Monroe → **JFK/RFK killed Marilyn**
- Felix Rohatyn and Lynne Cheney are leaders of a crypto-Nazi "Synarchist" plan to control world / jet contrails are U.S. government "chemtrails" → **government "chemtrails"**
- Freemasons/Illuminati control world / omnipotent God created and controls the universe → **omnipotent God**
- FDR complicit in Pearl Harbor attack / UN and WHO seek to criminalize health supplements → **FDR's Pearl Harbor**
- Bilderberg Group controls world / U.S. shot down TWA flight 800 → **TWA flight 800**
- U.S. hides truth about extraterrestrials / Teletubbies & SpongeBob are gay propaganda → **U.S. hides ETs**
- HIV/AIDS a genocidal U.S. government plot / Princess Diana murdered → **Di murdered**
- reptilian humanoids seek to control world / Diebold Inc. rigs voting machines for GOP → **Diebold vote rigging**
- Jews control world via media, finance, etc. / fluoride in drinking water a Soviet plot → **Jews control world**
- CIA behind crack cocaine trade / Vatican suppresses facts about early Christianity → **Vatican suppresses truth**
- U.S. officials complicit in JFK assassination / Pentagon's Alaskan HAARP facility → **JFK assassination**
- Hearst/Mellon cartel criminalized hemp / Oklahoma City bomb a government plot → **U.S. Oklahoma City plot**
- 9/11 a U.S./Enron/Saudi/Israeli inside job / extraterrestrials abduct earthlings → **9/11 a U.S. plot**
- Trilateral Commission controls world / Council on Foreign Relations controls world → **Council controls**
- Saddam Hussein complicit in 9/11 / Skull and Bones controls world → **Saddam Hussein complicit in 9/11**
- Waco actually a UN/U.S. mass murder / Avian flu a U.S. government hoax → **Waco coverup**

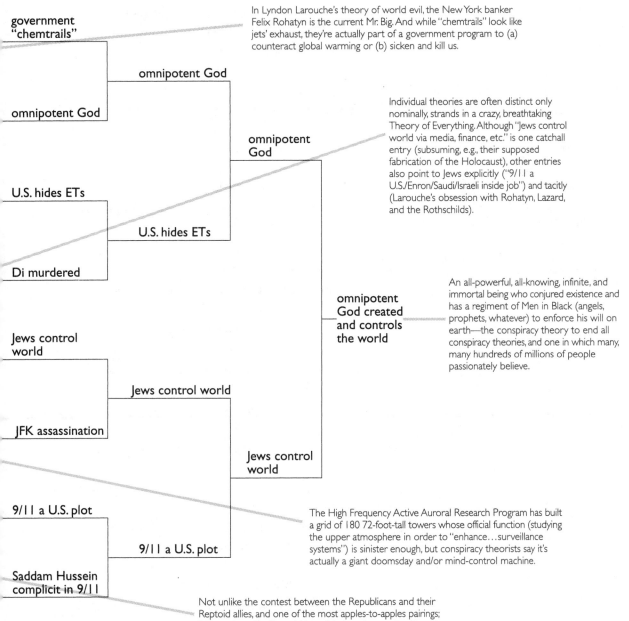

government
"chemtrails"

In Lyndon Larouche's theory of world evil, the New York banker Felix Rohatyn is the current Mr. Big. And while "chemtrails" look like jets' exhaust, they're actually part of a government program to (a) counteract global warming or (b) sicken and kill us.

omnipotent God

omnipotent God

omnipotent
God

Individual theories are often distinct only nominally, strands in a crazy, breathtaking Theory of Everything. Although "Jews control world via media, finance, etc." is one catchall entry (subsuming, e.g., their supposed fabrication of the Holocaust), other entries also point to Jews explicitly ("9/11 a U.S./Enron/Saudi/Israeli inside job") and tacitly (Larouche's obsession with Rohatyn, Lazard, and the Rothschilds).

U.S. hides ETs

U.S. hides ETs

Di murdered

omnipotent
God created
and controls
the world

An all-powerful, all-knowing, infinite, and immortal being who conjured existence and has a regiment of Men in Black (angels, prophets, whatever) to enforce his will on earth—the conspiracy theory to end all conspiracy theories, and one in which many, many hundreds of millions of people passionately believe.

Jews control
world

Jews control world

JFK assassination

Jews control
world

9/11 a U.S. plot

9/11 a U.S. plot

The High Frequency Active Auroral Research Program has built a grid of 180 72-foot-tall towers whose official function (studying the upper atmosphere in order to "enhance…surveillance systems") is sinister enough, but conspiracy theorists say it's actually a giant doomsday and/or mind-control machine.

Saddam Hussein
complicit in 9/11

Not unlike the contest between the Republicans and their Reptoid allies, and one of the most apples-to-apples pairings; 30 years ago, the Commission might have beaten the Council.

Corporate Jargon
by STANLEY BING

All cultures have their language, forged in common experience, and corporations are no different. Certain terms, however, have bubbled up from individual tar pits to form a sticky, unique, and singular argot, notable for its subtle use of euphemism, creative sleight of tongue and sly, vicious wit. The central tenet here is rather Zen: to speak without having spoken, to eschew clarity when mystery is required, to have a laugh at the various and sundry gods who run an irrational universe. Note: the higher the functional bullshit factor of any expression, the better the chance it will make it into permanent and useful parlance.

STANLEY BING is a columnist for *Fortune* magazine, the author of numerous bestselling books, and a corporate executive who has been impactful and effective at the big table for some years, and hopes to remain so in any conceivable outyear scenario.

Quality came first, in the 1930s, but by the mid-'80s had devolved into a weird amalgam of sensitivity training and self-criticism. Quality eventually became a business-world laughingstock, replaced by bizarre offspring like Six Sigma at General Electric. Excellence still remains a serviceable concept a generation after Tom Peters nearly destroyed it.

This is a case of a good idea facing what is possibly the workplace cosmology's most powerful mandatory requirement. Note the mingling of military verbiage and a baseball reference in the first phrase. Sports metaphors, once very favored, are now used only by those who like seeing people's eyeballs roll around in their heads when they are spoken to.

ramping it up	ramping it up
flying in tighter circles	spending more time with the family
pursue other opportunities	
spending more time with the family	
EBITDA (earnings before interest, taxes, depreciation, and amortization)	OIBITDA
OIBITDA (operating income before blah, blah, blah)	
re-engineering	key differentiator
key differentiator	
let's talk offline	let's talk offline
it's hands-in	
sharing best practices	sharing best practices
merger of equals	
scrubbing the numbers	scrubbing the numbers
drinking the Kool-Aid	
just the treetops, please	going granular
going granular	
excellence	excellence
quality	
playing in the same sandbox	off the reservation
off the reservation	
leverage	positioning
positioning	
synergistic	moving the cheese
moving the cheese	
micro/macromanagement	micro/macromanagement
phoning it in	
shoot for the fences	cover your ass
cover your ass	
brainstorming	blamestorming
blamestorming	
thinking outside the box	on the same page
on the same page	

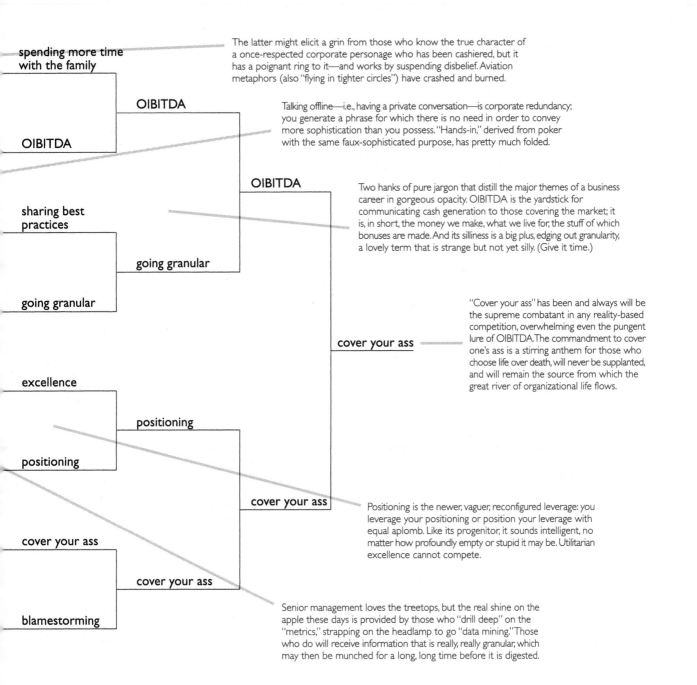

spending more time with the family

OIBITDA

OIBITDA

The latter might elicit a grin from those who know the true character of a once-respected corporate personage who has been cashiered, but it has a poignant ring to it—and works by suspending disbelief. Aviation metaphors (also "flying in tighter circles") have crashed and burned.

OIBITDA

Talking offline—i.e., having a private conversation—is corporate redundancy; you generate a phrase for which there is no need in order to convey more sophistication than you possess. "Hands-in," derived from poker with the same faux-sophisticated purpose, has pretty much folded.

sharing best practices

going granular

going granular

OIBITDA

Two hanks of pure jargon that distill the major themes of a business career in gorgeous opacity. OIBITDA is the yardstick for communicating cash generation to those covering the market; it is, in short, the money we make, what we live for, the stuff of which bonuses are made. And its silliness is a big plus, edging out granularity, a lovely term that is strange but not yet silly. (Give it time.)

excellence

positioning

positioning

cover your ass

cover your ass

"Cover your ass" has been and always will be the supreme combatant in any reality-based competition, overwhelming even the pungent lure of OIBITDA. The commandment to cover one's ass is a stirring anthem for those who choose life over death, will never be supplanted, and will remain the source from which the great river of organizational life flows.

cover your ass

cover your ass

blamestorming

Positioning is the newer, vaguer, reconfigured leverage: you leverage your positioning or position your leverage with equal aplomb. Like its progenitor, it sounds intelligent, no matter how profoundly empty or stupid it may be. Utilitarian excellence cannot compete.

Senior management loves the treetops, but the real shine on the apple these days is provided by those who "drill deep" on the "metrics," strapping on the headlamp to go "data mining." Those who do will receive information that is really, really granular, which may then be munched for a long, long time before it is digested.

25

Dogs for the Ages

by CLAUDIA KAWCZYNSKA and CAMERON WOO

Here at *Bark*, we adhere to the theory that humans coevolved with dogs. If wolves hadn't chosen to leave their packs and join our humble campfires, who knows what rung of the evolutionary ladder we would still be on. Not only did dogs teach us the hunt (Sirius), they guided us through icy storms (Buck, Balto), waited our return from adventures (Argos, Krypto), saved us from hair-raising travails (Checkers, Rin Tin Tin, Lassie, Snowy, Toto, and Asta), acted as our confidants (Charley, Fala, Gromit), served as our muses (Boatswain, Flush, Man Ray, Marley, and Tulip) and in the end, became what they are best known as—our truest and oldest friends (Earl, Old Yeller, Skip, and Snoopy).

CLAUDIA KAWCZYNSKA and CAMERON WOO are the cofounders of *Bark*, the acclaimed modern dog culture magazine. *Bark* grew from a dog-park newsletter started in 1997 in Berkeley, California, into an award-winning magazine and Web site (www.thebark.com). Its motto, "Dog Is My Co-Pilot," is also the title of its *New York Times* bestselling anthology, *Dog Is My Co-Pilot: Great Writers on the World's Oldest Friendship*. Their new book, *Howl*, a canine humor compilation, will be published in 2007 by Crown.

Lassie, the über-Collie, set the bar for canine exploits so high that all our dogs are doomed to pale in comparison. Rin Tin Tin, a scrappy German Shepherd, defined the rugged action hero. The tiebreaker? "Rinty" was a real dog discovered on a WWI battlefield, a dog's dog. Lassie was an actor. Besides, who can resist a dog in uniform?

These two heroes captured the world's attention—Balto in 1925, for his role in the Alaskan serum run, and Laika in 1957, for being the first earthling in space. Laika wins by a nose. Found on the streets of Moscow, the mongrel stray (dubbed Muttnik) wins points for her humble beginnings and her tragic end, while Balto tasted stardom.

A runoff between two notable presidential pets—on one ticket, we have Checkers, the Cocker Spaniel who saved Richard Nixon's career, and on the other, FDR's constant companion and confidant Fala, a Scottish Terrier who never missed a photo opportunity, accompanying the president by plane, limo, and ship—giving new meaning to dog-friendly travel. Fala in a landslide!

It's a battle of styles— Goofy, the lead dog in Walt Disney's cast of cuddly, sentimental characters, versus Tex Avery's gum-chewing, sarcastic barnyard beboppers, represented here by the deadpan Droopy. Sorry, Goof …

Argos	Argos
Sirius	
Krypto	Underdog
Underdog	
Lassie	Rin Tin Tin
Rin Tin Tin	
Old Yeller	Old Yeller
Buck	
Skip	Tulip
Tulip	
Charley	Charley
Marley	
Balto	Laika
Laika	
Checkers	Fala
Fala	
Asta	Asta
Toto	
Gromit	Gromit
Snowy	
Cujo	Cujo
Benji	
Greyfriars Bobby	Boatswain
Boatswain	
Flush	Man Ray
Man Ray	
Snoopy	Snoopy
Earl	
Goofy	Droopy
Droopy	
Santa's Little Helper	Santa's Little Helper
Barfy	

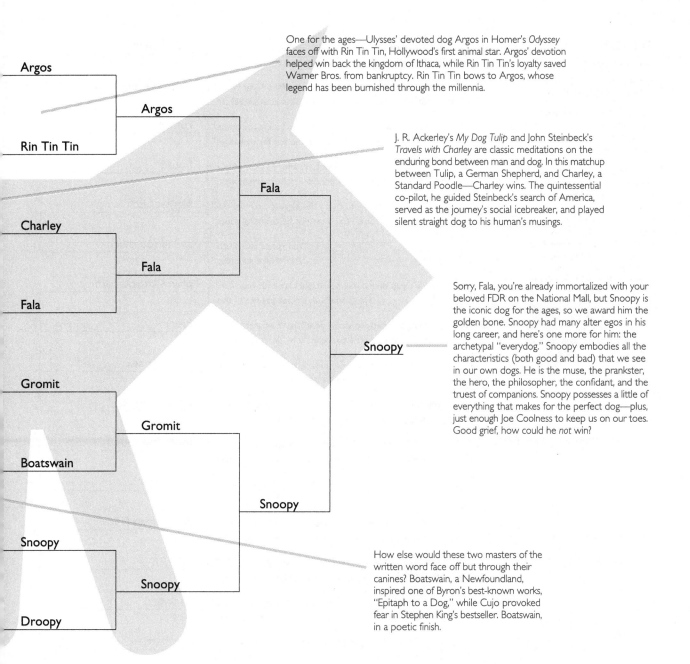

Argos

Rin Tin Tin

Argos

Charley

Fala

Fala

Fala

Snoopy

Gromit

Boatswain

Gromit

Snoopy

Snoopy

Droopy

Snoopy

One for the ages—Ulysses' devoted dog Argos in Homer's *Odyssey* faces off with Rin Tin Tin, Hollywood's first animal star. Argos' devotion helped win back the kingdom of Ithaca, while Rin Tin Tin's loyalty saved Warner Bros. from bankruptcy. Rin Tin Tin bows to Argos, whose legend has been burnished through the millennia.

J. R. Ackerley's *My Dog Tulip* and John Steinbeck's *Travels with Charley* are classic meditations on the enduring bond between man and dog. In this matchup between Tulip, a German Shepherd, and Charley, a Standard Poodle—Charley wins. The quintessential co-pilot, he guided Steinbeck's search of America, served as the journey's social icebreaker, and played silent straight dog to his human's musings.

Sorry, Fala, you're already immortalized with your beloved FDR on the National Mall, but Snoopy is the iconic dog for the ages, so we award him the golden bone. Snoopy had many alter egos in his long career, and here's one more for him: the archetypal "everydog." Snoopy embodies all the characteristics (both good and bad) that we see in our own dogs. He is the muse, the prankster, the hero, the philosopher, the confidant, and the truest of companions. Snoopy possesses a little of everything that makes for the perfect dog—plus, just enough Joe Coolness to keep us on our toes. Good grief, how could he *not* win?

How else would these two masters of the written word face off but through their canines? Boatswain, a Newfoundland, inspired one of Byron's best-known works, "Epitaph to a Dog," while Cujo provoked fear in Stephen King's bestseller. Boatswain, in a poetic finish.

26

Marital Arguments

by PHIL LEE, M.D., and
DIANE RUDOLPH, M.D.

You don't have be married to argue, but it seems you have to argue to be married. All arguments are not created equal, but how do you rate them? Most *destructive*, most *persistent*, most *common*, most *annoying*? You see the problem, right? The one thing we can agree on is that marital arguments rarely resolve conflict. They just prolong it, in a death spiral of humorless recrimination and domestic forensics that would make the *CSI* team proud. We've divided the entries here into he said/she said binaries, using the criterion: which argument, introduced by He or She, can actually lead to closure one way or the other?

PHIL LEE, M.D., and DIANE RUDOLPH, M.D., are the co-heads of marital therapy at Payne-Whitney Clinic of New York Presbyterian Hospital. Married in real life, they annually enact a feuding couple for the residents to interview. Some years demand more acting than others. Phil Lee is also the author of *Shrink Your Handicap*.

He: "That's the dumbest way to stack a dishwasher I've ever seen."
She: "How can you put the wineglasses with the plates?"
dishwasher

He: "Nobody told me I was marrying Miss Neat Freak."
She: "Do you have to make a mess in every room?"
mess in every room

She: "How come you never do anything romantic?"
He: "How about some sex for a change?"
romantic

He: "We can't afford a new house."
She: "Why don't you make more money?"
house

He: "Your mother's the biggest bitch I know."
She: "You must not be counting yours."
biggest bitch

He: "You spend too much."
She: "You're so cheap."
spend too much

She: "Couldn't you ever come home and play with your son?"
He: "Somebody's gotta pay for all this."
play with your son

He: "When are you going back to work, or is Pilates a career now?"
She: "Looking a little paunchy there, don't you think?"
Pilates

He: "Be nice if you'd initiate sex once in a while."
She: "Is it all about sex with you?"
all about sex

She: "Why don't you spend more time with me and the kids?"
He: "Why can't we spend more time by ourselves without the kids?"
me and the kids

He: "The kids need more religious education."
She: "They'd be okay if you set a better example."
more religious

She: "Are you listening to me?"
He: "Can I watch this in peace?"
listening

He: "Can't you even read a map, Kimberly?": (circa 1987)
She: "Can't you just stop and ask for directions?" (circa 1987)
read a map (1987)

He: "Can't you even read a map, Kimberly?" (circa 2007)
She: "Wouldn't have to if you'd bought the GPS." (circa 2007)
GPS

He: "I'm staying in the city. I hate commuting."
She: "Don't you want your kids to have a backyard?"
backyard

She: "When are we going to get married?"
He: "Huh?"
get married

dishwasher

romantic

dishwasher

Arguments about in-laws are like the in-laws themselves: they won't go away. The woman could have made it to the Final Four here if she had taken an undefensive approach: He: "Your mother is the biggest bitch I ever met." She: "I'll say! She's the biggest bitch anybody ever met. But I'm stuck with her, so could you possibly help me out and…" As easy as that, and the woman wins. But she doesn't do that. And the man moves on.

dishwasher

Withdrawing and self-absorbed fathers vs. mothers with an ax to grind is a typical midpoint between the euphoria of the wedding and the bitterness of the divorce. Things could go either way. He and She's problem is that they're mixing topics. She's worried about the children, He about money. The woman's advantage is temporary. Kids matter. So does paying the bills. Stalemate.

biggest bitch

Pilates

biggest bitch

He: "That's the dumbest way to stack a dishwasher I've ever seen."

While all marital arguments are a mistake, this truly can't be won, not against an expert. You say, "That's the most idiotic way to stack a dishwasher I've ever seen." Your other half says, "You're absolutely right, honey, I'm pathetic at that. You're the only one who can do it right, so could you help us out and do it from now on?" Checkmate. An argument guaranteed to create closure.

me and the kids

listening

me and the kids

He is introducing the subject of the kids' welfare, while She wants to be heard. The woman has a surefire argument starter, no matter what the response. "No" leaves her feeling neglected. "Yes" is worse. The man bringing religion and morality into marital debate provides a specific, highly charged valence, transforming the issue from the children's welfare to spousal behavior. He can win, however, by attending church. And thus fails to advance.

get married

GPS

get married

The woman's complaint induces guilt. But her victory is illusory. The man changes, becomes more devoted to family, but grumbling all the time—because he has been shamed into it, not permanently altered. She, on the other hand, is married.

get married

An early front-runner against all other marital arguments, but by definition it fades as fast as the wedding bells. What She leaves out is "… because then I'd be happy and we wouldn't have these arguments." This will morph into "I don't want to be forty before I have kids" and then, "We wouldn't have these problems if we had a bigger house." An illusory victory for the woman, hardly a permanent one.

27

Elmore Leonard Novels

by MARK REITER

Elmore Leonard novels are models of economy, snappy patter, and precise characterization. When he produces a clunker (and there are very few among his more than 40 novels), blame it on slack, why-should-I-care plotting. He started out writing westerns in the 1950s, updating to modern times in the 1970s, often with settings in Detroit or southern Florida. There's always a high-noon showdown, delayed as long as possible, often surprising you with who's drawing the guns. Leonard's biggest virtue in more than fifty years of writing is how hard he tries not to repeat himself in a familiar genre—and how often he succeeds. He is to fiction what Jack Nicholson is to acting: easy to mimic but impossible to duplicate.

MARK REITER, the coeditor of this book, rereads two or three Leonard novels a year—to remind himself how we all can survive without adverbs. Only one got an invite to this bracket.

Fifty-Two Pickup (1974)	Fifty-Two Pickup
The Switch (1978)	
Swag (1976)	Swag
Bandits (1987)	
Split Images (1981)	Mr. Majestyk
Mr. Majestyk (1974)	
Maximum Bob (1991)	Maximum Bob
Be Cool (1999)	
The Hot Kid (2005)	Touch
Touch (1987)	
Pronto (1993)	Hombre
Hombre (1961)	
City Primeval: High Noon in Detroit (1980)	City Primeval
The Bounty Hunters (1953)	
The Hunted (1977)	The Hunted
Mr. Paradise (2004)	
Freaky Deaky (1988)	Freaky Deaky
Valdez Is Coming (1970)	
Last Stand at Saber River (1959)	Last Stand
Glitz (1985)	
LaBrava (1983)	LaBrava
Escape from Five Shadows (1956)	
Gold Coast (1980)	Get Shorty
Get Shorty (1990)	
Unknown Man No. 89 (1977)	Unknown Man
Rum Punch (1992)	
Out of Sight (1996)	Out of Sight
Stick (1983)	
The Moonshine War (1969)	The Moonshine War
Forty Lashes Less One (1972)	
Killshot (1989)	Killshot
Cat Chaser (1982)	

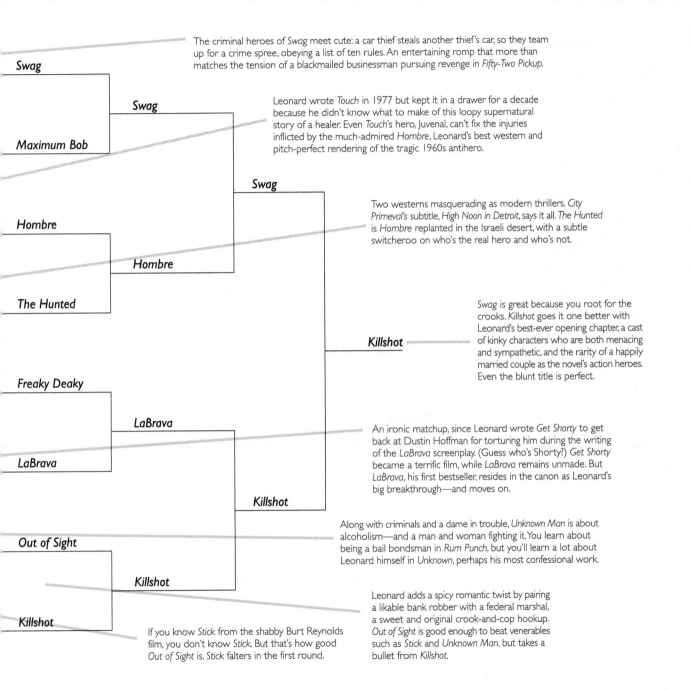

Swag

Maximum Bob

Swag

Hombre

The Hunted

Hombre

Swag

Swag

The criminal heroes of *Swag* meet cute: a car thief steals another thief's car, so they team up for a crime spree, obeying a list of ten rules. An entertaining romp that more than matches the tension of a blackmailed businessman pursuing revenge in *Fifty-Two Pickup*.

Leonard wrote *Touch* in 1977 but kept it in a drawer for a decade because he didn't know what to make of this loopy supernatural story of a healer. Even *Touch*'s hero, Juvenal, can't fix the injuries inflicted by the much-admired *Hombre*, Leonard's best western and pitch-perfect rendering of the tragic 1960s antihero.

Two westerns masquerading as modern thrillers. *City Primeval*'s subtitle, *High Noon in Detroit*, says it all. *The Hunted* is *Hombre* replanted in the Israeli desert, with a subtle switcheroo on who's the real hero and who's not.

Killshot

Swag is great because you root for the crooks. *Killshot* goes it one better with Leonard's best-ever opening chapter, a cast of kinky characters who are both menacing and sympathetic, and the rarity of a happily married couple as the novel's action heroes. Even the blunt title is perfect.

Freaky Deaky

LaBrava

LaBrava

Killshot

An ironic matchup, since Leonard wrote *Get Shorty* to get back at Dustin Hoffman for torturing him during the writing of the *LaBrava* screenplay. (Guess who's Shorty?) *Get Shorty* became a terrific film, while *LaBrava* remains unmade. But *LaBrava*, his first bestseller, resides in the canon as Leonard's big breakthrough—and moves on.

Out of Sight

Killshot

Killshot

Along with criminals and a dame in trouble, *Unknown Man* is about alcoholism—and a man and woman fighting it. You learn about being a bail bondsman in *Rum Punch*, but you'll learn a lot about Leonard himself in *Unknown*, perhaps his most confessional work.

Leonard adds a spicy romantic twist by pairing a likable bank robber with a federal marshal, a sweet and original crook-and-cop hookup. *Out of Sight* is good enough to beat venerables such as *Stick* and *Unknown Man*, but takes a bullet from *Killshot*.

If you know *Stick* from the shabby Burt Reynolds film, you don't know *Stick*. But that's how good *Out of Sight* is. *Stick* falters in the first round.

Elvis Costello Songs

by MARK REITER

Elvis Costello songs are all about smart beat, smarter lyrics, and sweet or sour mood. You don't hum his tunes; you sing his lyrics because you savor the sharp phrases popping off your tongue. The songs also vacillate in style between Elvis's artistic ambition (e.g., his forays into "classical" music) and his unabashed desire to write "hits." Which songs you prefer depends on whether you feel like dancing or drowning your sorrows.

MARK REITER, the coeditor of this book, has invested more money buying Elvis Costello recordings than those of any other artist, largely because many of them have been issued on vinyl, cassette, and CD, and reissued on CD not once but twice.

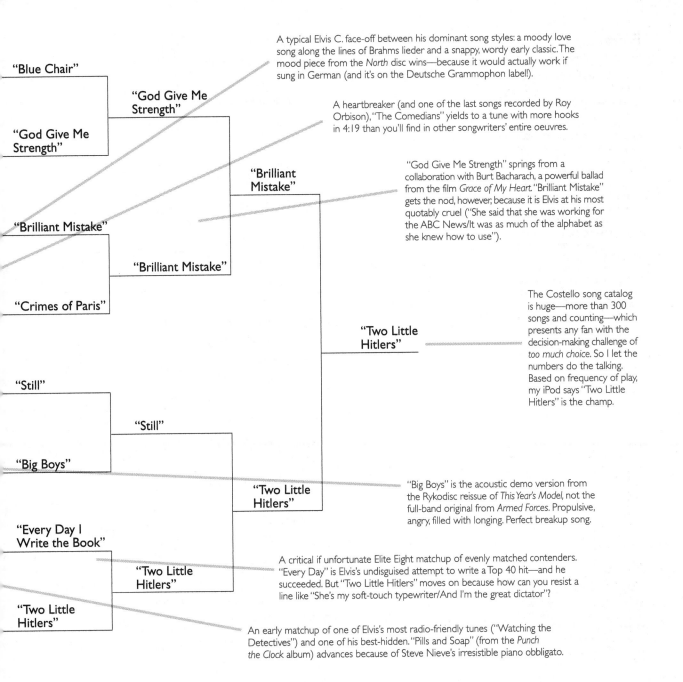

"Blue Chair"

"God Give Me Strength"

"God Give Me Strength"

A typical Elvis C. face-off between his dominant song styles: a moody love song along the lines of Brahms lieder and a snappy, wordy early classic. The mood piece from the *North* disc wins—because it would actually work if sung in German (and it's on the Deutsche Grammophon label!).

A heartbreaker (and one of the last songs recorded by Roy Orbison), "The Comedians" yields to a tune with more hooks in 4:19 than you'll find in other songwriters' entire oeuvres.

"Brilliant Mistake"

"Brilliant Mistake"

"God Give Me Strength" springs from a collaboration with Burt Bacharach, a powerful ballad from the film *Grace of My Heart*. "Brilliant Mistake" gets the nod, however, because it is Elvis at his most quotably cruel ("She said that she was working for the ABC News/It was as much of the alphabet as she knew how to use").

"Brilliant Mistake"

"Brilliant Mistake"

"Crimes of Paris"

"Two Little Hitlers"

The Costello song catalog is huge—more than 300 songs and counting—which presents any fan with the decision-making challenge of *too much choice*. So I let the numbers do the talking. Based on frequency of play, my iPod says "Two Little Hitlers" is the champ.

"Still"

"Still"

"Big Boys"

"Two Little Hitlers"

"Big Boys" is the acoustic demo version from the Rykodisc reissue of *This Year's Model*, not the full-band original from *Armed Forces*. Propulsive, angry, filled with longing. Perfect breakup song.

"Every Day I Write the Book"

"Two Little Hitlers"

A critical if unfortunate Elite Eight matchup of evenly matched contenders. "Every Day" is Elvis's undisguised attempt to write a Top 40 hit—and he succeeded. But "Two Little Hitlers" moves on because how can you resist a line like "She's my soft-touch typewriter/And I'm the great dictator"?

"Two Little Hitlers"

An early matchup of one of Elvis's most radio-friendly tunes ("Watching the Detectives") and one of his best-hidden. "Pills and Soap" (from the *Punch the Clock* album) advances because of Steve Nieve's irresistible piano obbligato.

29

Emoticons
by J. D. BIERSDORFER

In the disembodied world of bites and bytes, hundreds of emoticons roam the Internet and have done so since computer geeks, armed with a handful of common punctuation symbols, looked for simple ways to represent mood and facial expression in basic e-mail communications. (Tilt your head to the left to get the picture.) Emoticons can be annoying, even childish, but these rudimentary graphics provide necessary nuance and meaning to words that might be misinterpreted when read and not spoken. This is a battle to be the most recognizable and creative representations of voiceless conversations. (Keep your head tilted.)

J. D. BIERSDORFER writes about art and technology for the *New York Times* and is also the author of *iPod & iTunes: The Missing Manual* and coauthor of *The Internet: The Missing Manual*.

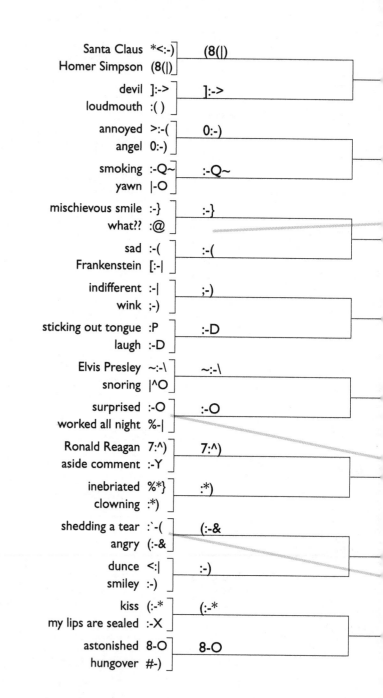

Santa Claus	*<:-)	(8(|)
Homer Simpson	(8(|)	
devil	]:->	]:->
loudmouth	:( )	
annoyed	>:-(	0:-)
angel	0:-)	
smoking	:-Q~	:-Q~
yawn	|-O	
mischievous smile	:-}	:-}
what??	:@	
sad	:-(	:-(
Frankenstein	[:-|	
indifferent	:-|	;-)
wink	;-)	
sticking out tongue	:P	:-D
laugh	:-D	
Elvis Presley	~:-\	~:-\
snoring	|^O	
surprised	:-O	:-O
worked all night	%-|	
Ronald Reagan	7:^)	7:^)
aside comment	:-Y	
inebriated	%*}	:*)
clowning	:*)	
shedding a tear	:`-(	(:-&
angry	(:-&	
dunce	<:|	:-)
smiley	:-)	
kiss	(:-*	(:-*
my lips are sealed	:-X	
astonished	8-O	8-O
hungover	#-)	

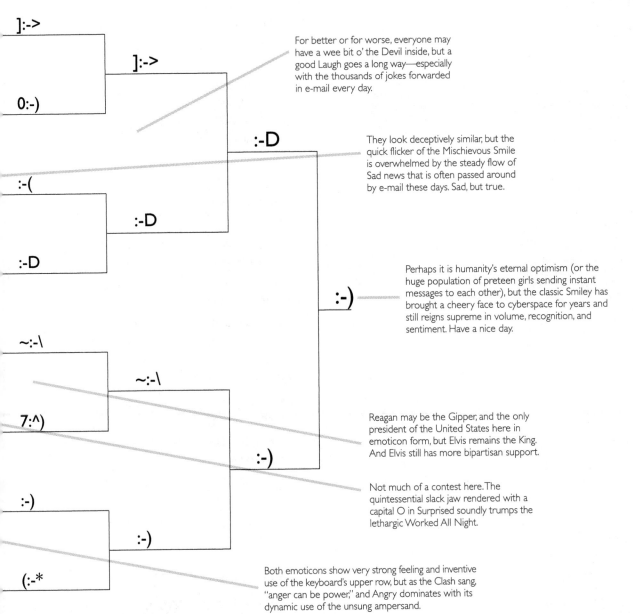

]:->

0:-)

]:->

For better or for worse, everyone may have a wee bit o' the Devil inside, but a good Laugh goes a long way—especially with the thousands of jokes forwarded in e-mail every day.

:-(

:-D

:-D

:-D

They look deceptively similar, but the quick flicker of the Mischievous Smile is overwhelmed by the steady flow of Sad news that is often passed around by e-mail these days. Sad, but true.

:-)

Perhaps it is humanity's eternal optimism (or the huge population of preteen girls sending instant messages to each other), but the classic Smiley has brought a cheery face to cyberspace for years and still reigns supreme in volume, recognition, and sentiment. Have a nice day.

~:-\

7:^)

~:-\

:-)

Reagan may be the Gipper, and the only president of the United States here in emoticon form, but Elvis remains the King. And Elvis still has more bipartisan support.

Not much of a contest here. The quintessential slack jaw rendered with a capital O in Surprised soundly trumps the lethargic Worked All Night.

:-)

(:-*

:-)

Both emoticons show very strong feeling and inventive use of the keyboard's upper row, but as the Clash sang, "anger can be power," and Angry dominates with its dynamic use of the unsung ampersand.

30

Endangered Species

by CHRISTOPHER L. JENKINS

To some people, endangered species are "perps" that halt industrial progress and inspire years of litigation. But we forget that when an endangered species disappears, it doesn't come back. Ever. In selecting this group of North American endangered species, I leaned heavily on the fish, amphibians, reptiles, birds, and mammals that, for whatever reason, have the most value in the public's eye. My criteria were the threat to the species, its public image, and its chance of recovery. Thus, the bracket is dominated by "charismatic megafauna" and could, with some irony, be titled Endangered Species at Lowest Risk. Or, put another way, the winner is the one most likely to leave you speechless and regretful when your grandchild points to a picture and asks you, "What's that?"

CHRIS JENKINS is a wildlife ecologist who works and lives in the Greater Yellowstone Ecosystem. He is an avid hunter and conservation biologist. He hopes to raise his children in a world where all endangered species win.

Most people hate snakes, so the rattler starts with a disadvantage here. "Shoot, shovel, and shut up" is most ranchers' solution for the unpopular ferret. Somehow the ridge-nosed rattler moves on.

When you consider that bighorn sheep are part of the "Grand Slam" of hunting (shooting one of each North American mountain sheep), the sheep squeak one out.

The ivory-billed woodpecker gained fame when it was recently found in the swamps of Arkansas. But this tiny population of woodpeckers can't stand up to a beloved reptile. That said, harvesting of eggs, development of nesting habitats, and mortality due to commercial fisheries doom the sea turtle in the next round against the grizzly bear.

black-footed ferret	ridge-nosed rattlesnake	
ridge-nosed rattlesnake		
American alligator	American alligator	
ocelot		
bog turtle	Canada lynx	
Canada lynx		
desert tortoise	desert tortoise	
bull trout		
gray wolf	gray wolf	
piping plover		
red-bellied turtle	California condor	
California condor		
sockeye salmon	sockeye salmon	
willow flycatcher		
pygmy rabbit	red-legged frog	
red-legged frog		
white sturgeon	bald eagle	
bald eagle		
indigo snake	Atlantic salmon	
Atlantic salmon		
marbled murrelet	bighorn sheep	
bighorn sheep		
chinook salmon	humpback whale	
humpback whale		
flatwoods salamander	spotted owl	
spotted owl		
Wyoming toad	Florida panther	
Florida panther		
stellar sea lion	grizzly bear	
grizzly bear		
ivory-billed woodpecker	hawksbill sea turtle	
hawksbill sea turtle		

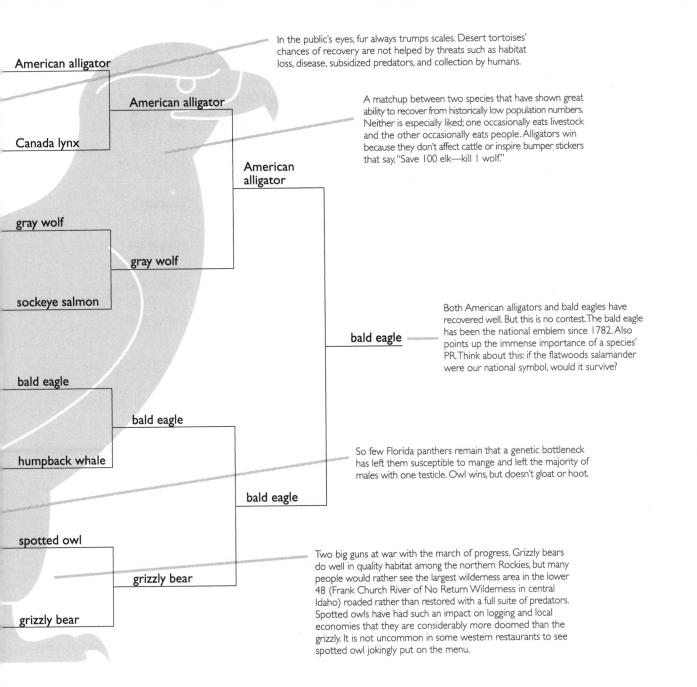

American alligator

American alligator

Canada lynx

American alligator

gray wolf

gray wolf

sockeye salmon

bald eagle

bald eagle

bald eagle

humpback whale

bald eagle

spotted owl

grizzly bear

grizzly bear

In the public's eyes, fur always trumps scales. Desert tortoises' chances of recovery are not helped by threats such as habitat loss, disease, subsidized predators, and collection by humans.

A matchup between two species that have shown great ability to recover from historically low population numbers. Neither is especially liked; one occasionally eats livestock and the other occasionally eats people. Alligators win because they don't affect cattle or inspire bumper stickers that say, "Save 100 elk—kill 1 wolf."

Both American alligators and bald eagles have recovered well. But this is no contest. The bald eagle has been the national emblem since 1782. Also points up the immense importance of a species' PR. Think about this: if the flatwoods salamander were our national symbol, would it survive?

So few Florida panthers remain that a genetic bottleneck has left them susceptible to mange and left the majority of males with one testicle. Owl wins, but doesn't gloat or hoot.

Two big guns at war with the march of progress. Grizzly bears do well in quality habitat among the northern Rockies, but many people would rather see the largest wilderness area in the lower 48 (Frank Church River of No Return Wilderness in central Idaho) roaded rather than restored with a full suite of predators. Spotted owls have had such an impact on logging and local economies that they are considerably more doomed than the grizzly. It is not uncommon in some western restaurants to see spotted owl jokingly put on the menu.

31

Cooking Tools
by BILL YOSSES

The greatest tool ever invented is the human hand, but it is *hors de concours* since it dwarfs other tools in its utility. You can do anything in the kitchen with your hands—and without hands most tools are simply not usable. A vicious circle. That said, we eliminated electrical devices, useful though they are, because they seem like cheating. What makes a tool essential is how much it improves the finished product, whether it's a simple stew or an elaborate dessert. As a baker and pastry chef, I have a slight fondness for the "weapons" that help me attack a diner's sweet tooth. But give me the tools that reach the semifinals here and I can satisfy any gastronomic urge.

For his work at restaurants such as Montrachet, Bouley, and Bouley Bakery, BILL YOSSES was named one of New York City's master pastry chefs by *New York* magazine. He is the coauthor, with Bryan Miller, of *Desserts for Dummies.*

Both have many uses and both give a "pro" touch to a meal. But the bag is dominant in more categories in the kitchen: any soft batter, dough, or filling, whether savory or sweet, benefits from it.

The funnel's unique utility is sketchy, since it can be replaced or jury-rigged so many ways. The side towel is a sleeper essential, taken for granted like water from a faucet. Keeps the scene clean, of course, but things pretty much stop without a way to grab a hot panhandle.

parchment paper	parchment paper
stainless steel rings	
wine key/corkscrew	spatulas
spatulas, hand scrapers	
pastry bag	pastry bag
Silpat and Flexipat sheets	
rubber mallet	veggie peeler set
vegetable peeler/melon baller/zester/reamer set	
blowtorch	blowtorch
box grater	
sieve/tamis/strainer	cookbooks
cookbooks	
metal tongs	metal tongs
chinois	
mandoline	rolling pin
rolling pin	
scissors/shears	scissors
thermometer	
funnel	side towel
side towel	
pots and pans	pots and pans
knife kit	
salad spinner	bowls
bowls, stainless and Pyrex	
Misono high-carbon knife	Misono knife
ring cutters	
refractometer/sugar density gauge	ring molds
stainless steel ring molds	
rubber cutting board	cutting board
whipped cream maker	
spoons	spoons
pasta maker/sheeter	

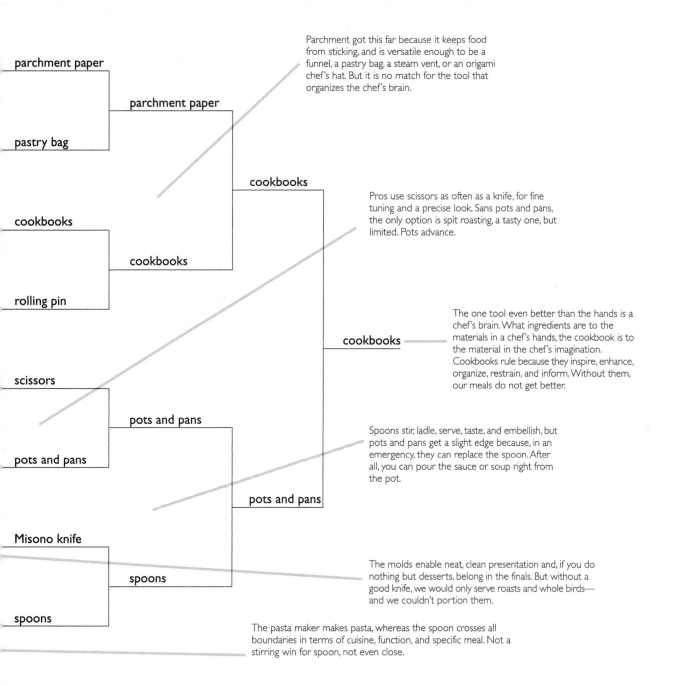

parchment paper

parchment paper

pastry bag

Parchment got this far because it keeps food from sticking, and is versatile enough to be a funnel, a pastry bag, a steam vent, or an origami chef's hat. But it is no match for the tool that organizes the chef's brain.

cookbooks

cookbooks

cookbooks

rolling pin

Pros use scissors as often as a knife, for fine tuning and a precise look. Sans pots and pans, the only option is spit roasting, a tasty one, but limited. Pots advance.

scissors

pots and pans

pots and pans

cookbooks

The one tool even better than the hands is a chef's brain. What ingredients are to the materials in a chef's hands, the cookbook is to the material in the chef's imagination. Cookbooks rule because they inspire, enhance, organize, restrain, and inform. Without them, our meals do not get better.

Spoons stir, ladle, serve, taste, and embellish, but pots and pans get a slight edge because, in an emergency, they can replace the spoon. After all, you can pour the sauce or soup right from the pot.

pots and pans

Misono knife

spoons

spoons

The molds enable neat, clean presentation and, if you do nothing but desserts, belong in the finals. But without a good knife, we would only serve roasts and whole birds—and we couldn't portion them.

The pasta maker makes pasta, whereas the spoon crosses all boundaries in terms of cuisine, function, and specific meal. Not a stirring win for spoon, not even close.

32

Economic Indicators

by TIM HARFORD

The professional economic forecasters plug dozens of variables into their equations, but—as my champion economic indicator suggests—they have an undistinguished record. So I tried to keep things simple, with four categories: the everyday, such as the number of cranes on the horizon; the incestuous, where you forecast by looking at other people's forecasts; the global, which attempts to predict which economies will grow rich and which will stay poor; and the wonkish, about which the less said the better. I was impressed by and privately rooting for the taxi drivers, but in the end there is a simple purity about the champ that demands recognition.

TIM HARFORD is the only economist in the world to have his own problem-page column, Dear Economist, in the *Financial Times*. He is the author of the business bestseller *The Undercover Economist: Exposing Why the Rich Are Rich, the Poor Are Poor—and Why You Can Never Buy a Decent Used Car!*

EVERYDAY REGIONAL

cranes on the Manhattan skyline — cranes
thickness of brokers' reports
hemlines — hemlines
cardboard box orders
people drinking beer not wine — taxi drivers
taxi drivers offer stock tips
commute time in Silicon Valley — commute time
Wall Street champagne expenses

INCESTUOUS REGIONAL

"consensus" of economic forecasts — consensus
mutterings from the Fed
IMF World Economic Outlook — last year's forecast
whatever last year's forecast was
Time magazine says Ben Bernanke is Man of the Year — *Time* magazine
Business Week "new economy" word count
Wall Street Journal "recession" word count — *Washington Post*
Washington Post help wanted section

GLOBAL REGIONAL

distance from equator — equator
average trade barriers
infant mortality rate — infant mortality
population at university
number of days to legally start a new business — new business
perceptions of corruption
size of manufacturing sector — oil sector
size of oil sector

WONKISH REGIONAL

extra cost of premium gasoline — gasoline
presidential approval rating
bilateral trade deficit with China — Michigan
Michigan consumer sentiment
purchasing managers index — PMI
monthly jobless figures
Ten-year treasury yield minus two-year yield — yield curve
stocks down yesterday

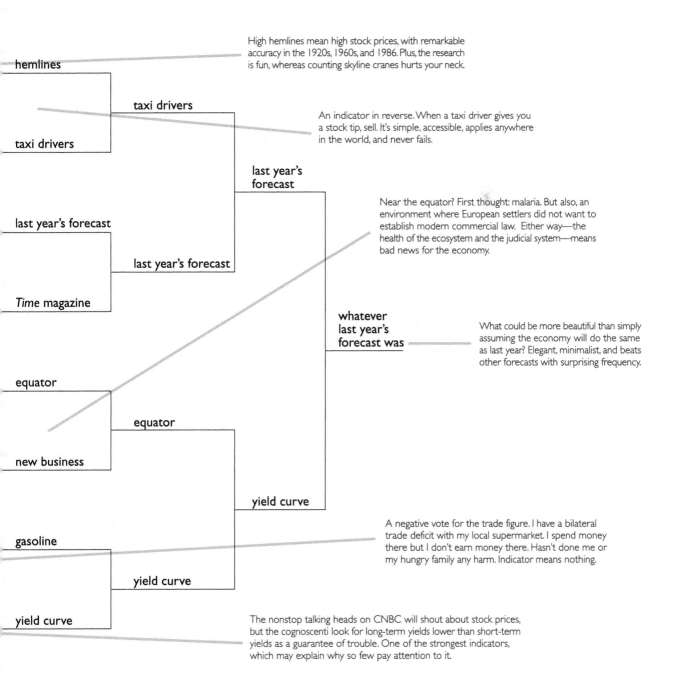

hemlines

High hemlines mean high stock prices, with remarkable accuracy in the 1920s, 1960s, and 1986. Plus, the research is fun, whereas counting skyline cranes hurts your neck.

taxi drivers

taxi drivers

An indicator in reverse. When a taxi driver gives you a stock tip, sell. It's simple, accessible, applies anywhere in the world, and never fails.

last year's forecast

last year's forecast

last year's forecast

Time magazine

Near the equator? First thought: malaria. But also, an environment where European settlers did not want to establish modern commercial law. Either way—the health of the ecosystem and the judicial system—means bad news for the economy.

whatever last year's forecast was

What could be more beautiful than simply assuming the economy will do the same as last year? Elegant, minimalist, and beats other forecasts with surprising frequency.

equator

equator

new business

yield curve

gasoline

A negative vote for the trade figure. I have a bilateral trade deficit with my local supermarket. I spend money there but I don't earn money there. Hasn't done me or my hungry family any harm. Indicator means nothing.

yield curve

yield curve

The nonstop talking heads on CNBC will shout about stock prices, but the cognoscenti look for long-term yields lower than short-term yields as a guarantee of trouble. One of the strongest indicators, which may explain why so few pay attention to it.

33

Film Deaths
by MATTHEW SHEPATIN

You don't need to be Freud to figure out why movie audiences would voluntarily watch people be shot, slashed, poisoned, eaten by a shark, disemboweled by an alien, or decapitated by plate glass. Then again, the best screen fatalities deliver an emotional wallop. They are visually compelling. They spark a visceral response: fear, disgust, laughter, sorrow, or even faith. For all those reasons, it's not surprising to find 16 Oscar nominees for Best Picture here (and 7 winners). While horror film directors make a living serving up spectacular killings, accomplished directors such as Steven Spielberg, who has 2 entries (sorry, kids, E.T. lives), know the tremendous power expelled in that final breath.

MATTHEW SHEPATIN, ace researcher on this book, is a freelance writer whose articles have appeared in the *Los Angeles Times*, *Playboy*, the *Village Voice*, and *Time Out New York*.

King Kong falls from Empire State Building
cancer-stricken Debra Winger dies in hospital

Bonnie and Clyde riddled with bullets
Walken loses Russian roulette in *The Deer Hunter*

Titanic sinks and DiCaprio drowns
Bambi's mom shot by hunters

Alec Guinness blows up *The Bridge Over the River Kwai*
Susan Hayward gets the chair in *I Want To Live!*

Nazis melt in *Raiders of the Lost Ark*
dirty cop suffocates in corn silo in *Witness*

Scarface goes out with a bang
Wicked Witch melts

Alan Rickman's skyscraper plunge in *Die Hard*
Cagney goes up in flames in *White Heat*

Wallace Shawn's wine poisoning in *The Princess Bride*
Robocop criminal gets toxic waste bath

David Warner's decapitation in *The Omen*
John Hurt's bursting stomach in *Alien*

telekinetic Carrie sends knives into her mom
Travolta shoots backseat passenger in *Pulp Fiction*

airbag accidentally deploys, killing *Final Destination* girl
Mr. Big expands and pops in *Live and Let Die*

Psycho shower scene
shark attack on female swimmer in *Jaws* opener

Sonny Corleone gunned down at tollbooth
Darth Vader strikes down Obi-Wan Kenobi

Dr. Strangelove's Slim Pickens rides nuclear bomb
babes chase sexist off cliff in Python's *Meaning of Life*

Willem Dafoe's fatal battlefield collapse in *Platoon*
Tom Hanks shot on bridge in *Saving Private Ryan*

Thelma and Louise drive car off edge of Grand Canyon
Russell Crowe's death match in Roman coliseum

King Kong falls

Bonnie and Clyde shot

Bambi's mom shot

Hayward gets chair

Nazis melt

Wicked Witch melts

Rickman's fall

Shawn's poisoning

Hurt's bursting stomach

Travolta shoots passenger

airbag in *Final Destination*

Psycho shower scene

Vader kills Obi-Wan

Pickens rides bomb

Dafoe dies in battle

Crowe stabbed

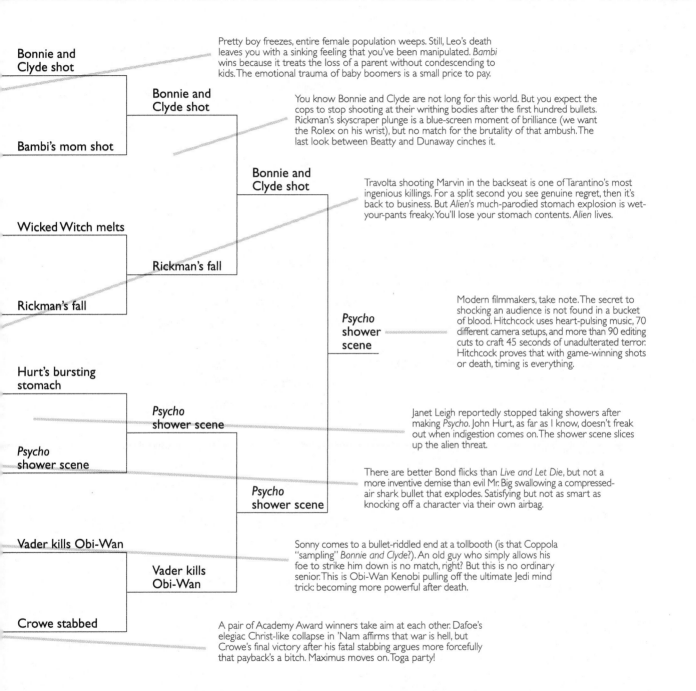

Bonnie and Clyde shot

Bambi's mom shot

Wicked Witch melts

Rickman's fall

Hurt's bursting stomach

Psycho shower scene

Vader kills Obi-Wan

Crowe stabbed

Bonnie and Clyde shot

Rickman's fall

Psycho shower scene

Psycho shower scene

Vader kills Obi-Wan

Bonnie and Clyde shot

Bonnie and Clyde shot

Psycho shower scene

Pretty boy freezes, entire female population weeps. Still, Leo's death leaves you with a sinking feeling that you've been manipulated. *Bambi* wins because it treats the loss of a parent without condescending to kids. The emotional trauma of baby boomers is a small price to pay.

You know Bonnie and Clyde are not long for this world. But you expect the cops to stop shooting at their writhing bodies after the first hundred bullets. Rickman's skyscraper plunge is a blue-screen moment of brilliance (we want the Rolex on his wrist), but no match for the brutality of that ambush. The last look between Beatty and Dunaway cinches it.

Travolta shooting Marvin in the backseat is one of Tarantino's most ingenious killings. For a split second you see genuine regret, then it's back to business. But *Alien*'s much-parodied stomach explosion is wet-your-pants freaky. You'll lose your stomach contents. *Alien* lives.

Modern filmmakers, take note. The secret to shocking an audience is not found in a bucket of blood. Hitchcock uses heart-pulsing music, 70 different camera setups, and more than 90 editing cuts to craft 45 seconds of unadulterated terror. Hitchcock proves that with game-winning shots or death, timing is everything.

Janet Leigh reportedly stopped taking showers after making *Psycho*. John Hurt, as far as I know, doesn't freak out when indigestion comes on. The shower scene slices up the alien threat.

There are better Bond flicks than *Live and Let Die*, but not a more inventive demise than evil Mr. Big swallowing a compressed-air shark bullet that explodes. Satisfying but not as smart as knocking off a character via their own airbag.

Sonny comes to a bullet-riddled end at a tollbooth (is that Coppola "sampling" *Bonnie and Clyde*?). An old guy who simply allows his foe to strike him down is no match, right? But this is no ordinary senior. This is Obi-Wan Kenobi pulling off the ultimate Jedi mind trick: becoming more powerful after death.

A pair of Academy Award winners take aim at each other. Dafoe's elegiac Christ-like collapse in 'Nam affirms that war is hell, but Crowe's final victory after his fatal stabbing argues more forcefully that payback's a bitch. Maximus moves on. Toga party!

34

Frank Sinatra Songs

by DAVID McCLINTICK

Frank Sinatra recorded more than 1,200 songs during his 60-year career. The profusion of styles and moods in the Sinatra repertoire is astonishing. Along with a number of classics, the 32 contenders here include some little-known treasures such as "Weep They Will," which is Tony Bennett's favorite Sinatra recording; "If You Are but a Dream," which Woody Allen featured in *Radio Days*; and the Brechtian romp "Mack the Knife," which Sinatra got to only late in life and then overdubbed even later because he wasn't happy with his first try. He believed in plumbing songs until he'd mastered them, which is why we list the years of recording to pinpoint the preferred rendition. Consider his reconsiderations of George Harrison's "Something" and Sondheim's "Send in the Clowns," rerecorded with new arrangements after he'd sung them hundreds of times in concert. Sinatra couldn't take "yes" for an answer.

DAVID McCLINTICK, a former staff writer for the *Wall Street Journal*, is the award-winning author of *Indecent Exposure* and *Swordfish*. He won a Grammy Award for Best Album Notes for Frank Sinatra's *Trilogy*.

"All or Nothing at All" (1966)
"Luck Be a Lady" (1963) — "Luck Be a Lady"

"Weep They Will" (1955)
"In the Wee Small Hours" (1955) — "Wee Small Hours"

"All of Me" (1954)
"I've Got You Under My Skin" (1956) — "I've Got You"

"From This Moment On" (1956)
"Mack the Knife" (1986) — "From This Moment On"

"At Long Last Love" (1956)
"Fly Me to the Moon" (1964) — "At Long Last Love"

"Something" (1979)
"I Only Have Eyes for You" (1962) — "Something"

"I'll Only Miss Her When I Think of Her" (1965)
"If You Are but a Dream" (1944) — "I'll Only Miss Her"

"The Birth of the Blues" (1952)
"The Lady Is a Tramp" (1956) — "The Lady Is a Tramp"

"One for My Baby (And One More for the Road)" (1958)
"Drinking Again" (1967) — "One for My Baby"

"I Have Dreamed" (1963)
"The Cradle Song (Brahms' Lullaby)" (1944) — "I Have Dreamed"

"The Best Is Yet to Come" (1964)
"Come Rain or Come Shine" (1961) — "Come Rain"

"I Get Along Without You Very Well" (1955)
"Mood Indigo" (1955) — "I Get Along"

"Blues in the Night" (1958)
"Here's That Rainy Day" (1959) — "Blues in the Night"

"Last Night When We Were Young" (1954)
"My One and Only Love" (1953) — "Last Night"

"Spring Is Here" (1958)
"What's New" (1958) — "Spring Is Here"

"Send in the Clowns" (1976)
"It Was a Very Good Year" (1965) — "It Was a Very Good Year"

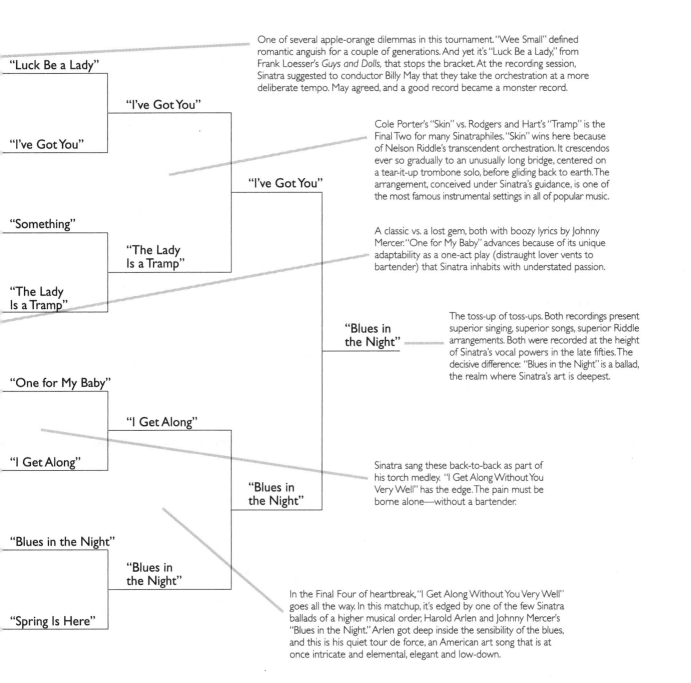

"Luck Be a Lady"

"I've Got You"

"I've Got You"

"Something"

"The Lady Is a Tramp"

"The Lady Is a Tramp"

"One for My Baby"

"I Get Along"

"I Get Along"

"Blues in the Night"

"Blues in the Night"

"Blues in the Night"

"Spring Is Here"

"I've Got You"

"Blues in the Night"

One of several apple-orange dilemmas in this tournament. "Wee Small" defined romantic anguish for a couple of generations. And yet it's "Luck Be a Lady," from Frank Loesser's *Guys and Dolls,* that stops the bracket. At the recording session, Sinatra suggested to conductor Billy May that they take the orchestration at a more deliberate tempo. May agreed, and a good record became a monster record.

Cole Porter's "Skin" vs. Rodgers and Hart's "Tramp" is the Final Two for many Sinatraphiles. "Skin" wins here because of Nelson Riddle's transcendent orchestration. It crescendos ever so gradually to an unusually long bridge, centered on a tear-it-up trombone solo, before gliding back to earth. The arrangement, conceived under Sinatra's guidance, is one of the most famous instrumental settings in all of popular music.

A classic vs. a lost gem, both with boozy lyrics by Johnny Mercer. "One for My Baby" advances because of its unique adaptability as a one-act play (distraught lover vents to bartender) that Sinatra inhabits with understated passion.

The toss-up of toss-ups. Both recordings present superior singing, superior songs, superior Riddle arrangements. Both were recorded at the height of Sinatra's vocal powers in the late fifties. The decisive difference: "Blues in the Night" is a ballad, the realm where Sinatra's art is deepest.

Sinatra sang these back-to-back as part of his torch medley. "I Get Along Without You Very Well" has the edge. The pain must be borne alone—without a bartender.

In the Final Four of heartbreak, "I Get Along Without You Very Well" goes all the way. In this matchup, it's edged by one of the few Sinatra ballads of a higher musical order, Harold Arlen and Johnny Mercer's "Blues in the Night." Arlen got deep inside the sensibility of the blues, and this is his quiet tour de force, an American art song that is at once intricate and elemental, elegant and low-down.

35

Freshwater and Saltwater Flies

by PETER KAMINSKY

In fly-fishing, the fly you use says a lot about you as a person. Snobbish gentlemen firmly believed if it wasn't a dry fly, you weren't fly-fishing. A better yardstick, and the one employed here, is "Does it catch fish?" This is a defiantly utilitarian approach in a sport where aesthetes still judge a fly on whether or not it contains such exotic materials as urine-stained vixen belly and eye of jungle cock. You show me a store where they sell vixen belly and I'll show you a place in need of a better rack jobber. Fooling fish is what it's all about: their small brain against your—presumably—bigger one.

PETER KAMINSKY first took up fishing as a method to preserve his mental and spiritual well-being while serving as managing editor of *National Lampoon*. He is the author of *The Moon Pulled Up an Acre of Bass, Pig Perfect, American Waters, The Fly Fisherman's Guide to the Meaning of Life,* and *Fly Fishing for Dummies.* His Outdoors column has appeared in the *New York Times* for two decades.

Perhaps the prettiest, most glamorous fly of the bunch, the Coachman is rarely as effective as the less tarted-up Royal Wulff, a much more floatable fly.

Royal Coachman / Royal Wulff	Royal Wulff
Irresistible / Humpy	Humpy
Usual / Ausable Wulff	Usual
Griffith's Gnat / Trico Spinner	Griffith's Gnat
Comparadun / Light Hendricksen	Comparadun
Parachute Adams / Adams	Parachute Adams
Henryville Special / Elk Hair Caddis	Elk Hair Caddis
Gold-Ribbed Hare's Ear / Pheasant Tail Nymph	Gold-Ribbed Hare's Ear
Prince Bead Head / Madame X	Prince Bead Head
Dave's Hopper / Chernobyl Ant	Dave's Hopper
Stimulator / Muddler Minnow	Muddler Minnow
Clouser / Bunny Leech	Clouser
Wooly Bugger / San Juan Worm	Wooly Bugger
Gotcha / Crazy Charly	Gotcha
Crease Fly / Popping Bug	Crease Fly
Lefty's Deceiver / Surf Candy	Lefty's Deceiver

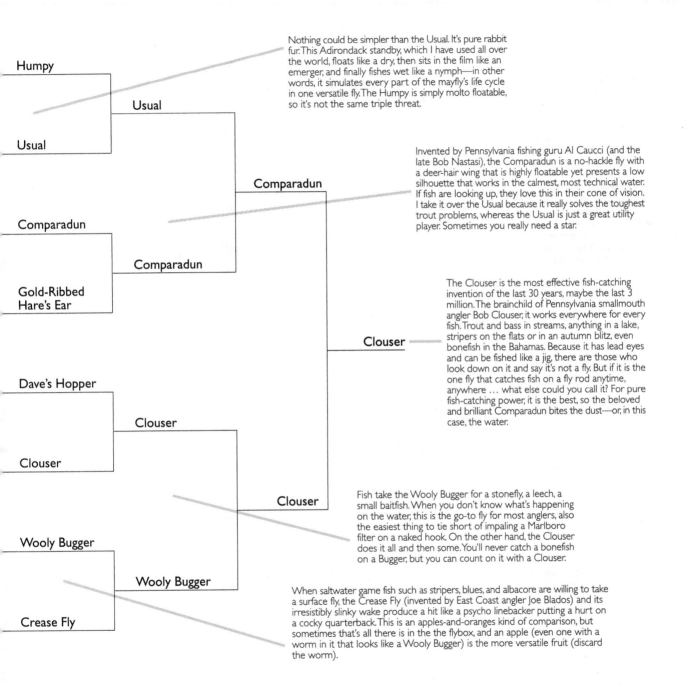

Humpy

Usual

Usual

Comparadun

Comparadun

Comparadun

Gold-Ribbed
Hare's Ear

Clouser

Dave's Hopper

Clouser

Clouser

Clouser

Wooly Bugger

Wooly Bugger

Wooly Bugger

Crease Fly

Nothing could be simpler than the Usual. It's pure rabbit fur. This Adirondack standby, which I have used all over the world, floats like a dry, then sits in the film like an emerger, and finally fishes wet like a nymph—in other words, it simulates every part of the mayfly's life cycle in one versatile fly. The Humpy is simply molto floatable, so it's not the same triple threat.

Invented by Pennsylvania fishing guru Al Caucci (and the late Bob Nastasi), the Comparadun is a no-hackle fly with a deer-hair wing that is highly floatable yet presents a low silhouette that works in the calmest, most technical water. If fish are looking up, they love this in their cone of vision. I take it over the Usual because it really solves the toughest trout problems, whereas the Usual is just a great utility player. Sometimes you really need a star.

The Clouser is the most effective fish-catching invention of the last 30 years, maybe the last 3 million. The brainchild of Pennsylvania smallmouth angler Bob Clouser, it works everywhere for every fish. Trout and bass in streams, anything in a lake, stripers on the flats or in an autumn blitz, even bonefish in the Bahamas. Because it has lead eyes and can be fished like a jig, there are those who look down on it and say it's not a fly. But if it is the one fly that catches fish on a fly rod anytime, anywhere … what else could you call it? For pure fish-catching power, it is the best, so the beloved and brilliant Comparadun bites the dust—or, in this case, the water.

Fish take the Wooly Bugger for a stonefly, a leech, a small baitfish. When you don't know what's happening on the water, this is the go-to fly for most anglers, also the easiest thing to tie short of impaling a Marlboro filter on a naked hook. On the other hand, the Clouser does it all and then some. You'll never catch a bonefish on a Bugger, but you can count on it with a Clouser.

When saltwater game fish such as stripers, blues, and albacore are willing to take a surface fly, the Crease Fly (invented by East Coast angler Joe Blados) and its irresistibly slinky wake produce a hit like a psycho linebacker putting a hurt on a cocky quarterback. This is an apples-and-oranges kind of comparison, but sometimes that's all there is in the the flybox, and an apple (even one with a worm in it that looks like a Wooly Bugger) is the more versatile fruit (discard the worm).

36

Fruit

by NEIL AMDUR

Fruit is in our cereal, our yogurt, our drinks, our salads, even our Coronas. We pour it into our blenders, buy it in bulk at Costco, and enrich Jamba Juice with our smoothie orders. But when was the last time you appreciated a piece of fruit as you would a slice of Godiva cheesecake or an exotic appetizer? Each fruit has its own texture and sweetness, taste and lusciousness, health benefits and dependability. Indeed, the personality of your preferred fruit can define who you are.

Stalwarts that require peeling before eating. The grapefruit is at a disadvantage, even when represented by its most potent variety, Indian River, which pushes the banana to its limits. But the banana survives for its universality, while Indian River is at its best when freshly squeezed and served in lightly chilled crystal.

NEIL AMDUR has spent a lifetime covering tournaments of all kinds—from tennis to the Olympics—as a reporter and then as sports editor of the *New York Times* for 12 years. One of the last questions he would routinely ask a recruit applying for a job was "If you were a fruit, what would you be?" Amdur is an apricot. More important, he has a doctorate in fruitology, whatever that means.

Round 1	Round 2
apple / lime	apple
pineapple / lemon	pineapple
fig / plum	plum
raspberry / strawberry	strawberry
kumquat / apricot	apricot
papaya / cantaloupe	cantaloupe
guava / pomegranate	pomegranate
avocado / grape	grape
banana / grapefruit	banana
mango / blueberry	mango
tangerine / pear	pear
cranberry / watermelon	watermelon
nectarine / honeydew	honeydew
blackberry / peach	peach
date / cherry	cherry
kiwi / orange	orange

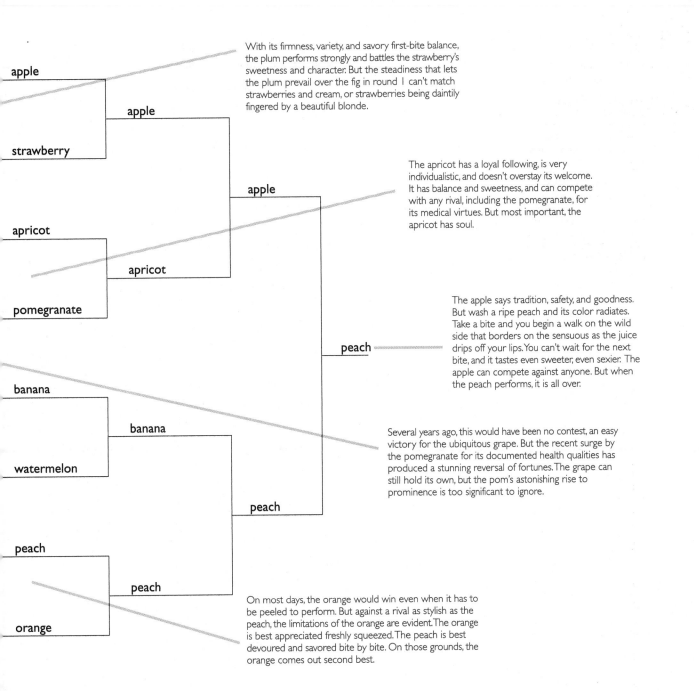

apple

apple

strawberry

apricot

apricot

pomegranate

apple

With its firmness, variety, and savory first-bite balance, the plum performs strongly and battles the strawberry's sweetness and character. But the steadiness that lets the plum prevail over the fig in round 1 can't match strawberries and cream, or strawberries being daintily fingered by a beautiful blonde.

The apricot has a loyal following, is very individualistic, and doesn't overstay its welcome. It has balance and sweetness, and can compete with any rival, including the pomegranate, for its medical virtues. But most important, the apricot has soul.

peach

The apple says tradition, safety, and goodness. But wash a ripe peach and its color radiates. Take a bite and you begin a walk on the wild side that borders on the sensuous as the juice drips off your lips. You can't wait for the next bite, and it tastes even sweeter, even sexier. The apple can compete against anyone. But when the peach performs, it is all over.

banana

banana

watermelon

peach

Several years ago, this would have been no contest, an easy victory for the ubiquitous grape. But the recent surge by the pomegranate for its documented health qualities has produced a stunning reversal of fortunes. The grape can still hold its own, but the pom's astonishing rise to prominence is too significant to ignore.

peach

peach

orange

On most days, the orange would win even when it has to be peeled to perform. But against a rival as stylish as the peach, the limitations of the orange are evident. The orange is best appreciated freshly squeezed. The peach is best devoured and savored bite by bite. On those grounds, the orange comes out second best.

37

Game Show Catchphrases

by KEN JENNINGS

Since the early days of radio, the American idiom has borrowed heavily from the repeated phrases and taglines on the nation's game shows. When catchphrases from 32 different shows, divorced from the dapper hosts who coined them, square off mano-a-mano, who will emerge undefeated and who will go home with lovely parting gifts and a copy of our home game? Ah, that's the $64,000 question.

KEN JENNINGS was a Salt Lake City software engineer in 2004 when he rose to unlikely celebrity for his 74-game, $2.52-million-winning streak on the quiz show *Jeopardy!* He now lives in Seattle and is the author of *Brainiac*, a book on American trivia culture.

Is it bigger than a breadbox? — **breadbox**
We'll take the physical challenge.

You are the weakest link. Goodbye. — **prize chosen**
Here's a prize chosen especially for you.

Get ready to match the stars! — **match the stars**
Here is your first subject. Go.

Joker! Joker! Joker! — **final answer?**
Is that your final answer?

Get Tic and Tac, and you automatically get the dough. — **Survey said…!**
Survey said…!

Not a match; the board goes back. — **Not a match**
We stop the clock, you beat the clock.

Would you like to be queen for a day? — **queen for a day**
Let's see what's behind Door Number Two!

(The password is…) — **The password is…**
Let's make it a true Daily Double.

Circle gets the square. — **Circle gets the square**
I'm putting $5,000 of *my* money on the line.

Big bucks, no whammies, STOP! — **no whammies**
Deal, or no deal?

Aces are high, deuces are low, call them right and win the dough! — **I've got a secret!**
My name is _____, and I've got a secret!

Do you feel the need for greed? — **secret woid**
Say the secret woid and win $100.

Bachelor Number One? — **please stand up**
Will the real _____ please stand up?

You didn't tell the truth, so you must pay the consequences. — **Come on down!**
Come on down!

Here's your toss-up. — **buy a vowel**
I'd like to buy a vowel.

Going once…going twice…no sale! — **name that tune**
I can name that tune in _____ notes.

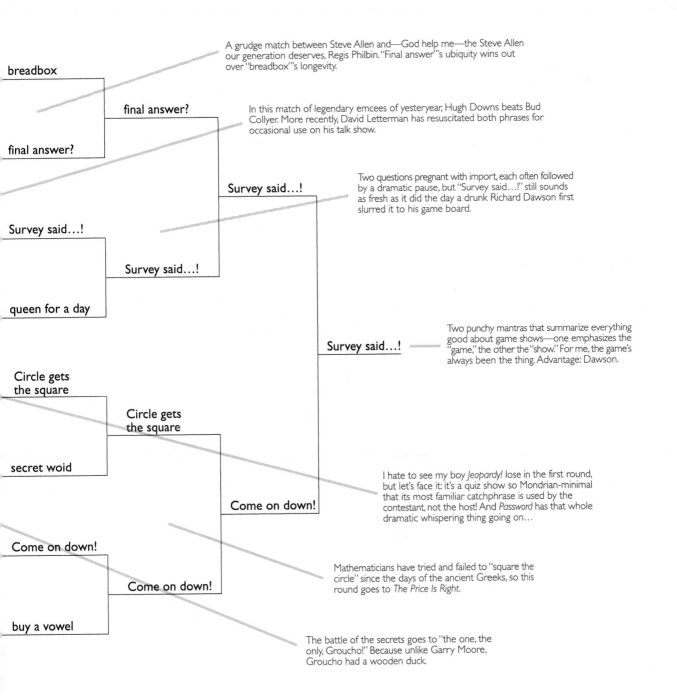

breadbox

final answer?

final answer?

Survey said…!

Survey said…!

Survey said…!

queen for a day

Survey said…!

Circle gets
the square

Circle gets
the square

secret woid

Come on down!

Come on down!

Come on down!

Come on down!

buy a vowel

A grudge match between Steve Allen and—God help me—the Steve Allen our generation deserves, Regis Philbin. "Final answer?"'s ubiquity wins out over "breadbox"'s longevity.

In this match of legendary emcees of yesteryear, Hugh Downs beats Bud Collyer. More recently, David Letterman has resuscitated both phrases for occasional use on his talk show.

Two questions pregnant with import, each often followed by a dramatic pause, but "Survey said…!" still sounds as fresh as it did the day a drunk Richard Dawson first slurred it to his game board.

Two punchy mantras that summarize everything good about game shows—one emphasizes the "game," the other the "show." For me, the game's always been the thing. Advantage: Dawson.

I hate to see my boy *Jeopardy!* lose in the first round, but let's face it: it's a quiz show so Mondrian-minimal that its most familiar catchphrase is used by the contestant, not the host! And *Password* has that whole dramatic whispering thing going on…

Mathematicians have tried and failed to "square the circle" since the days of the ancient Greeks, so this round goes to *The Price Is Right*.

The battle of the secrets goes to "the one, the only, Groucho!" Because unlike Garry Moore, Groucho had a wooden duck.

38

Sportscaster Signature Calls

by RICHARD SANDOMIR

Sportscasters can transcend time and their own deaths. They can make great calls at just the right moment and use phrases that will stick to them beyond the grave. The great play call offers the excitement and eloquence that leads to an indelible place on the eternal highlight reel. The trademark phrase blends simplicity, timelessness, and personality, which allows it to be repeated for decades and adopted by fans of every sport.

RICHARD SANDOMIR, the coeditor of this book, has been paid since 1991 by the *New York Times* to watch sports on television and dispense his opinions. The job has pretty much wrecked his enjoyment of sports, because, after all, how many fans sit around with a steno pad and pen, jotting down what the announcers are saying and counting how much network airtime Tiger Woods receives?

"The Giants win the pennant!" **Russ Hodges** — Giants win
"Down goes Frazier!" **Howard Cosell**

"The thrill of victory and the agony of defeat" **Jim McKay** — thrill of victory
"The Colts are the champions! Ameche scores!" **Bob Wolff**

"The Red Sox have won baseball's world championship. Can you believe it?" **Joe Castiglione** — He shoots
"He shoots, he scores!" **Foster Hewitt**

"Havlicek stole the ball!" **Johnny Most** — It gets through Buckner!
"A little roller up along first. Behind the bag! It gets through Buckner!" **Vin Scully**

"Holy cow!" **Phil Rizzuto** — Holy cow!
"It's awesome, baby!" **Dick Vitale**

"Gooooooaaaaaaal!" **Andrés Cantor** — Gooooooaaaaaaal!
"Kick save and a beauty." **Lloyd Petit**

"He's in the catbird seat." **Red Barber** — Two and two
"Two and two to Harvey Kuenn." **Vin Scully**

"Going, going, gone!" **Mel Allen** — Going, going, gone!
"It might be, it could be, it is…a home run!" **Harry Caray**

"Back, back, back, back, back…Oh-ho doctor!" **Red Barber** — Oh-ho doctor!
"Juuuust a bit outside." **Bob Uecker in** *Major League*

"Yes!" **Marv Albert** — Yes!
"Let's get ready to rumble." **Michael Buffer**

"There's a new home run champion of all time, and it's Henry Aaron." **Milo Hamilton** — Henry Aaron
"Touch first, Mark, you are the new single-season home run king!" **Joe Buck**

"Swish!" **Marty Glickman** — Swish!
"Whoa, Nellie!" **Keith Jackson**

"Go crazy!" **Jack Buck** — the band is out…
"They're down to the 20. Oh, the band is out on the field!" **Joe Starkey**

"Secretariat is alone. He is moving like a tremendous machine." **Chick Anderson** — Secretariat is alone
"There it is, a win for the ages." **Jim Nantz**

"They're all gone." **Jim McKay** — They're all gone
"He put him in the popcorn machine." **Chick Hearn**

"I don't believe what I just saw." **Jack Buck** — Do you believe?
"Do you believe in miracles? Yes!" **Al Michaels**

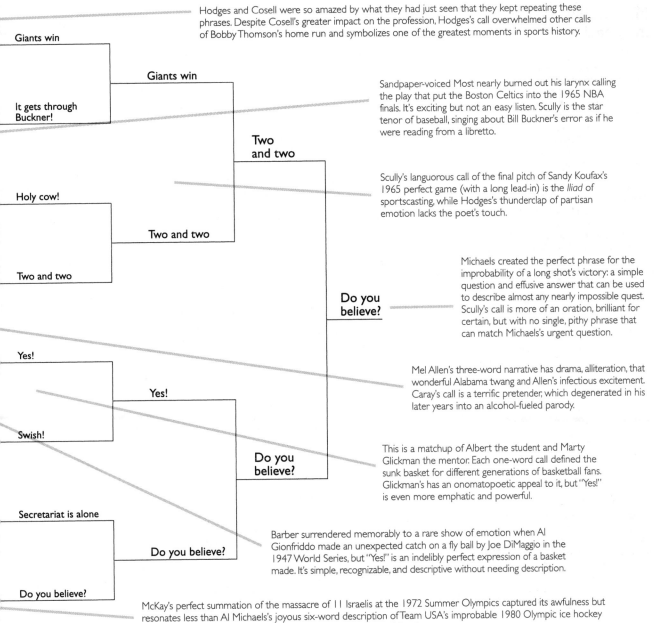

Hodges and Cosell were so amazed by what they had just seen that they kept repeating these phrases. Despite Cosell's greater impact on the profession, Hodges's call overwhelmed other calls of Bobby Thomson's home run and symbolizes one of the greatest moments in sports history.

Giants win

Giants win

It gets through Buckner!

Sandpaper-voiced Most nearly burned out his larynx calling the play that put the Boston Celtics into the 1965 NBA finals. It's exciting but not an easy listen. Scully is the star tenor of baseball, singing about Bill Buckner's error as if he were reading from a libretto.

Two and two

Holy cow!

Scully's languorous call of the final pitch of Sandy Koufax's 1965 perfect game (with a long lead-in) is the *Iliad* of sportscasting, while Hodges's thunderclap of partisan emotion lacks the poet's touch.

Two and two

Two and two

Michaels created the perfect phrase for the improbability of a long shot's victory: a simple question and effusive answer that can be used to describe almost any nearly impossible quest. Scully's call is more of an oration, brilliant for certain, but with no single, pithy phrase that can match Michaels's urgent question.

Do you believe?

Yes!

Mel Allen's three-word narrative has drama, alliteration, that wonderful Alabama twang and Allen's infectious excitement. Caray's call is a terrific pretender, which degenerated in his later years into an alcohol-fueled parody.

Yes!

Swish!

This is a matchup of Albert the student and Marty Glickman the mentor. Each one-word call defined the sunk basket for different generations of basketball fans. Glickman's has an onomatopoetic appeal to it, but "Yes!" is even more emphatic and powerful.

Do you believe?

Secretariat is alone

Barber surrendered memorably to a rare show of emotion when Al Gionfriddo made an unexpected catch on a fly ball by Joe DiMaggio in the 1947 World Series, but "Yes!" is an indelibly perfect expression of a basket made. It's simple, recognizable, and descriptive without needing description.

Do you believe?

Do you believe?

McKay's perfect summation of the massacre of 11 Israelis at the 1972 Summer Olympics captured its awfulness but resonates less than Al Michaels's joyous six-word description of Team USA's improbable 1980 Olympic ice hockey victory over the Soviets, and translated cold war angst into celebration.

39

Memorable Lines in Speeches

by JEFF SHESOL

A sound bite is like a smoke ring: a neat trick, maybe, but it's gone in an instant; it dissolves in the air. A truly great line, however, transcends its time and place. And it does more than simply endure. The very best lines redefine reality, changing the way people think or act. Most of the first-round entries here are from political speeches, the majority of them from the mouths of presidents (because presidents weigh in on vital issues and people pay a lot of attention). But a few civilian speeches make the cut—some with cinematic origins—because they have the same effect: they redefine your reality, bury themselves in your brain, and get you talking.

JEFF SHESOL, a former speechwriter for President Bill Clinton, is disappointed that none of his own best lines made the opening round. Shesol is the author of *Mutual Contempt: Lyndon Johnson, Robert Kennedy and the Feud That Defined a Decade*, and of a forthcoming book on Franklin Roosevelt.

"I want a kinder and gentler nation"—George H.W. Bush, 1988
"Either you are with us, or you are with the terrorists"—George W. Bush, 2001
— with the terrorists

"Those who hate you don't win unless you hate them; and then you destroy yourself"—Nixon, 1974
"You like me—right now, you like me!"—Sally Field, 1985
— Those who hate you

"It is not the critic who counts…the credit belongs to the man who is actually in the arena"—T. Roosevelt, 1910
"We must not confuse dissent with disloyalty"—Edward R. Murrow, 1954
— dissent

"We have nothing to fear but fear itself"—FDR, 1933
"Our long national nightmare is over"—Gerald Ford, 1974
— We have nothing to fear

"Give me liberty or give me death!"—Patrick Henry, 1775
"Extremism in the defense of liberty is no vice"—Barry Goldwater, 1964
— Give me liberty

"With malice toward none; with charity for all"—Lincoln, 1865
"This nation, under God, shall have a new birth of freedom"—Lincoln, 1863
— new birth of freedom

"The world must be made safe for democracy"—W. Wilson, 1917
"Peace, commerce, and honest friendship with all nations; entangling alliances with none"—Jefferson, 1801
— safe for democracy

"We must guard against…unwarranted influence…by the military-industrial complex"—Eisenhower, 1961
"Battle is the most magnificent competition in which a human being can indulge"—Patton, 1943
— military-industrial complex

"Each time a man stands up for an ideal…he sends forth a tiny ripple of hope"—Robert F. Kennedy, 1966
"I still believe in a place called Hope"—Bill Clinton, 1992
— tiny ripple of hope

"Some of us are becoming the men we wanted to marry"—Gloria Steinem, 1981
"Women would rather be loved than liberated"—Phyllis Schlafly, 1979
— men we wanted to marry

"I have a dream"—M.L.K. Jr., 1963
"We shall be as a city upon a hill"—John Winthrop, 1630
— dream

"Political power grows out of the barrel of a gun"—Mao, 1938
"Let it be the ballot or the bullet"—Malcolm X, 1964
— ballot or the bullet

"I have nothing to offer but blood, toil, tears, and sweat"—Churchill, 1940
"This was their finest hour"—Churchill, 1940
— blood, toil, tears

"You all think I'm licked…well, I'm not licked"—Sen. Jefferson Smith, *Mr. Smith Goes to Washington*, 1939
"They're not going to lick me…I'll never go hungry again!"—Scarlett O'Hara, *Gone with the Wind*, 1939
— I'll never go hungry again!

"This administration… declares unconditional war on poverty"—LBJ, 1964
"Government is not the solution to our problem; government is the problem"—Reagan, 1981
— government is the problem

"Ask not what your country can do for you; ask what you can do for your country"—JFK, 1961
"Greed…is good"—Gordon Gekko, *Wall Street*, 1987
— Ask not

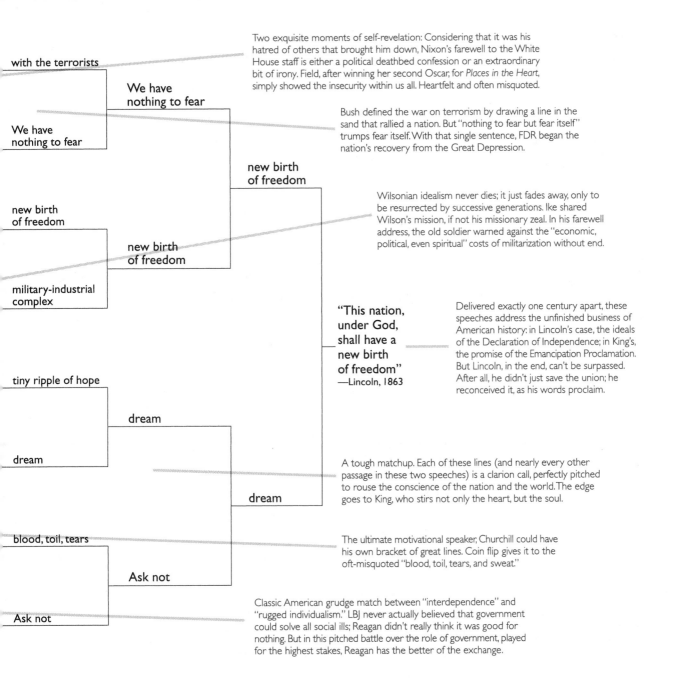

with the terrorists

We have
nothing to fear

We have
nothing to fear

Two exquisite moments of self-revelation: Considering that it was his hatred of others that brought him down, Nixon's farewell to the White House staff is either a political deathbed confession or an extraordinary bit of irony. Field, after winning her second Oscar, for *Places in the Heart*, simply showed the insecurity within us all. Heartfelt and often misquoted.

Bush defined the war on terrorism by drawing a line in the sand that rallied a nation. But "nothing to fear but fear itself" trumps fear itself. With that single sentence, FDR began the nation's recovery from the Great Depression.

new birth
of freedom

new birth
of freedom

new birth
of freedom

military-industrial
complex

Wilsonian idealism never dies; it just fades away, only to be resurrected by successive generations. Ike shared Wilson's mission, if not his missionary zeal. In his farewell address, the old soldier warned against the "economic, political, even spiritual" costs of militarization without end.

"This nation, under God, shall have a new birth of freedom"
—Lincoln, 1863

Delivered exactly one century apart, these speeches address the unfinished business of American history: in Lincoln's case, the ideals of the Declaration of Independence; in King's, the promise of the Emancipation Proclamation. But Lincoln, in the end, can't be surpassed. After all, he didn't just save the union; he reconceived it, as his words proclaim.

tiny ripple of hope

dream

dream

dream

A tough matchup. Each of these lines (and nearly every other passage in these two speeches) is a clarion call, perfectly pitched to rouse the conscience of the nation and the world. The edge goes to King, who stirs not only the heart, but the soul.

blood, toil, tears

Ask not

Ask not

The ultimate motivational speaker, Churchill could have his own bracket of great lines. Coin flip gives it to the oft-misquoted "blood, toil, tears, and sweat."

Classic American grudge match between "interdependence" and "rugged individualism." LBJ never actually believed that government could solve all social ills; Reagan didn't really think it was good for nothing. But in this pitched battle over the role of government, played for the highest stakes, Reagan has the better of the exchange.

40

Golf Swing Thoughts

by CHRISTOPHER SMITH

Golf is a game played mostly between the ears. So your thoughts just before you swing matter. Any given golfer could have a thousand swing thoughts running through his brain as he heads to the course. Nine hundred of those are worthless. The other hundred, while useful at times, must be managed. If the experts are right, you can only have one dominant thought during a swing. That thought might change, depending on the strengths and weaknesses of your game. Thirty-two possibilities are listed here.

CHRISTOPHER SMITH, a teaching pro at Pumpkin Ridge Golf Club in North Plains, Oregon, was the Northwest PGA Teacher of the Year in 2004. He is a champion speed golfer (the ultimate "thought-free" golf), once shooting 65 in 44 minutes carrying only 6 clubs. His book, *I've Got 99 Swing Thoughts but Hit the Ball Ain't One*, will be published in 2007.

head stays behind the ball through impact
keep head still
— head stays behind ball

cover the ball with chest at impact
shift weight to left side on downswing
— cover at impact

hit ball first and then turf
on downswing drop the club inside the backswing plane
— hit ball first and then turf

keep hands ahead of the ball at impact
swing the handle, not the clubhead
— hands ahead of ball

hit the ball in the middle of the clubface
release the club through impact area
— middle of the clubface

finish facing the target
roll the clubface over through impact
— finish facing target

stay smooth and balanced throughout
extend arms toward target through impact
— smooth and balanced

finish with your hands high
shift weight to left side
— weight on left side

keep spine angle constant
turn left shoulder behind the ball
— spine angle constant

stay connected and stop backswing short of parallel
clear hips on the downswing
— stay connected

focus on your target and ball flight
keep the clubhead in front of your body
— focus on target

hinge wrists on backswing when hands reach waist high
coil upper body around lower body like a spring
— hinge wrists

one-piece takeaway
start downswing by pushing off your right foot
— one-piece takeaway

keep your forearms close together throughout
keep your left arm straight
— forearms together

constant, light grip pressure throughout
don't let your right arm overpower your left
— light grip

take clubhead back low to the ground the first 18 inches
load your weight on your right leg at top of backswing
— clubhead low

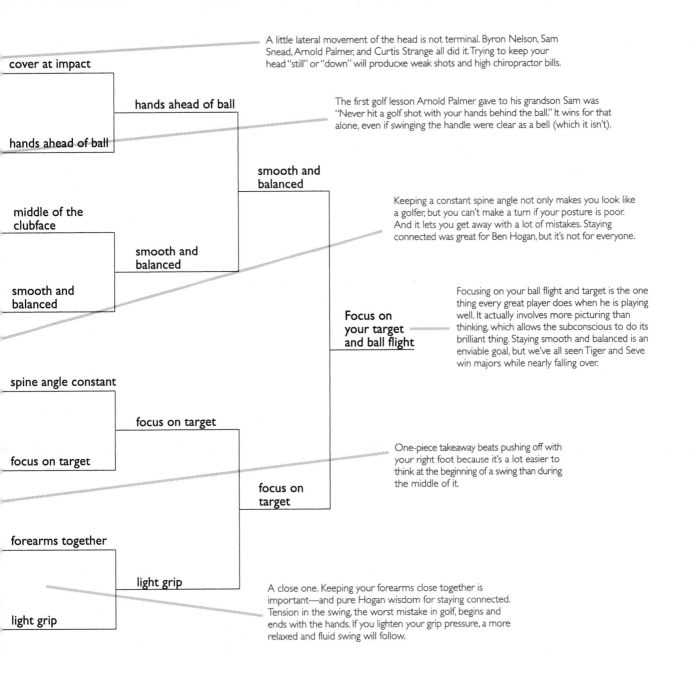

cover at impact

A little lateral movement of the head is not terminal. Byron Nelson, Sam Snead, Arnold Palmer, and Curtis Strange all did it. Trying to keep your head "still" or "down" will producxe weak shots and high chiropractor bills.

hands ahead of ball

The first golf lesson Arnold Palmer gave to his grandson Sam was "Never hit a golf shot with your hands behind the ball." It wins for that alone, even if swinging the handle were clear as a bell (which it isn't).

hands ahead of ball

smooth and balanced

middle of the clubface

Keeping a constant spine angle not only makes you look like a golfer, but you can't make a turn if your posture is poor. And it lets you get away with a lot of mistakes. Staying connected was great for Ben Hogan, but it's not for everyone.

smooth and balanced

smooth and balanced

Focus on your target and ball flight

Focusing on your ball flight and target is the one thing every great player does when he is playing well. It actually involves more picturing than thinking, which allows the subconscious to do its brilliant thing. Staying smooth and balanced is an enviable goal, but we've all seen Tiger and Seve win majors while nearly falling over.

spine angle constant

focus on target

focus on target

focus on target

One-piece takeaway beats pushing off with your right foot because it's a lot easier to think at the beginning of a swing than during the middle of it.

forearms together

light grip

light grip

A close one. Keeping your forearms close together is important—and pure Hogan wisdom for staying connected. Tension in the swing, the worst mistake in golf, begins and ends with the hands. If you lighten your grip pressure, a more relaxed and fluid swing will follow.

41

Horses for the Ages

by WILLIAM NACK

The horse has been man's guide, inspiration, fellow warrior, costar, and beast of burden since the first hominid caught him with a length of prehistoric ivy, tamed and domesticated him, and climbed on board for his first ride into the antediluvian sunset. For centuries steeds have carried men to the finish line and off to war, most famously Alexander the Great's Bucephalus and Richard III's Surrey, whose demise spurred Richard to cry: "My kingdom for a horse!" All 32 entries here were chosen for the bright and pleasant images they conjure, for the part they played in our culture and history, and for their endurance as equine icons.

WILLIAM NACK has been a thoroughbred racing writer since 1972, the last 23 years for *Sports Illustrated*. He has won seven Eclipse Awards for excellence in turf writing. His book *Secretariat: The Making of a Champion* was hailed by Britain's distinguished *Racing Post* as "the greatest equine biography ever written." His personal memoir of Ruffian will be published in 2007.

Two TV partners go at it. Tonto's horse, Scout, was the homely, blue-collar pinto routinely upstaged by the Lone Ranger's steed, Silver, preening on his hind legs to the blaring of the *William Tell* Overture. Here the world's most famous pinto gets his revenge.

Secretariat
Dan Patch — Secretariat

Scout
Silver — Scout

Wing Commander
Trigger — Wing Commander

Trojan Horse
Flicka — Trojan Horse

Little Sorrel
Traveller — Little Sorrel

Cigar
The Pie — The Pie

Black Beauty
Mr. Ed — Mr. Ed

Pegasus
Ruffian — Ruffian

Greyhound
Phar Lap — Greyhound

Man o' War
Paul Revere's horse — Man o' War

Surrey
Henry the Horse — Surrey

Upset
Eclipse — Upset

Barbaro
Smarty Jones — Barbaro

Champion
Bucephalus — Bucephalus

Go Man Go
Swaps — Swaps

The Old Gray Mare
Rocinante — The Old Gray Mare

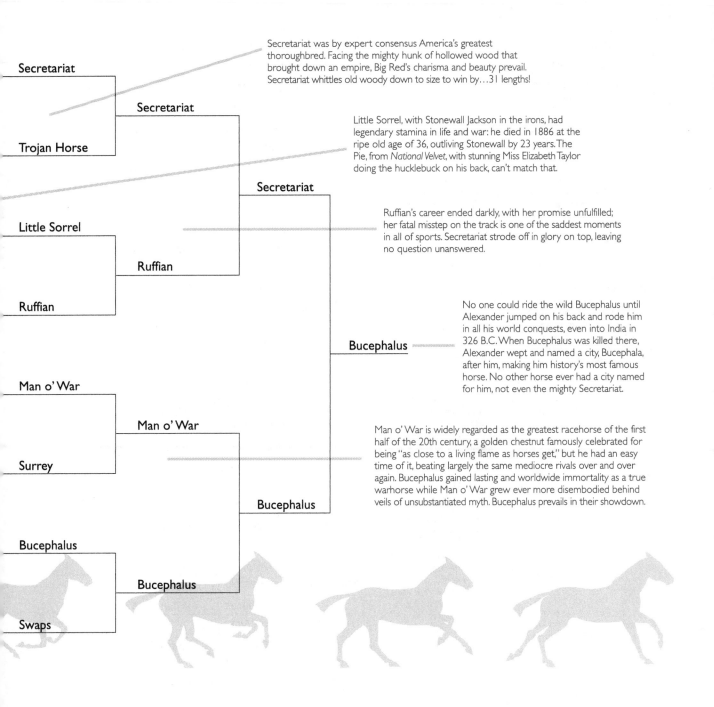

Secretariat

Trojan Horse

Secretariat

Secretariat was by expert consensus America's greatest thoroughbred. Facing the mighty hunk of hollowed wood that brought down an empire, Big Red's charisma and beauty prevail. Secretariat whittles old woody down to size to win by…31 lengths!

Little Sorrel, with Stonewall Jackson in the irons, had legendary stamina in life and war: he died in 1886 at the ripe old age of 36, outliving Stonewall by 23 years. The Pie, from *National Velvet*, with stunning Miss Elizabeth Taylor doing the hucklebuck on his back, can't match that.

Secretariat

Little Sorrel

Ruffian

Ruffian

Ruffian's career ended darkly, with her promise unfulfilled; her fatal misstep on the track is one of the saddest moments in all of sports. Secretariat strode off in glory on top, leaving no question unanswered.

Bucephalus

No one could ride the wild Bucephalus until Alexander jumped on his back and rode him in all his world conquests, even into India in 326 B.C. When Bucephalus was killed there, Alexander wept and named a city, Bucephala, after him, making him history's most famous horse. No other horse ever had a city named for him, not even the mighty Secretariat.

Man o' War

Man o' War

Surrey

Man o' War is widely regarded as the greatest racehorse of the first half of the 20th century, a golden chestnut famously celebrated for being "as close to a living flame as horses get," but he had an easy time of it, beating largely the same mediocre rivals over and over again. Bucephalus gained lasting and worldwide immortality as a true warhorse while Man o' War grew ever more disembodied behind veils of unsubstantiated myth. Bucephalus prevails in their showdown.

Bucephalus

Bucephalus

Bucephalus

Swaps

42

Jock Films
by RICHARD SANDOMIR

Ever notice that the best sports films are about baseball and boxing? Fourteen were invited to this year's tournament, and one from each sport moved to the final. Pool, horse racing, and even swordplay in the Roman Colosseum got invites too, but major sports like football and basketball (*The Fish That Saved Pittsburgh* couldn't make a Division III tourney) rarely achieve greatness. Comedies are rare; *Caddyshack* advanced because Bill Murray's Carl Spackler played golf with the Dalai Lama. To make it beyond round 1, a sports film must follow rule 1: The actors must look like they could actually play the sport. *Pride of the Yankees*, with Gary Cooper's lame at-bats and fielding, is the exception that proves the rule.

RICHARD SANDOMIR, the coeditor of this book, watches sports on television for a living as a columnist for the *New York Times*. He has watched one film in the tournament more than any other: *A League of Their Own*.

Nazi documentary about the 1936 Berlin Olympics up against baseball parable by quintessential Jewish novelist Bernard Malamud. Director Barry Levinson sugar-coated the rise, fall, and rise of slugger Roy Hobbs, but he was working for TriStar Pictures, not Der Führer. Redford's smooth swing trumps Hitler's stiff-armed salute.

A De Niro faceoff. His wussy, dim-witted, dying catcher in *Bang* proves the young Don Corleone could do "sensitive," but his Oscar-winning portrayal of the nasty, relentless boxer Jake LaMotta is the signature De Niro character.

A matchup of athletes dying young: one by incurable disease (Gary Cooper's Lou Gehrig in *Pride*), the other Hilary Swank's paralyzed boxer who begs her trainer to end it all. *Pride* goes to the next round on dignity points. Gehrig dies off-screen while *Baby's* Maggie bites her tongue.

Rocky — Rocky
Bend It Like Beckham
Chariots of Fire — Chariots of Fire
Jerry Maguire
The Color of Money — The Color of Money
Grand Prix
Hoop Dreams — Hoop Dreams
The Bad News Bears
Olympia — The Natural
The Natural
Bull Durham — Bull Durham
Damn Yankees
Field of Dreams — Field of Dreams
A League of Their Own
Slap Shot — Slap Shot
Breaking Away
The Hustler — The Hustler
The Program
Raging Bull — Raging Bull
Bang the Drum Slowly
Million Dollar Baby — Pride of the Yankees
Pride of the Yankees
Gladiator — Gladiator
Rollerball
Caddyshack — Caddyshack
One Day in September
Hoosiers — Hoosiers
Requiem for a Heavyweight
Seabiscuit — When We Were Kings
When We Were Kings
Eight Men Out — Brian's Song
Brian's Song

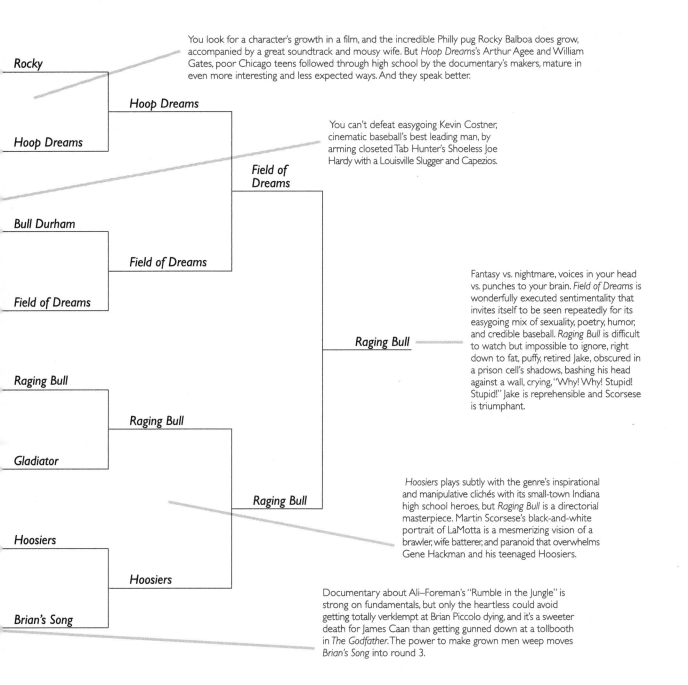

Rocky

Hoop Dreams

Hoop Dreams

Bull Durham

Field of Dreams

Field of Dreams

Raging Bull

Raging Bull

Gladiator

Hoosiers

Hoosiers

Brian's Song

Field of Dreams

Raging Bull

Raging Bull

You look for a character's growth in a film, and the incredible Philly pug Rocky Balboa does grow, accompanied by a great soundtrack and mousy wife. But *Hoop Dreams*'s Arthur Agee and William Gates, poor Chicago teens followed through high school by the documentary's makers, mature in even more interesting and less expected ways. And they speak better.

You can't defeat easygoing Kevin Costner, cinematic baseball's best leading man, by arming closeted Tab Hunter's Shoeless Joe Hardy with a Louisville Slugger and Capezios.

Fantasy vs. nightmare, voices in your head vs. punches to your brain. *Field of Dreams* is wonderfully executed sentimentality that invites itself to be seen repeatedly for its easygoing mix of sexuality, poetry, humor, and credible baseball. *Raging Bull* is difficult to watch but impossible to ignore, right down to fat, puffy, retired Jake, obscured in a prison cell's shadows, bashing his head against a wall, crying, "Why! Why! Stupid! Stupid!" Jake is reprehensible and Scorsese is triumphant.

Hoosiers plays subtly with the genre's inspirational and manipulative clichés with its small-town Indiana high school heroes, but *Raging Bull* is a directorial masterpiece. Martin Scorsese's black-and-white portrait of LaMotta is a mesmerizing vision of a brawler, wife batterer, and paranoid that overwhelms Gene Hackman and his teenaged Hoosiers.

Documentary about Ali–Foreman's "Rumble in the Jungle" is strong on fundamentals, but only the heartless could avoid getting totally verklempt at Brian Piccolo dying, and it's a sweeter death for James Caan than getting gunned down at a tollbooth in *The Godfather*. The power to make grown men weep moves *Brian's Song* into round 3.

43

Guilty Pleasures

by SIMON TREWIN,
TOM BROMLEY, and
MICHAEL MORAN

Guilty pleasures are those indulgences that you confess only to your closest friends (if at all). They fill us with shame and pleasure in equal measure. We prefer to celebrate them. Using a geek logic equation—the Employment Frequency Algorithm (how often do you do this?) times Social Scorn Ratio (how many peers do it too?) plus Ironic Boastfulness Factor (would you actually brag about it after four beers?) divided by Happiness Quota (do you smile during the deed?), we came up with these 32. Think of the process as the first step down the rocky road toward cultural rehabilitation. You'll find comfort knowing you are not alone in your appalling lapses in taste and judgment?

SIMON, TOM, and MICHAEL are the coauthors collectively of the UK bestseller *The Encyclopaedia of Guilty Pleasures: 1001 Things You Hate to Love*. They invite you (yes, you) to confess your secrets at 1001guiltypleasures.com. C'mon, you know you want to.

looking in people's bathroom cabinets — bathroom cabinets
not waking people up on last train home

able-bodied use of disabled bathrooms — first-class upgrade
getting an upgrade to first class

faking out dogs with pretend ball throws — faking out dogs
having a fat pet

DVD extras (wasting time watching) — DVD extras
dirty images on Google (wasting time searching for)

e-mail offering free money from Nigeria — Nigerian e-mail
e-mail (pretending to be someone else when sending)

insisting on English wherever you are — misdirecting tourists
misdirecting tourists

finding and taking last seat on bus or train — farting in elevator
farting in the elevator (just before getting out)

telling truth about a girlfriend's appearance — peeing in shower
peeing in the shower

gym (not going to the) — gym (not going)
gym (going to the)

Hair straighteners — nostril hair trimmers
nostril hair trimmers

lying about having met heroes — heroes
kissing and telling

Paris Hilton — Paris Hilton
Donald Trump

faking it — masturbation
masturbation

stealing from hotel rooms — cheating on expenses
cheating on expenses (petty or not)

Molly Ringwald in *The Breakfast Club* — Molly Ringwald
Romy and Michele's High School Reunion

diet fads (believing in) — Krispy Kreme donuts
Krispy Kreme donuts (consumption of)

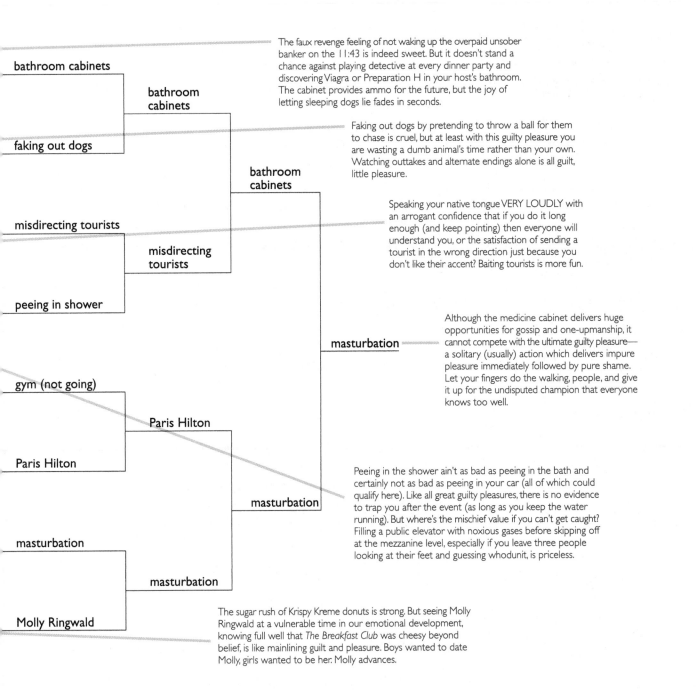

bathroom cabinets

bathroom cabinets

faking out dogs

The faux revenge feeling of not waking up the overpaid unsober banker on the 11:43 is indeed sweet. But it doesn't stand a chance against playing detective at every dinner party and discovering Viagra or Preparation H in your host's bathroom. The cabinet provides ammo for the future, but the joy of letting sleeping dogs lie fades in seconds.

Faking out dogs by pretending to throw a ball for them to chase is cruel, but at least with this guilty pleasure you are wasting a dumb animal's time rather than your own. Watching outtakes and alternate endings alone is all guilt, little pleasure.

bathroom cabinets

misdirecting tourists

misdirecting tourists

peeing in shower

Speaking your native tongue VERY LOUDLY with an arrogant confidence that if you do it long enough (and keep pointing) then everyone will understand you, or the satisfaction of sending a tourist in the wrong direction just because you don't like their accent? Baiting tourists is more fun.

masturbation

Although the medicine cabinet delivers huge opportunities for gossip and one-upmanship, it cannot compete with the ultimate guilty pleasure—a solitary (usually) action which delivers impure pleasure immediately followed by pure shame. Let your fingers do the walking, people, and give it up for the undisputed champion that everyone knows too well.

gym (not going)

Paris Hilton

Paris Hilton

Peeing in the shower ain't as bad as peeing in the bath and certainly not as bad as peeing in your car (all of which could qualify here). Like all great guilty pleasures, there is no evidence to trap you after the event (as long as you keep the water running). But where's the mischief value if you can't get caught? Filling a public elevator with noxious gases before skipping off at the mezzanine level, especially if you leave three people looking at their feet and guessing whodunit, is priceless.

masturbation

masturbation

masturbation

Molly Ringwald

The sugar rush of Krispy Kreme donuts is strong. But seeing Molly Ringwald at a vulnerable time in our emotional development, knowing full well that The Breakfast Club was cheesy beyond belief, is like mainlining guilt and pleasure. Boys wanted to date Molly, girls wanted to be her. Molly advances.

44

Guitar Solos
by ALLEN ST. JOHN

In *This Is Spinal Tap*, when a bare-chested Nigel Tufnel is left alone on stage, eyes closed, his amp turned up to 11, choking a riff out of his squealing Gibson Flying V by rubbing a violin across the fretboard, he might as well be engaged in another brand of, um, soloing. But at its best, the guitar solo rises well above self-parody, blending melody and groove in a way that even the human voice can't match. To provide a field that rises above the usual air-guitar fodder, I'm employing a broad definition of "solo." You'll find jazzers, bluesmen, and country pickers as well as rockers; instruments electric and acoustic; and solos that last minutes while others are more like riffs on steroids. Only one solo to a customer, or the champ might be facing off against himself in the finals.

ALLEN ST. JOHN is the author of *Clapton's Guitar: Watching Wayne Henderson Build the Perfect Instrument* (Free Press, 2005). He's currently working on a solo acoustic version of "Smoke on the Water."

Jimmy Page, "Stairway to Heaven" (Led Zeppelin)
Chuck Berry, "Johnny B. Goode" — "Johnny B. Goode"

Freddie King, "Hide Away"
Joe Walsh/Don Felder, "Hotel California" (The Eagles) — "Hide Away"

George Harrison, "And Your Bird Can Sing" (The Beatles)
Steve Cropper, "Soul Man" (Sam & Dave) — "And Your Bird Can Sing"

John Fogerty, "Born on the Bayou" (Creedence Clearwater Revival)
Skunk Baxter, "My Old School" (Steely Dan) — "My Old School"

Carlos Santana, "Black Magic Woman" (Santana)
Robbie Robertson, "King Harvest" (The Band) — "King Harvest"

David Gilmour, "Comfortably Numb" (Pink Floyd)
Wes Montgomery, "Four on Six" — "Comfortably Numb"

Doc Watson, "Black Mountain Rag"
Gary Rossington/Allen Collins, "Free Bird" (Lynyrd Skynyrd) — "Black Mountain Rag"

Charlie Christian, "Solo Flight"
Jimi Hendrix, "Voodoo Child (Slight Return)" — "Voodoo Child"

Duane Allman, "Layla" (Derek and the Dominoes)
Albert Collins, "Frosty" — "Layla"

Merle Travis, "Cannon Ball Rag"
Frank Zappa, "Zoot Allures" — "Cannon Ball Rag"

Jeff Beck, "Goodbye Porkpie Hat"
Eric Clapton, "Crossroads" (Cream) — "Crossroads" (Clapton)

Robert Johnson, "Crossroads"
Keith Richards, "Sympathy for the Devil" (The Rolling Stones) — "Crossroads" (Johnson)

Prince, "Little Red Corvette"
Richard Thompson, "Calvary Cross" — "Calvary Cross"

Eddie Van Halen, "Eruption" (Van Halen)
Django Reinhardt, "Minor Swing" — "Minor Swing"

Kirk Hammett, "One" (Metallica)
Stevie Ray Vaughan, "Texas Flood" — "Texas Flood"

Kurt Cobain, "Smells Like Teen Spirit:" (Nirvana)
Mark Knopfler, "Sultans of Swing" (Dire Straits) — "Sultans of Swing"

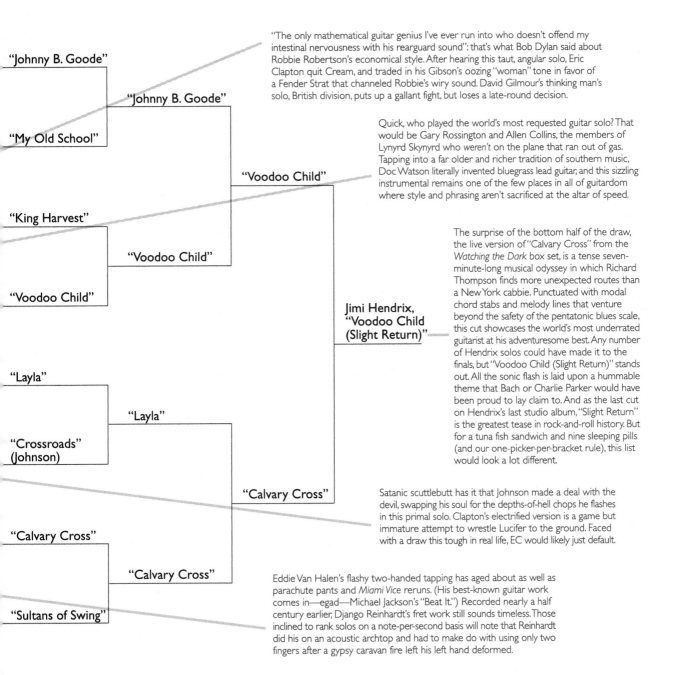

"Johnny B. Goode"

"Johnny B. Goode"

"My Old School"

"Voodoo Child"

"King Harvest"

"Voodoo Child"

"Voodoo Child"

Jimi Hendrix, "Voodoo Child (Slight Return)"

"Layla"

"Layla"

"Crossroads" (Johnson)

"Calvary Cross"

"Calvary Cross"

"Calvary Cross"

"Sultans of Swing"

"The only mathematical guitar genius I've ever run into who doesn't offend my intestinal nervousness with his rearguard sound": that's what Bob Dylan said about Robbie Robertson's economical style. After hearing this taut, angular solo, Eric Clapton quit Cream, and traded in his Gibson's oozing "woman" tone in favor of a Fender Strat that channeled Robbie's wiry sound. David Gilmour's thinking man's solo, British division, puts up a gallant fight, but loses a late-round decision.

Quick, who played the world's most requested guitar solo? That would be Gary Rossington and Allen Collins, the members of Lynyrd Skynyrd who weren't on the plane that ran out of gas. Tapping into a far older and richer tradition of southern music, Doc Watson literally invented bluegrass lead guitar, and this sizzling instrumental remains one of the few places in all of guitardom where style and phrasing aren't sacrificed at the altar of speed.

The surprise of the bottom half of the draw, the live version of "Calvary Cross" from the Watching the Dark box set, is a tense seven-minute-long musical odyssey in which Richard Thompson finds more unexpected routes than a New York cabbie. Punctuated with modal chord stabs and melody lines that venture beyond the safety of the pentatonic blues scale, this cut showcases the world's most underrated guitarist at his adventuresome best. Any number of Hendrix solos could have made it to the finals, but "Voodoo Child (Slight Return)" stands out. All the sonic flash is laid upon a hummable theme that Bach or Charlie Parker would have been proud to lay claim to. And as the last cut on Hendrix's last studio album, "Slight Return" is the greatest tease in rock-and-roll history. But for a tuna fish sandwich and nine sleeping pills (and our one-picker-per-bracket rule), this list would look a lot different.

Satanic scuttlebutt has it that Johnson made a deal with the devil, swapping his soul for the depths-of-hell chops he flashes in this primal solo. Clapton's electrified version is a game but immature attempt to wrestle Lucifer to the ground. Faced with a draw this tough in real life, EC would likely just default.

Eddie Van Halen's flashy two-handed tapping has aged about as well as parachute pants and Miami Vice reruns. (His best-known guitar work comes in—egad—Michael Jackson's "Beat It.") Recorded nearly a half century earlier, Django Reinhardt's fret work still sounds timeless. Those inclined to rank solos on a note-per-second basis will note that Reinhardt did his on an acoustic archtop and had to make do with using only two fingers after a gypsy caravan fire left his left hand deformed.

45

Hairstyles
by GERSH KUNTZMAN

Clothes make the man? That hasn't been true since the ancient Egyptians tried to cure baldness by spreading a salve of burnt mice on the naked pate. Millennia later, mankind is finally ready to realize something my wife taught me on our first date: hairstyle is vital (in my personal case, she told me she would not have a second date with me unless I got rid of my Jewfro, which to that point in my life had been my pride and joy). The right hairstyle can help its wearer achieve power (the Caesar, the Hillary), show a devotion to a cause (the tonsure), or start a revolution (the moptop). Can a suit do that?

Despite sporting a full head of hair, GERSH KUNTZMAN is the author of HAIR! Mankind's Historic Quest to End Baldness (Random House, 2001). Since one piece of hack work just wouldn't do, he also wrote Chrismukkah: The Official Guide to the World's Most-Beloved Holiday (Sasquatch Books, 2006). Gersh also was a columnist for Newsweek and the New York Post and is editor in chief of the Brooklyn Papers, a chain of weeklies.

Tournament bracket:

- the Aniston / the beehive → Aniston
- the combover / the tonsure → tonsure
- the Mohawk / the rattail → Mohawk
- the Hillary / the pageboy → Hillary
- the crew cut / the bouffant → crew cut
- the ponytail / Rick James's greasy Jheri Curl → Rick James
- that glam metal crap like Flock of Seagulls / the Caesar → Caesar
- French braids / the mullet → French braids
- the Afro / the Farrah → Afro
- the Jewfro / Grace Jones's high-top fade → Jewfro
- the bob / the moptop → moptop
- the pompadour / pigtails → pompadour
- cornrows / punk → cornrows
- payos / cowlick → payos
- the bowl cut / dreadlocks → dreadlocks
- the Cyndi Lauper (multicolored) / the bun → Cyndi Lauper

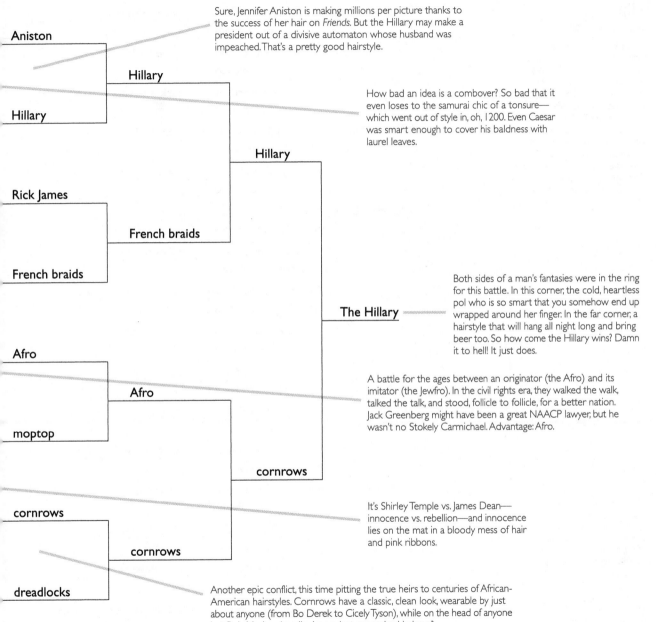

Aniston

Hillary

Hillary

Sure, Jennifer Aniston is making millions per picture thanks to the success of her hair on *Friends*. But the Hillary may make a president out of a divisive automaton whose husband was impeached. That's a pretty good hairstyle.

Hillary

How bad an idea is a combover? So bad that it even loses to the samurai chic of a tonsure—which went out of style in, oh, 1200. Even Caesar was smart enough to cover his baldness with laurel leaves.

Rick James

French braids

French braids

The Hillary

Both sides of a man's fantasies were in the ring for this battle. In this corner, the cold, heartless pol who is so smart that you somehow end up wrapped around her finger. In the far corner, a hairstyle that will hang all night long and bring beer too. So how come the Hillary wins? Damn it to hell! It just does.

Afro

Afro

moptop

A battle for the ages between an originator (the Afro) and its imitator (the Jewfro). In the civil rights era, they walked the walk, talked the talk, and stood, follicle to follicle, for a better nation. Jack Greenberg might have been a great NAACP lawyer, but he wasn't no Stokely Carmichael. Advantage: Afro.

cornrows

cornrows

cornrows

It's Shirley Temple vs. James Dean—innocence vs. rebellion—and innocence lies on the mat in a bloody mess of hair and pink ribbons.

dreadlocks

Another epic conflict, this time pitting the true heirs to centuries of African-American hairstyles. Cornrows have a classic, clean look, wearable by just about anyone (from Bo Derek to Cicely Tyson), while on the head of anyone but Bob Marley, dreadlocks are just uncombed hair, no?

46

Hip
by JOHN LELAND

What is hip? You could create brackets just on the etymology. Some linguists cite the West African words *hipi* or *hepi*, meaning "to see" or "to open your eyes." Others think it came from the Prohibition-era use of hip flasks, or the telltale bruises on the hips of recumbent opium smokers. We yield to the Bay Area funk band Tower of Power: "Hipness is what it is/And sometimes hipness is/What it ain't."

JOHN LELAND is a reporter at the *New York Times* and author of *Hip: The History.* He is writing a book about Jack Kerouac's *On the Road,* to appear in fall 2007. He has been a hip-hop DJ and a new wave drummer, and briefly attended a school for professional wrestlers.

Bob Dylan in the '60s ┐ young Dylan
Bugs Bunny ┘

Charlie "Yardbird" Parker ┐ Charlie Parker
Béla Bartók ┘

Jack Kerouac ┐ Jack Kerouac
iPod nano ┘

Herman Melville's *The Confidence-Man* ┐ *The Confidence-Man*
TV's *The Prisoner* ┘

Bob Dylan in his 60s ┐ old Dylan
the Jewfro ┘

The Velvet Underground & Nico vinyl LP ┐ *The Velvet Underground & Nico*
ironic retro furniture ┘

black turtleneck ┐ black turtleneck
boxy architect's glasses ┘

Bathing Ape clothing ┐ low-fi 7-inch singles
low-fi 7-inch singles ┘

dead bluesmen ┐ dead rappers
dead rappers ┘

rock stars ┐ porn stars
porn stars ┘

skater/snowboard kids ┐ pimps
pimps ┘

hard-boiled detective fiction ┐ underground hip-hop
underground hip-hop ┘

weird collectible kitsch from Japan ┐ Gil Evans
Gil Evans ┘

Miles Davis ┐ Miles Davis
Machinima ┘

Paul Bowles ┐ Paul Bowles
Mark Twain ┘

Dennis Hopper's oeuvre ┐ Dennis Hopper's oeuvre
Billy Wilder's oeuvre ┘

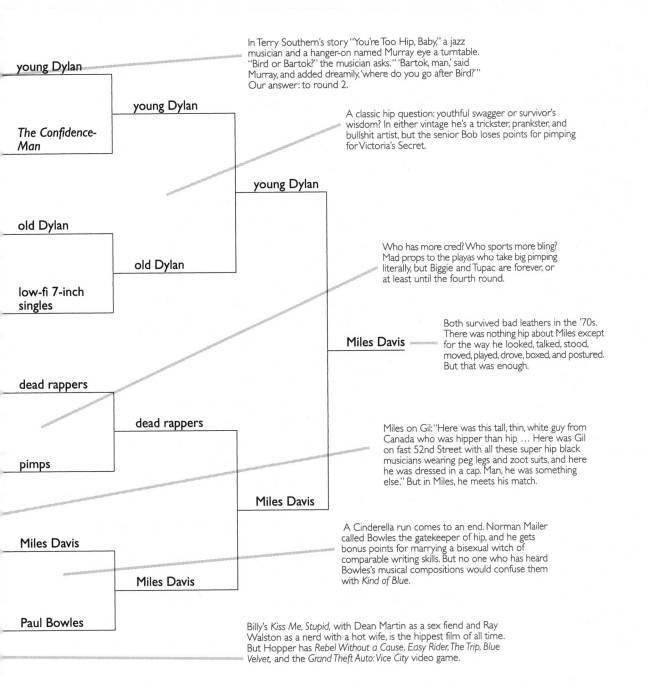

young Dylan

The Confidence-Man

In Terry Southern's story "You're Too Hip, Baby," a jazz musician and a hanger-on named Murray eye a turntable. "Bird or Bartok?" the musician asks. "'Bartok, man,' said Murray, and added dreamily, 'where do you go after Bird?'" Our answer: to round 2.

young Dylan

A classic hip question: youthful swagger or survivor's wisdom? In either vintage he's a trickster, prankster, and bullshit artist, but the senior Bob loses points for pimping for Victoria's Secret.

young Dylan

old Dylan

low-fi 7-inch singles

old Dylan

Who has more cred? Who sports more bling? Mad props to the playas who take big pimping literally, but Biggie and Tupac are forever, or at least until the fourth round.

Miles Davis

Both survived bad leathers in the '70s. There was nothing hip about Miles except for the way he looked, talked, stood, moved, played, drove, boxed, and postured. But that was enough.

dead rappers

pimps

dead rappers

Miles on Gil: "Here was this tall, thin, white guy from Canada who was hipper than hip … Here was Gil on fast 52nd Street with all these super hip black musicians wearing peg legs and zoot suits, and here he was dressed in a cap. Man, he was something else." But in Miles, he meets his match.

Miles Davis

Miles Davis

Paul Bowles

Miles Davis

A Cinderella run comes to an end. Norman Mailer called Bowles the gatekeeper of hip, and he gets bonus points for marrying a bisexual witch of comparable writing skills. But no one who has heard Bowles's musical compositions would confuse them with *Kind of Blue*.

Billy's *Kiss Me, Stupid*, with Dean Martin as a sex fiend and Ray Walston as a nerd with a hot wife, is the hippest film of all time. But Hopper has *Rebel Without a Cause, Easy Rider, The Trip, Blue Velvet*, and the *Grand Theft Auto: Vice City* video game.

47

Indie Rock Albums

by JOHN SELLERS

Indie rock—that musical genre that has long been underserved by mainstream radio and is also known as alternative, modern, or college rock—came into prominence in the early 1980s, when self-funded labels sprang up to put out records by quirky, cultish, cool bands that the majors wouldn't touch. These days, what makes a band alternative is a matter of opinion, and indeed many major-label acts "feel" indie (e.g., Weezer, the White Stripes). To eliminate all argument, only albums initially released on truly independent labels in the U.S. or U.K. have been considered here. Also, some indie outfits have issued multiple albums that would rank in the top 32 of all time; in the interest of diversity, the rule is only one release per artist. Lame, I know.

JOHN SELLERS is the author of *Perfect From Now On: How Indie Rock Saved My Life* (Simon & Schuster). He has contributed to *GQ, Spin,* and the *New York Times,* and half-assedly maintains the blog Angry John Sellers. The first concert he ever attended, in 1987, was in no way indie: Duran Duran. Please don't hold it against him.

My Bloody Valentine, *Loveless* (Creation, 1991) — *Loveless*
Slint, *Spiderland* (Touch and Go, 1991)

Big Star, *#1 Record* (Ardent, 1972) — *Bandwagonesque*
Teenage Fanclub, *Bandwagonesque* (Creation, 1991)

Minutemen, *Double Nickels on the Dime* (SST, 1984) — *Zen Arcade*
Hüsker Dü, *Zen Arcade* (SST, 1984)

The Replacements, *Let It Be* (Twin/Tone, 1984) — *Let It Be*
Archers of Loaf, *Icky Mettle* (Alias, 1993)

Sonic Youth, *Daydream Nation* (Blast First, 1988) — *Daydream Nation*
Mission of Burma, *Vs.* (Ace of Hearts, 1982)

Dinosaur Jr., *You're Living All Over Me* (SST, 1987) — *You're Living All Over Me*
Nirvana, *Bleach* (Sub Pop, 1989)

Yo La Tengo, *I Can Hear the Heart Beating As One* (Matador, 1997) — *The Head on the Door*
The Cure, *The Head on the Door* (Fiction, 1985)

Sebadoh, *Bakesale* (Sub Pop, 1994) — *Surfer Rosa*
Pixies, *Surfer Rosa* (4AD, 1988)

Pavement, *Slanted and Enchanted* (Matador, 1992) — *Slanted and Enchanted*
Silver Jews, *American Water* (Drag City, 1998)

R.E.M., *Reckoning* (I.R.S., 1984) — *Reckoning*
Uncle Tupelo, *Still Feel Gone* (Rockville, 1991)

The Arcade Fire, *Funeral* (Merge, 2004) — *Funeral*
Belle & Sebastian, *Tigermilk* (Electric Honey, 1996)

Joy Division, *Closer* (Factory, 1980) — *Closer*
Interpol, *Turn on the Bright Lights* (Matador, 2002)

Guided By Voices, *Bee Thousand* (Scat, 1994) — *Bee Thousand*
Neutral Milk Hotel, *In the Aeroplane over the Sea* (Merge, 1998)

They Might Be Giants, *Lincoln* (Bar/None, 1988) — *No Pocky for Kitty*
Superchunk, *No Pocky for Kitty* (Matador, 1991)

The Shins, *Chutes Too Narrow* (Sub Pop, 2003) — *There's Nothing…*
Built to Spill, *There's Nothing Wrong with Love* (Up, 1994)

Magnetic Fields, *69 Love Songs* (Merge, 1999) — *The Queen Is Dead*
The Smiths, *The Queen Is Dead* (Rough Trade, 1986)

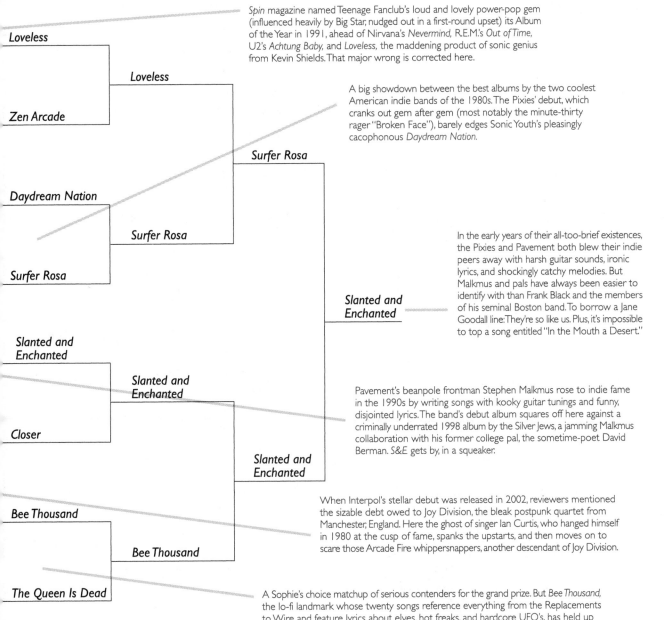

Loveless

Zen Arcade

Loveless

Daydream Nation

Surfer Rosa

Surfer Rosa

Surfer Rosa

Spin magazine named Teenage Fanclub's loud and lovely power-pop gem (influenced heavily by Big Star, nudged out in a first-round upset) its Album of the Year in 1991, ahead of Nirvana's *Nevermind*, R.E.M.'s *Out of Time*, U2's *Achtung Baby*, and *Loveless*, the maddening product of sonic genius from Kevin Shields. That major wrong is corrected here.

A big showdown between the best albums by the two coolest American indie bands of the 1980s. The Pixies' debut, which cranks out gem after gem (most notably the minute-thirty rager "Broken Face"), barely edges Sonic Youth's pleasingly cacophonous *Daydream Nation*.

Slanted and Enchanted

Closer

Slanted and Enchanted

Bee Thousand

Bee Thousand

The Queen Is Dead

Slanted and Enchanted

In the early years of their all-too-brief existences, the Pixies and Pavement both blew their indie peers away with harsh guitar sounds, ironic lyrics, and shockingly catchy melodies. But Malkmus and pals have always been easier to identify with than Frank Black and the members of his seminal Boston band. To borrow a Jane Goodall line: They're so like us. Plus, it's impossible to top a song entitled "In the Mouth a Desert."

Pavement's beanpole frontman Stephen Malkmus rose to indie fame in the 1990s by writing songs with kooky guitar tunings and funny, disjointed lyrics. The band's debut album squares off here against a criminally underrated 1998 album by the Silver Jews, a jamming Malkmus collaboration with his former college pal, the sometime-poet David Berman. *S&E* gets by, in a squeaker.

Slanted and Enchanted

When Interpol's stellar debut was released in 2002, reviewers mentioned the sizable debt owed to Joy Division, the bleak postpunk quartet from Manchester, England. Here the ghost of singer Ian Curtis, who hanged himself in 1980 at the cusp of fame, spanks the upstarts, and then moves on to scare those Arcade Fire whippersnappers, another descendant of Joy Division.

A Sophie's choice matchup of serious contenders for the grand prize. But *Bee Thousand*, the lo-fi landmark whose twenty songs reference everything from the Replacements to Wire and feature lyrics about elves, hot freaks, and hardcore UFO's, has held up better than Morrissey and Marr's mopey masterpiece.

48

Innovations In Sports

by JAMES BOICE

It's easy to forget that sports were different once. We talk trade deadlines, injuries, draft picks, ego, scandal. Rarely do we sit at Fenway and think back to a time when baseball was played without curveballs or bunts. Soccer hooligans rarely stop rioting in order to consider that their sport had similarly savage origins. Canadians forget that the first goalie to put on a face mask was derided off the ice. In putting the greatest sports innovations to the test, the criteria for victory were this: Does the innovation endure today? Was the innovation radical? Did the innovation (pardon the pun) take balls?

Basketball used to be a game played with a peach basket nailed to the top of a pole. It went from a game to a sport when someone cut out the bottom of the basket. The superspeedway is the big oval track in NASCAR— all left turns, so fast and dangerous they limit speeds with restrictor plates on the carburetors. It's a question of back-and-forth versus round-and-round.

In the late 1860s Candy Cummings broke his wrist trying to invent (debatably) what was then called the skewball. Dickey Pearce is credited with first bunting in 1866. It must have been an exciting time for baseball. Nevertheless, the scores of games went from like 47–40 before the curveball to like 3–1 thereafter. Influential? You think?

JAMES BOICE's debut novel, *MVP*, is being published in May 2007 by Scribner. He is *Esquire*'s "New Voice" and a *McSweeney's* New Author. He is a young man from northern Virginia who lives in Somerville, MA, and is unfortunately a Washington Redskins fan.

slam dunk
jump shot — jump shot

the dome
lights — lights

triangle offense
West Coast offense — West Coast offense

soccer-style kickers
forward pass — forward pass

the Mesoamerican Ballgame Ritual (MBR)
Pheidippides' first marathon — the MBR

official review
the mulligan — the mulligan

Gatorade
beer — beer

big, baggy shorts
the sports bra — the sports bra

the superspeedway
the hole in the peach basket — the hole in the peach basket

free agency
the salary cap — free agency

the Fosbury flop
jumping from the top rope — the Fosbury flop

the sideline reporter
the color commentator — the color commentator

the curveball
the bunt — the curveball

the Vardon grip
the caddy — the Vardon grip

the pick and roll
run and shoot — the pick and roll

integration
hockey goalie face mask — integration

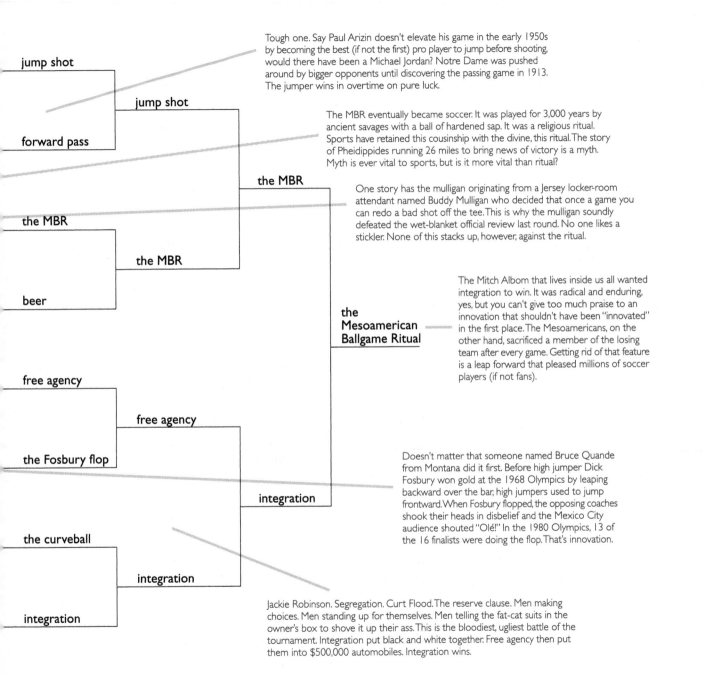

jump shot

jump shot

forward pass

Tough one. Say Paul Arizin doesn't elevate his game in the early 1950s by becoming the best (if not the first) pro player to jump before shooting, would there have been a Michael Jordan? Notre Dame was pushed around by bigger opponents until discovering the passing game in 1913. The jumper wins in overtime on pure luck.

the MBR

The MBR eventually became soccer. It was played for 3,000 years by ancient savages with a ball of hardened sap. It was a religious ritual. Sports have retained this cousinship with the divine, this ritual. The story of Pheidippides running 26 miles to bring news of victory is a myth. Myth is ever vital to sports, but is it more vital than ritual?

the MBR

the MBR

beer

One story has the mulligan originating from a Jersey locker-room attendant named Buddy Mulligan who decided that once a game you can redo a bad shot off the tee. This is why the mulligan soundly defeated the wet-blanket official review last round. No one likes a stickler. None of this stacks up, however, against the ritual.

the Mesoamerican Ballgame Ritual

The Mitch Albom that lives inside us all wanted integration to win. It was radical and enduring, yes, but you can't give too much praise to an innovation that shouldn't have been "innovated" in the first place. The Mesoamericans, on the other hand, sacrificed a member of the losing team after every game. Getting rid of that feature is a leap forward that pleased millions of soccer players (if not fans).

free agency

free agency

the Fosbury flop

integration

Doesn't matter that someone named Bruce Quande from Montana did it first. Before high jumper Dick Fosbury won gold at the 1968 Olympics by leaping backward over the bar, high jumpers used to jump frontward. When Fosbury flopped, the opposing coaches shook their heads in disbelief and the Mexico City audience shouted "Olé!" In the 1980 Olympics, 13 of the 16 finalists were doing the flop. That's innovation.

the curveball

integration

integration

Jackie Robinson. Segregation. Curt Flood. The reserve clause. Men making choices. Men standing up for themselves. Men telling the fat-cat suits in the owner's box to shove it up their ass. This is the bloodiest, ugliest battle of the tournament. Integration put black and white together. Free agency then put them into $500,000 automobiles. Integration wins.

49

Inventions
by ADI IGNATIUS

How do you rank innovation? How do you compare one invention's contribution to society against another's? What's more worthy, birth control or Viagra? The guillotine or Prozac? Paper or plastic? The fact is, a great invention doesn't have to be a great leap forward technologically. It has to improve our lives and help us in that most meaningful activity: the pursuit of happiness. Marvelous as some of these innovations are, it's hard to see how airplanes—or even TVs and PCs—truly make us happier. The former is as much an agent of destruction as a means of transportation, the latter two perhaps the biggest time wasters in history.

ADI IGNATIUS is an executive editor of *Time* magazine, and a former *Wall Street Journal* bureau chief in Beijing and Moscow. His favorite childhood innovations involved adapting baseball for the backyard. None of his friends or siblings could keep these straight, particularly the one where you hit the ball with a tennis racket off the roof.

Paper or plastic? To some it's an important line of questioning at the supermarket, to others a sly pickup line in a bar. But without paper Americans don't need the printing press, can't bid adieu to George III and the British Empire, and can't debate *any* interpretation of the Constitution (because it wouldn't exist). Paper rolls on.

Two marvels of modern transportation go at it, but the airplane has the edge (largely because more people die in cars than planes; what's that say about the airbag's utility?). If someone could just invent a decent airbag for an airplane, it would top both.

Gunpowder made us more hostile. Sliced bread made us happy. Consider the life-affirming sector of the food industry that begat PB&J, lunch meats, packaged cheese slices, Spamwiches. Can you imagine life without grilled cheese sandwiches? No sliced bread, no happy childhood.

Round 1	Round 2
automobile / Segway	automobile
paper / plastic	paper
airplane / airbag	airplane
radio / television	television
indoor plumbing / cat litter	indoor plumbing
abacus / computer	computer
birth control / Viagra	birth control
cotton gin / polyester	cotton gin
elevator / stairs	elevator
guillotine / Prozac	Prozac
assembly line / chaos theory	assembly line
air-conditioning / microwave	air-conditioning
coins / ATM	ATM
electric light / electric guitar	electric light
gunpowder / sliced bread	sliced bread
printing press / Internet	printing press

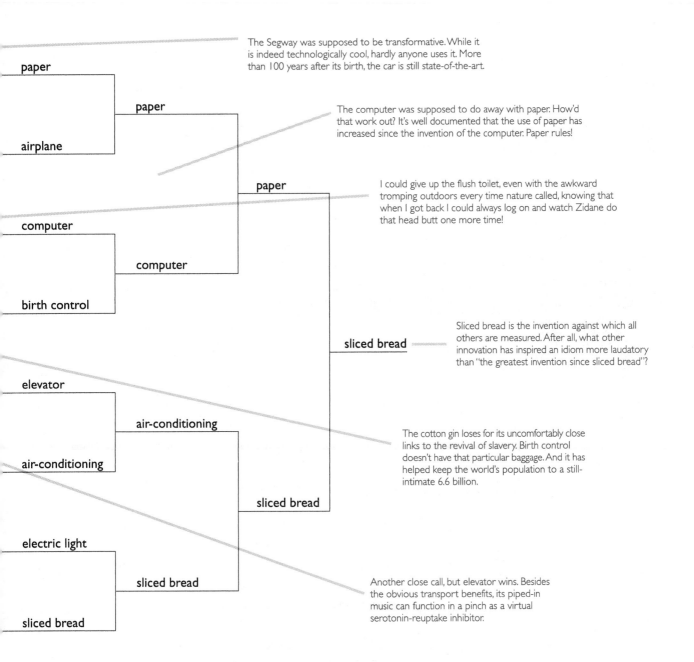

paper

paper

airplane

paper

The Segway was supposed to be transformative. While it is indeed technologically cool, hardly anyone uses it. More than 100 years after its birth, the car is still state-of-the-art.

The computer was supposed to do away with paper. How'd that work out? It's well documented that the use of paper has increased since the invention of the computer. Paper rules!

computer

computer

birth control

paper

I could give up the flush toilet, even with the awkward tromping outdoors every time nature called, knowing that when I got back I could always log on and watch Zidane do that head butt one more time!

sliced bread

Sliced bread is the invention against which all others are measured. After all, what other innovation has inspired an idiom more laudatory than "the greatest invention since sliced bread"?

elevator

air-conditioning

air-conditioning

The cotton gin loses for its uncomfortably close links to the revival of slavery. Birth control doesn't have that particular baggage. And it has helped keep the world's population to a still-intimate 6.6 billion.

sliced bread

electric light

sliced bread

sliced bread

Another close call, but elevator wins. Besides the obvious transport benefits, its piped-in music can function in a pinch as a virtual serotonin-reuptake inhibitor.

50

Investment Strategies
by CLARK WINTER

There is no such thing as a "best" investment. There is what is best for you at the moment. So we're talking about 2007. But if you look at capital flows, the investments that perform the best over time are those that provide the most leverage—that is, allow you to use a small amount of your own money in order to make a great deal more. When you (a) borrow money, (b) buy real estate, and (c) use that property to fund more real estate—that's leverage. It's the guiding criterion here as we assess 32 investments, some of them risky (certain hedge funds), some extremely prudent (cash, U.S. mega-caps), some requiring sophisticated tools and industry expertise (derivatives). Go forth and multiply. But be careful out there.

In high-interest-rate environments, and in situations when fear of losing it all drives investor thinking, cash is king. Nothing is safer than doing nothing with your money. But event-driven hedge funds, which invest in companies whose future is changed by events in the marketplace, such as merger activity in a company's sector, or exogenous happenings such as hurricanes, or a change in the regulatory environment, have the edge in both up and down environments.

In the carry trade, you are borrowing at a low rate to buy high-yielding investments. This was great when Japanese and U.S. interest rates were near zero and Brazil was in the high double digits. But as interest rates rise, it loses some of its allure. Oil and gas futures, on the other hand, can be profitable whether prices are rising or falling, if you study the trends carefully.

CLARK WINTER is global chief investment strategist for Citigroup Global Wealth Management. He is the author of The Either/Or Investor (Random House).

Round 1	Round 2
U.S. mega-caps	U.S. mega-caps
U.S. Treasury bills	
global equities	derivatives
derivatives	
U.S. mid-caps	U.S. mid-caps
commodities	
U.S. small caps	U.S. small caps
puts	
Japanese equities	Japanese equities
calls	
European equities	high-yield corporate bonds
high-yield corporate bonds	
Latin American equities	Latin American equities
high-rated U.S. corporate bonds	
Asian equities	Asian equities
preferred stocks	
Middle Eastern equities	M&A funds
M&A funds	
other emerging market equities	other emerging market equities
private equity	
long/short hedge funds	long/short hedge funds
capital market plays	
event-driven hedge funds	event-driven hedge funds
cash	
oil/gas futures	oil/gas futures
carry trade	
metal commodities (except gold)	metals (except gold)
gold	
emerging market sovereign bonds	real estate
real estate	
foreign currencies	foreign currencies
distressed equity hedge funds	

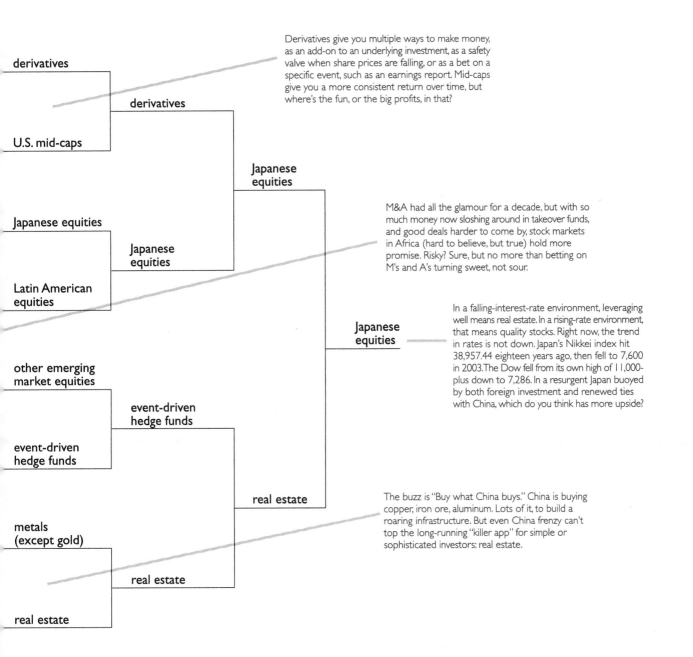

derivatives

derivatives

U.S. mid-caps

Japanese
equities

Derivatives give you multiple ways to make money,
as an add-on to an underlying investment, as a safety
valve when share prices are falling, or as a bet on a
specific event, such as an earnings report. Mid-caps
give you a more consistent return over time, but
where's the fun, or the big profits, in that?

Japanese equities

Japanese
equities

Latin American
equities

Japanese
equities

M&A had all the glamour for a decade, but with so
much money now sloshing around in takeover funds,
and good deals harder to come by, stock markets
in Africa (hard to believe, but true) hold more
promise. Risky? Sure, but no more than betting on
M's and A's turning sweet, not sour.

other emerging
market equities

event-driven
hedge funds

event-driven
hedge funds

In a falling-interest-rate environment, leveraging
well means real estate. In a rising-rate environment,
that means quality stocks. Right now, the trend
in rates is not down. Japan's Nikkei index hit
38,957.44 eighteen years ago, then fell to 7,600
in 2003. The Dow fell from its own high of 11,000-
plus down to 7,286. In a resurgent Japan buoyed
by both foreign investment and renewed ties
with China, which do you think has more upside?

real estate

metals
(except gold)

real estate

real estate

The buzz is "Buy what China buys." China is buying
copper, iron ore, aluminum. Lots of it, to build a
roaring infrastructure. But even China frenzy can't
top the long-running "killer app" for simple or
sophisticated investors: real estate.

51

Most Likely to Survive the 21st Century

by MICHAEL ROGERS

When you're considering what single artifact is likely to survive until January 1, 2100, remember what has disappeared in the past century: the passenger pigeon, celluloid, radium health tonics, singing telegrams, smallpox. Now, try to imagine what elements of today are sturdy enough to persist another 93 years—keeping in mind that the pace of change has accelerated a hundred-fold since the calendar read 1900. That's the sole criterion here: which extant thing today is most likely to be extant in 2100. An impossible task? Of course. That's why we have so many futurists: if enough of us keep guessing, somebody is bound to get it right. And yet, if you're so confounded by the challenge that you end up looking down at your feet, you're probably staring at the winner.

MICHAEL ROGERS is a novelist, journalist, and interactive media pioneer. He is futurist-in-residence for the New York Times Company and writes the Practical Futurist column for MSNBC.com.

Sexy as music videos are, most teens now spend several hours a day as pop stars in alternate online realities. Call it music virtual, but it dooms videos. Spam, on the other hand, continues to flow, still awaiting the final international adoption of secure online identities through ratification of the Global Internet Treaty.

You think EZ Pass is the greatest invention ever? By 2070 the entire highway is intelligent, billing drivers based on speed, vehicle occupancy, time of day, fuel conservation, and adherence to traffic laws.

Round 1	Round 2
Post-it notes	Post-it notes
nuclear power	
plate glass	plate glass
organic food	
hallucinogens	hallucinogens
wild polar bears	
tongue piercing	DVDs
DVDs	
spam (electronic)	spam
music videos	
artificial sweetener	hybrid cars
hybrid cars	
self-serve gas stations	self-serve gas stations
pennies	
silk	silk
silicon chips	
compasses	shoelaces
shoelaces	
contact lenses	contact lenses
decoupage	
sunscreen	sunscreen
paintball	
cubic zirconia	water parks
water parks	
margarine	laser surgery
laser surgery	
earphones	earphones
massage chairs	
rubber boots	rubber boots
AAA batteries	
tollbooths	binoculars
binoculars	

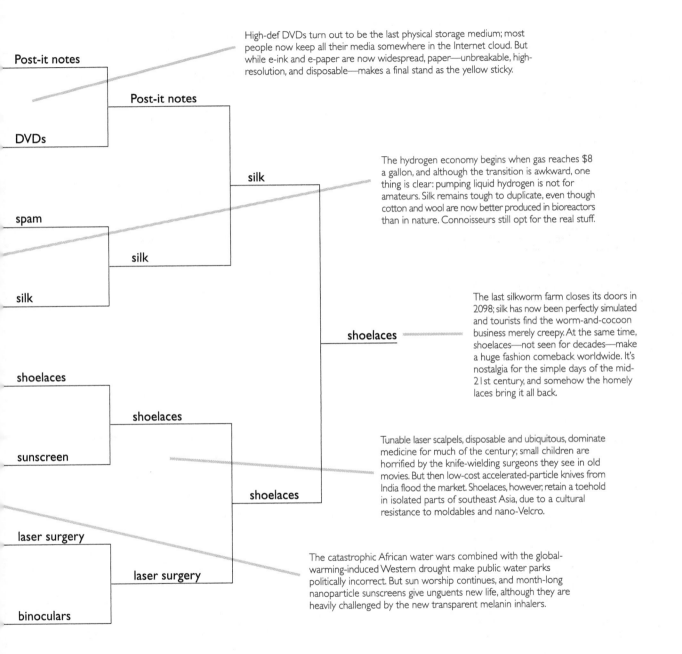

Post-it notes

Post-it notes

DVDs

High-def DVDs turn out to be the last physical storage medium; most people now keep all their media somewhere in the Internet cloud. But while e-ink and e-paper are now widespread, paper—unbreakable, high-resolution, and disposable—makes a final stand as the yellow sticky.

silk

spam

silk

silk

The hydrogen economy begins when gas reaches $8 a gallon, and although the transition is awkward, one thing is clear: pumping liquid hydrogen is not for amateurs. Silk remains tough to duplicate, even though cotton and wool are now better produced in bioreactors than in nature. Connoisseurs still opt for the real stuff.

shoelaces

The last silkworm farm closes its doors in 2098; silk has now been perfectly simulated and tourists find the worm-and-cocoon business merely creepy. At the same time, shoelaces—not seen for decades—make a huge fashion comeback worldwide. It's nostalgia for the simple days of the mid-21st century, and somehow the homely laces bring it all back.

shoelaces

shoelaces

sunscreen

shoelaces

Tunable laser scalpels, disposable and ubiquitous, dominate medicine for much of the century; small children are horrified by the knife-wielding surgeons they see in old movies. But then low-cost accelerated-particle knives from India flood the market. Shoelaces, however, retain a toehold in isolated parts of southeast Asia, due to a cultural resistance to moldables and nano-Velcro.

laser surgery

laser surgery

binoculars

The catastrophic African water wars combined with the global-warming-induced Western drought make public water parks politically incorrect. But sun worship continues, and month-long nanoparticle sunscreens give unguents new life, although they are heavily challenged by the new transparent melanin inhalers.

52

Jew/Not a Jew
by MICHAEL SOLOMON

Some are born Jewish. Others have it thrust upon them—either by conversion (*Shalom*, Marilyn Monroe! *Shalom*, Sammy Davis Jr!), by a drop of Hebrew hemoglobin in the bloodline (*L'chaim*, John Kerry! *L'chaim*, Madeleine Albright!), or simply because they *seem* Jewish (surely Joy Behar's real name is Simcha). Then there are those, like Kathie Lee Gifford, who got skittish about being Yiddish and opted out altogether. In this tournament the contestants are either Jews who are not thought of as Jewish, or people who are thought of as Chosen People but are, in fact, not. Victory goes to the person displaying the biggest gap between perception and reality. A Jew who is not a Jew—or vice versa. May the best *mensch* win.

A mismatch: There is no evidence that Mel Gibson is Jewish or has ever even played a Jew, although lots of Jewish men are named Max—and they often get mad. Whereas the Italian-born Behar has worked the Jewish shtick for so long—"No, I'm not Jewish. I'm not Jewish. *I keep telling you, Ma, I'm not Jewish!*"—that Mel never had a chance.

Anne Bancroft, also born Italian, was married to Mel Brooks for more than 40 years, which explains the confusion. Portraying Golda Meir on Broadway didn't hurt either. Meanwhile, *goyishe* Charlton Heston played *two* great movie Jews—Moses and Ben-Hur—but fooled no one. Also, can Jews even belong to the NRA? Mrs. Robinson wins this shootout.

MICHAEL SOLOMON is an editor at ESPN Books and the coauthor of *Blank: The Power of Not Actually Thinking at All.* His paternal great-grandmother was Catholic and his last name is often mistaken for Sullivan, but he was bar mitzvahed, can read Hebrew, and regards Abraham Lincoln as the first Jewish president.

CHOSEN PEOPLE

- Michael Douglas / Jack Black → Jack Black
- Rupert Murdoch / Walter Mosley → Rupert Murdoch
- William Shatner / Leonard Nimoy → William Shatner
- James Caan / Scarlett Johansson → Scarlett Johansson

OPTED OUT

- Bob Dylan / Gustav Mahler → Bob Dylan
- Bobby Fischer / Paul of Tarsus → Bobby Fischer
- Caspar Weinberger / David Berkowitz → David Berkowitz
- Kathie Lee Gifford / Jesus → Jesus

CONVERTED IN

- Marilyn Monroe / Connie Chung → Marilyn Monroe
- Nell Carter / Tom Arnold → Nell Carter
- Elizabeth Taylor / Mary Hart → Elizabeth Taylor
- Madonna / Sammy Davis Jr. → Sammy Davis Jr.

NOT CHOSEN

- Ethel Merman / Norman Jewison → Norman Jewison
- Joy Behar / Mel Gibson → Joy Behar
- Anne Bancroft / Charlton Heston → Anne Bancroft
- Whoopi Goldberg / Abraham Lincoln → Abraham Lincoln

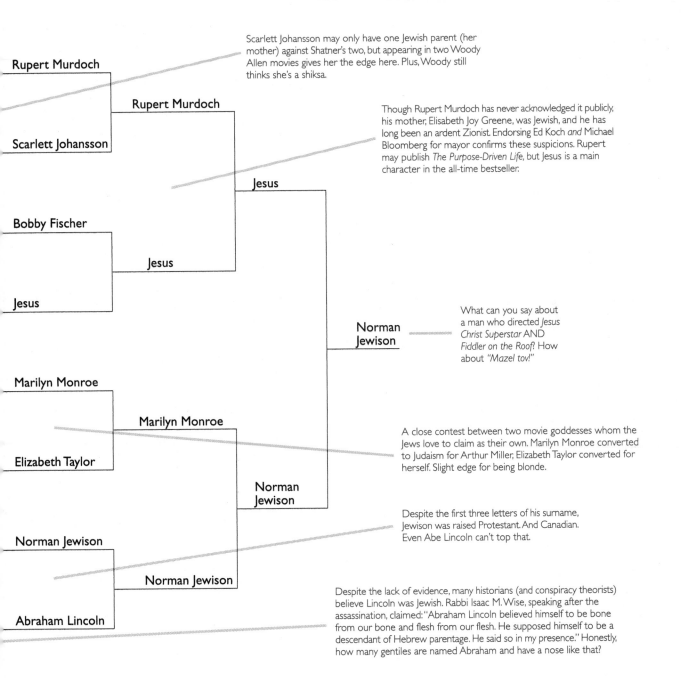

Rupert Murdoch

Scarlett Johansson

Scarlett Johansson may only have one Jewish parent (her mother) against Shatner's two, but appearing in two Woody Allen movies gives her the edge here. Plus, Woody still thinks she's a shiksa.

Rupert Murdoch

Though Rupert Murdoch has never acknowledged it publicly, his mother, Elisabeth Joy Greene, was Jewish, and he has long been an ardent Zionist. Endorsing Ed Koch *and* Michael Bloomberg for mayor confirms these suspicions. Rupert may publish *The Purpose-Driven Life*, but Jesus is a main character in the all-time bestseller.

Jesus

Bobby Fischer

Jesus

Jesus

Norman Jewison

What can you say about a man who directed *Jesus Christ Superstar* AND *Fiddler on the Roof*? How about "*Mazel tov!*"

Marilyn Monroe

Marilyn Monroe

Elizabeth Taylor

A close contest between two movie goddesses whom the Jews love to claim as their own. Marilyn Monroe converted to Judaism for Arthur Miller; Elizabeth Taylor converted for herself. Slight edge for being blonde.

Norman Jewison

Despite the first three letters of his surname, Jewison was raised Protestant. And Canadian. Even Abe Lincoln can't top that.

Norman Jewison

Norman Jewison

Abraham Lincoln

Despite the lack of evidence, many historians (and conspiracy theorists) believe Lincoln was Jewish. Rabbi Isaac M. Wise, speaking after the assassination, claimed: "Abraham Lincoln believed himself to be bone from our bone and flesh from our flesh. He supposed himself to be a descendant of Hebrew parentage. He said so in my presence." Honestly, how many gentiles are named Abraham and have a nose like that?

53

Kings and Queens of England

by CLIVE ASLET

My apologies, as a loyal subject, to Henry I, Richard the Lionheart, Edward VI, and George II, who did not reach the short list. That's the cruelty of life at the top. No kings of Scotland either (before James I of England, who was also James VI of Scotland and united the thrones). A great monarch must be the dominant figure of the age, a feat more difficult the nearer we get to our own time because kings and queens have inexorably lost power to their prime ministers. He or she must be a national figurehead, leaving a permanent stamp on Britain's character. He or she must preside over, or lay the foundations for, a period of peace and prosperity. He or she must repel invasion (no King Harold, then) and successfully prosecute any foreign wars. Extra points for encouragement of the arts, music, literature, education, and connoisseurship. Most choices made themselves.

From 1993 till 2006 CLIVE ASLET was the award-winning editor of *Country Life* magazine, where he is now editor at large. He is the author of many books; his most recent, *The Landmarks of Britain*, examines 500 places where history was made. He is married with three children, and lives in London and Kent.

Alfred the Great	Alfred the Great
Edward the Confessor	
William I	William I
Henry I	
John	Henry III
Henry III	
Edward I	Edward I
Edward II	
Edward III	Edward III
Richard II	
Henry IV	Henry V
Henry V	
Henry VI	Edward IV
Edward IV	
Richard III	Henry VIII
Henry VIII	
Mary I	Elizabeth I
Elizabeth I	
James I	James I
Charles I	
Charles II	Charles II
James II	
William and Mary	William and Mary
Anne	
George I	George III
George III	
George IV	Victoria
Victoria	
Edward VII	Edward VII
George V	
George VI	Elizabeth II
Elizabeth II	

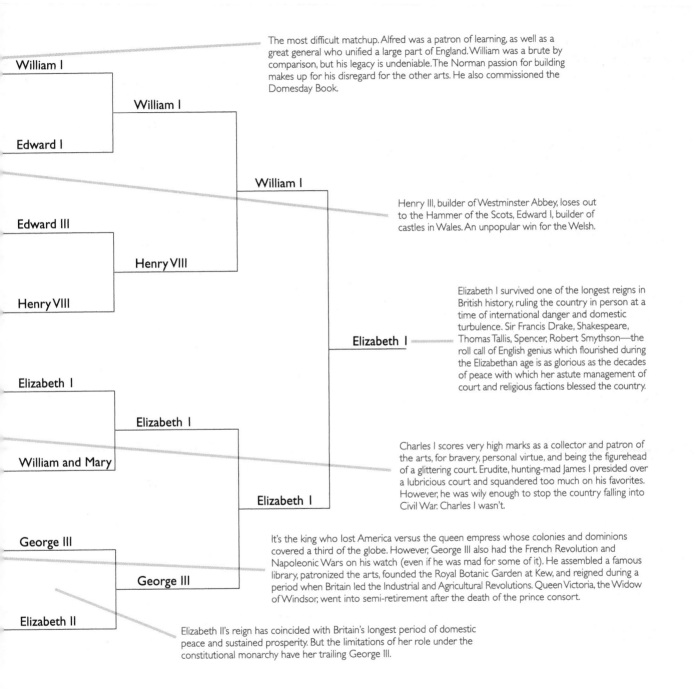

William I

Edward I

William I

Edward III

Henry VIII

Henry VIII

Elizabeth I

William and Mary

George III

Elizabeth II

William I

Henry VIII

Elizabeth I

George III

William I

Elizabeth I

William I

Elizabeth I

The most difficult matchup. Alfred was a patron of learning, as well as a great general who unified a large part of England. William was a brute by comparison, but his legacy is undeniable. The Norman passion for building makes up for his disregard for the other arts. He also commissioned the Domesday Book.

Henry III, builder of Westminster Abbey, loses out to the Hammer of the Scots, Edward I, builder of castles in Wales. An unpopular win for the Welsh.

Elizabeth I survived one of the longest reigns in British history, ruling the country in person at a time of international danger and domestic turbulence. Sir Francis Drake, Shakespeare, Thomas Tallis, Spencer, Robert Smythson—the roll call of English genius which flourished during the Elizabethan age is as glorious as the decades of peace with which her astute management of court and religious factions blessed the country.

Charles I scores very high marks as a collector and patron of the arts, for bravery, personal virtue, and being the figurehead of a glittering court. Erudite, hunting-mad James I presided over a lubricious court and squandered too much on his favorites. However, he was wily enough to stop the country falling into Civil War. Charles I wasn't.

It's the king who lost America versus the queen empress whose colonies and dominions covered a third of the globe. However, George III also had the French Revolution and Napoleonic Wars on his watch (even if he was mad for some of it). He assembled a famous library, patronized the arts, founded the Royal Botanic Garden at Kew, and reigned during a period when Britain led the Industrial and Agricultural Revolutions. Queen Victoria, the Widow of Windsor, went into semi-retirement after the death of the prince consort.

Elizabeth II's reign has coincided with Britain's longest period of domestic peace and sustained prosperity. But the limitations of her role under the constitutional monarchy have her trailing George III.

54

Latin Grammar

by HENRY BEARD

As anyone who has ever studied Latin knows, there are usually at least two ways to say anything, and both of the competing constructions are often equally correct. Thus, when Julius Caesar was assassinated during the Ides of March madness in the original Forum (no sky boxes, lots of columns), he probably needed a moment or two to compose the immortal line, *"Et tu, Brute?"* After all, he could have chosen an accusative of exclamation—*te*—instead of the more mundane nominative *tu* to address his killer. And, of course, he had to keep his mind off his multiple stab wounds long enough to remember to employ the tricky vocative case of his murderer's second-declension name. As a practical matter, the syntactical crowd-pleasers I chose to feature in the later rounds of this epic matchup rarely go head-to-head in actual Latin composition, and I have no idea whether Caesar, who was an accomplished prose stylist in his own right, would have gone along with my arbitrary final linguistic picks (although I know for a fact that the ablative absolute was a personal favorite of his), but I'm pretty sure about one thing: he and his friends, fellow Romans, and countrymen would all have taken the lions over the Christians in a heartbeat, even with that huge point spread.

HENRY BEARD was a cofounder of *National Lampoon* and served as its editor during its heyday in the 1970s. He is the author or coauthor of more than forty humorous books, including the improbable dead-language bestsellers *Latin for All Occasions* and *X-treme Latin*, as well as a pair of titles written in the debased patois of the decadent descendants of the defeated Gauls, *French for Cats* and *French Cats Don't Get Fat.*

Bracket

- ablative absolute / temporal, causal, or concessive clauses → **ablative absolute**
- active voice / passive voice → **active voice**
- contracted verb endings / regular verb endings → **contracted endings**
- gerund / supine → **gerund**
- indirect statement after verbs of emotion / *quod* with the indicative after verbs of emotion → **indirect statement**
- subjunctive with *ut* / infinitive → **subjunctive**
- accusative singular neuter adjective used as adverb / adverb → **adverb**
- poetic dative of motion / double accusative of motion → **double accusative**
- impersonal verbs expressing obligation or necessity / future passive periphrastic → **passive periphrastic**
- present historic infinitive / perfect indicative → **present historic**
- *velutsi* and conditional rules in imaginary comparisons / *quasi* and rules of sequence in imaginary comparisons → ***velutsi***
- ablative with a comparative / nominative or accusative with *quam* → **ablative**
- present participle / relative clause → **present participle**
- dative of possession / genitive of possession → **dative of possession**
- genitive of person and accusative of thing with *memini* and *obliviscor* / genitive of person and genitive of thing with *memini* and *obliviscor* → **accusative of thing**
- second person prohibitions using *ne* plus subjunctive / second person prohibitions using *noli* plus infinitive → ***noli* plus infinitive**

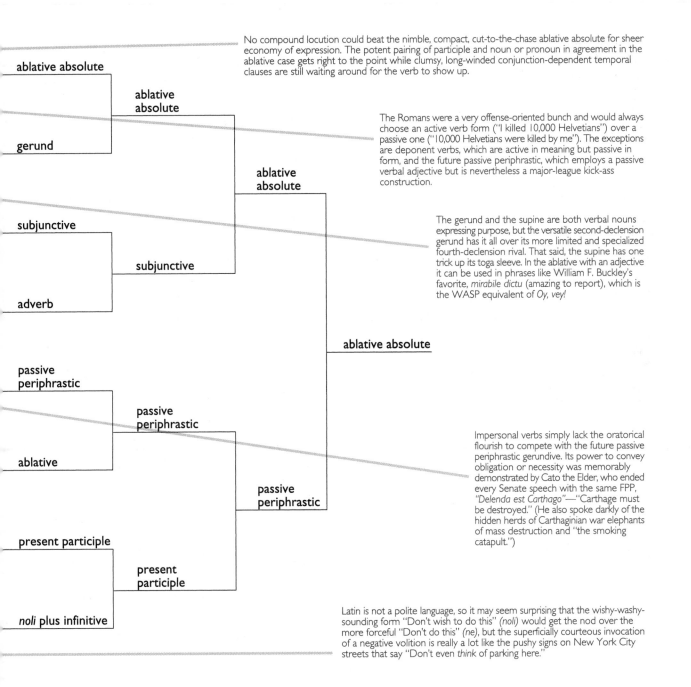

ablative absolute

ablative
absolute

gerund

ablative
absolute

subjunctive

subjunctive

adverb

ablative
absolute

ablative absolute

**passive
periphrastic**

passive
periphrastic

ablative

passive
periphrastic

present participle

present
participle

noli plus infinitive

No compound locution could beat the nimble, compact, cut-to-the-chase ablative absolute for sheer economy of expression. The potent pairing of participle and noun or pronoun in agreement in the ablative case gets right to the point while clumsy, long-winded conjunction-dependent temporal clauses are still waiting around for the verb to show up.

The Romans were a very offense-oriented bunch and would always choose an active verb form ("I killed 10,000 Helvetians") over a passive one ("10,000 Helvetians were killed by me"). The exceptions are deponent verbs, which are active in meaning but passive in form, and the future passive periphrastic, which employs a passive verbal adjective but is nevertheless a major-league kick-ass construction.

The gerund and the supine are both verbal nouns expressing purpose, but the versatile second-declension gerund has it all over its more limited and specialized fourth-declension rival. That said, the supine has one trick up its toga sleeve. In the ablative with an adjective it can be used in phrases like William F. Buckley's favorite, *mirabile dictu* (amazing to report), which is the WASP equivalent of *Oy, vey!*

Impersonal verbs simply lack the oratorical flourish to compete with the future passive periphrastic gerundive. Its power to convey obligation or necessity was memorably demonstrated by Cato the Elder, who ended every Senate speech with the same FPP, *"Delenda est Carthago"*—"Carthage must be destroyed." (He also spoke darkly of the hidden herds of Carthaginian war elephants of mass destruction and "the smoking catapult.")

Latin is not a polite language, so it may seem surprising that the wishy-washy-sounding form "Don't wish to do this" *(noli)* would get the nod over the more forceful "Don't do this" *(ne)*, but the superficially courteous invocation of a negative volition is really a lot like the pushy signs on New York City streets that say "Don't even *think* of parking here."

55

Long Songs
by JENS CARSTENSEN

Behold the epic. At least 10 minutes long. Cherished by stoners, reviled by a few punkers, regarded as ego trips to detractors, and just plain confusing to those with short attention spans, these little *Moby Dicks* are exalted by the bands' hard-core fans. But like 'em or hate 'em, this cavalcade of guitar solos spinning out of control, slow seething numbers, tightly constructed suites, noise-fests with punishing climaxes, and logorrheic frontmen shows there's much more than one way to create something memorably long.

Only *studio* versions qualify here (sorry Deadheads, so long "Whipping Post"). At least seven well-known epics fell between :30 and :05 short of the 10-minute cutoff. So, for once in your freakin' life, no requests for "Free Bird."

JENS CARSTENSEN was a writer with VH1's *Pop-Up Videos* show back in the day.

Sonic Youth, "The Diamond Sea" — "The Diamond Sea"
Neil Young, "Cowgirl in the Sand"

Spiritualized, "Cop Shoot Cop" — "Pass the Hatchet"
Yo La Tengo, "Pass the Hatchet, I Think I'm Goodkind"

Frank Zappa, "Billy the Mountain" — "Sister Ray"
The Velvet Underground, "Sister Ray"

Boz Scaggs, "Loan Me a Dime" — "Phoenix"
Isaac Hayes, "By the Time I Get to Phoenix"

Jimi Hendrix, "Voodoo Chile" — "Marquee Moon"
Television, "Marquee Moon"

Al Stewart, "Love Chronicles" — "Sad Eyed Lady"
Bob Dylan, "Sad Eyed Lady of the LowLands"

Jane's Addiction, "Three Days" — "Three Days"
Led Zeppelin, "Achilles Last Stand"

Meat Loaf, "I Would Do Anything For Love (But I Won't Do That)" — "Ancient Mariner"
Iron Maiden, "Rime of the Ancient Mariner"

Yes, "Heart of the Sunrise" — "Heart of the Sunrise"
The Mars Volta, "Cicatriz ESP"

Rush, "The Camera Eye" — "Echoes"
Pink Floyd, "Echoes"

Emerson, Lake & Palmer, "Take a Pebble" — "Take a Pebble"
Traffic, "The Low Spark of High-Heeled Boys"

Genesis, "Supper's Ready" — "Starless and Bible Black"
King Crimson, "Starless and Bible Black"

Lou Reed, "Street Hassle" — "Street Hassle"
Suicide, "Frankie Teardrop"

Iron Butterfly, "In-a-Gadda-Da-Vida" — "Mother Sky"
Can, "Mother Sky"

The Stooges, "We Will Fall" — "The End"
The Doors, "The End"

Cheater Slicks, "Thinkin' Some More" — "Grapevine"
Creedence Clearwater Revival, "I Heard It Through the Grapevine"

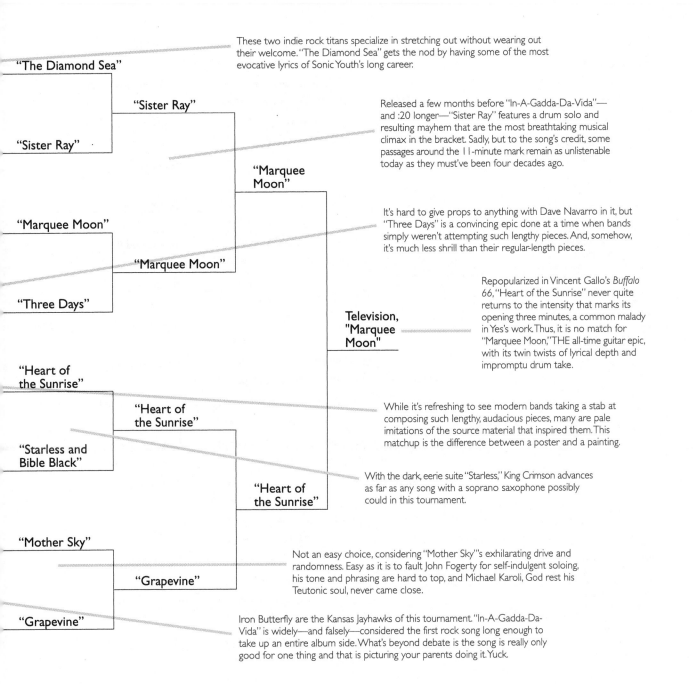

"The Diamond Sea"

"Sister Ray"

"Sister Ray"

"Marquee Moon"

"Marquee Moon"

"Marquee Moon"

"Three Days"

"Heart of the Sunrise"

"Heart of the Sunrise"

"Starless and Bible Black"

"Heart of the Sunrise"

"Mother Sky"

"Grapevine"

"Grapevine"

Television, "Marquee Moon"

These two indie rock titans specialize in stretching out without wearing out their welcome. "The Diamond Sea" gets the nod by having some of the most evocative lyrics of Sonic Youth's long career.

Released a few months before "In-A-Gadda-Da-Vida"—and :20 longer—"Sister Ray" features a drum solo and resulting mayhem that are the most breathtaking musical climax in the bracket. Sadly, but to the song's credit, some passages around the 11-minute mark remain as unlistenable today as they must've been four decades ago.

It's hard to give props to anything with Dave Navarro in it, but "Three Days" is a convincing epic done at a time when bands simply weren't attempting such lengthy pieces. And, somehow, it's much less shrill than their regular-length pieces.

Repopularized in Vincent Gallo's *Buffalo 66*, "Heart of the Sunrise" never quite returns to the intensity that marks its opening three minutes, a common malady in Yes's work. Thus, it is no match for "Marquee Moon," THE all-time guitar epic, with its twin twists of lyrical depth and impromptu drum take.

While it's refreshing to see modern bands taking a stab at composing such lengthy, audacious pieces, many are pale imitations of the source material that inspired them. This matchup is the difference between a poster and a painting.

With the dark, eerie suite "Starless," King Crimson advances as far as any song with a soprano saxophone possibly could in this tournament.

Not an easy choice, considering "Mother Sky"'s exhilarating drive and randomness. Easy as it is to fault John Fogerty for self-indulgent soloing, his tone and phrasing are hard to top, and Michael Karoli, God rest his Teutonic soul, never came close.

Iron Butterfly are the Kansas Jayhawks of this tournament. "In-A-Gadda-Da-Vida" is widely—and falsely—considered the first rock song long enough to take up an entire album side. What's beyond debate is the song is really only good for one thing and that is picturing your parents doing it. Yuck.

56

Longevity Strategies

by DAVID J. LEFFELL, M.D.

Everyone wants to live forever and still be healthy. Who can blame them? I specialize in skin cancer and skin aging, but two out of three patients visiting me ask about some aspect of longevity. While there are many ways to enhance the lifespan blueprint encoded in our genes, there's no single panacea. The 32 entries here fall into four regionals based on activity and diet, lifestyle choices, prescription medication, and my favorite, antioxidants (always popular, almost valid). Each strategy has some science to back it up—in some cases not very good science, but it is in the public consciousness. I end up with a champion that is hard to argue with and maybe harder to pursue consistently. Enjoy your walk!

DAVID J. LEFFELL, M.D., a world-renowned dermatologist, skin cancer expert, researcher, and writer, is professor of dermatology and surgery and deputy dean for clinical affairs at the Yale School of Medicine. Leffell is board-certified in internal medicine and dermatology. He is the author of *Total Skin* (Hyperion, 2000) and numerous scientific and popular articles.

FITNESS & DIET REGIONAL

- walk 30 to 60 minutes a day → walk daily
- cut out sugar
- endurance exercise → endurance exercise
- low-carbohydrate diet
- low trans fat diet → calorie-restricted diet
- calorie-restricted diet
- meditation → meditation
- yoga

LIFESTYLE REGIONAL

- use seat belts → use seat belts
- avoid skydiving
- obey speed limit → obey speed limit
- wear motorcycle helmet
- no drinking → no smoking
- no smoking
- sun protection → daily aspirin
- daily aspirin

PRESCRIPTION MEDS REGIONAL

- anti-hypertension medication → cholesterol medication
- cholesterol-lowering medication (e.g. Lipitor)
- serotonin reuptake inhibitor (e.g. Zoloft) → serotonin reuptake inhibitor
- vitamin B12 (injectable)
- sleep medication (e.g. Ambien) → sleep medication
- human growth hormone (HGH)
- testosterone or estrogen replacement → testosterone
- anti-ulcer medication

ANTIOXIDANTS REGIONAL

- fish oil (omega-3 fatty acids) → fish oil
- N-acetyl cysteine
- isoflavonoids → isoflavonoids
- alpha lipoic acid
- grape seed extract → green tea extract
- green tea extract
- coenzyme Q10 → coenzyme Q10
- lycopene

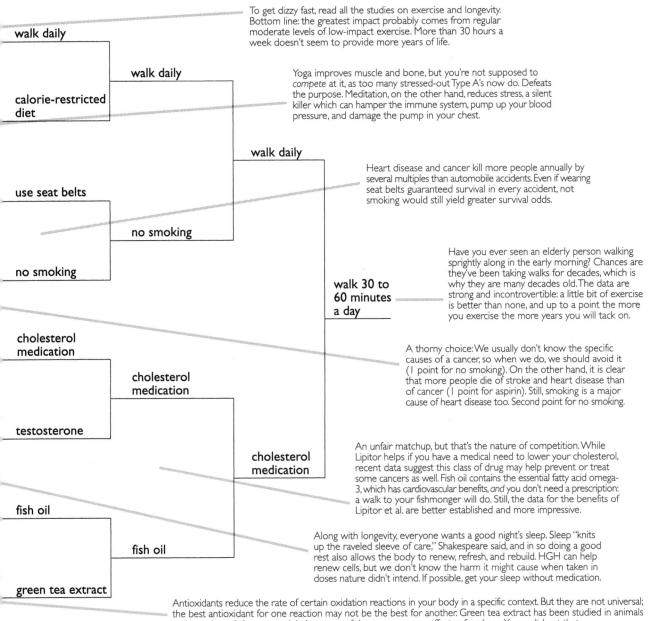

walk daily

calorie-restricted diet

walk daily

To get dizzy fast, read all the studies on exercise and longevity. Bottom line: the greatest impact probably comes from regular moderate levels of low-impact exercise. More than 30 hours a week doesn't seem to provide more years of life.

Yoga improves muscle and bone, but you're not supposed to *compete* at it, as too many stressed-out Type A's now do. Defeats the purpose. Meditation, on the other hand, reduces stress, a silent killer which can hamper the immune system, pump up your blood pressure, and damage the pump in your chest.

walk daily

use seat belts

no smoking

no smoking

Heart disease and cancer kill more people annually by several multiples than automobile accidents. Even if wearing seat belts guaranteed survival in every accident, not smoking would still yield greater survival odds.

walk 30 to 60 minutes a day

Have you ever seen an elderly person walking sprightly along in the early morning? Chances are they've been taking walks for decades, which is why they are many decades old. The data are strong and incontrovertible: a little bit of exercise is better than none, and up to a point the more you exercise the more years you will tack on.

cholesterol medication

cholesterol medication

testosterone

A thorny choice: We usually don't know the specific causes of a cancer, so when we do, we should avoid it (1 point for no smoking). On the other hand, it is clear that more people die of stroke and heart disease than of cancer (1 point for aspirin). Still, smoking is a major cause of heart disease too. Second point for no smoking.

cholesterol medication

An unfair matchup, but that's the nature of competition. While Lipitor helps if you have a medical need to lower your cholesterol, recent data suggest this class of drug may help prevent or treat some cancers as well. Fish oil contains the essential fatty acid omega-3, which has cardiovascular benefits, *and* you don't need a prescription: a walk to your fishmonger will do. Still, the data for the benefits of Lipitor et al. are better established and more impressive.

fish oil

fish oil

green tea extract

Along with longevity, everyone wants a good night's sleep. Sleep "knits up the raveled sleeve of care," Shakespeare said, and in so doing a good rest also allows the body to renew, refresh, and rebuild. HGH can help renew cells, but we don't know the harm it might cause when taken in doses nature didn't intend. If possible, get your sleep without medication.

Antioxidants reduce the rate of certain oxidation reactions in your body in a specific context. But they are not universal; the best antioxidant for one reaction may not be the best for another. Green tea extract has been studied in animals and people and shown to minimize some of the precancerous effects of sunburn. You can't beat that.

57

Magical Sports Numbers

by RICHARD SANDOMIR

Sports fans are obsessed with numbers, figures that cannot be paroled from their brains: uniform numbers (Willie Mays's 24), unique records (Wilt Chamberlain's 100 points in a game), memorable years (1941 or 1968), improbably long and durable streaks (Joe DiMaggio's 56), sport-altering equipment advances (the 24-second clock), and race distances (the 26.2-mile marathon). The criterion here is simple: the broader the significance of a single number, the more magical it is. If you need to think about a number, it ain't magical.

You'd think that having the best batting average since 1941 would give the lean, handsome, pre-frozen Ted Williams a runaway win, but the all-star combo wearing 24 steals the win while Teddy Ballgame bones his bat.

RICHARD SANDOMIR, the coeditor of this book, grew up a Mickey Mantle fan, and while he tried to manipulate this bracket to advance 7 beyond the second round, he ultimately recognized a superior number when he saw it.

3 (Babe Ruth, Dale Earnhardt, et al.; strikes and outs; most common score for birdies and eagles)

III (Jets win Super Bowl, change NFL)

26.2 (marathon miles)

61 (Roger Maris's single-season home run total)

755 (Hank Aaron's career home run record)

31 (Denny McLain's wins in 1968)

7 (Mickey Mantle, John Elway, David Beckham with Manchester United)

23 (Michael Jordan, LeBron James, Beckham with Real Madrid)

29 2¹/₂ (feet and inches of Bob Beamon's 1968 long jump)

500 (mileage of great auto races; standard for home run greatness)

60 (Babe Ruth's home runs in 1927)

32 (Jim Brown, Dr. J, Sandy Koufax, Magic Johnson)

4,256 (Pete Rose's all-time hits total)

1941 (Ted Williams hit .406, Joe DiMaggio hit in 56 consecutive games, Billy Conn nearly beat Joe Louis)

2,130 (consecutive games played by Lou Gehrig)

158.3 (perfect NFL passer rating)

.406 (Williams's feat is last time a major leaguer hit .400)

24 (Mays, Ken Griffey Jr., Jeff Gordon, Bill Bradley, Rickey Henderson)

511 (Cy Young's career wins, Mel Ott's home runs)

56 (DiMaggio's hitting streak, Lawrence Taylor)

5 (DiMaggio, Paul Hornung, Hank Greenberg, Brooks Robinson)

1968 (both Olympics; Year of the Pitcher)

44 (Aaron, Jerry West, Willie McCovey, Reggie Jackson)

49–0 (Rocky Marciano's unbeaten career wins)

8 (Yogi Berra, Bill Dickey, Cal Ripken Jr., Kobe Bryant, Steve Young, Troy Aikman)

100 (Wilt Chamberlain's one-game scoring record, standard length of many races; pitch velocity ideal)

4 (Lou Gehrig, Bobby Orr, Brett Favre, Mel Ott; balls needed for a walk)

92 (Wayne Gretzky's one-season goals mark)

1919 (Black Sox scandal, Jack Dempsey beats Jess Willard, Green Bay Packers formed)

73 (Barry Bonds's tainted home run record)

33 (Larry Bird, Kareem Abdul-Jabbar, Tony Dorsett)

1927 (Bronx Bombers, Dempsey–Tunney Long Count)

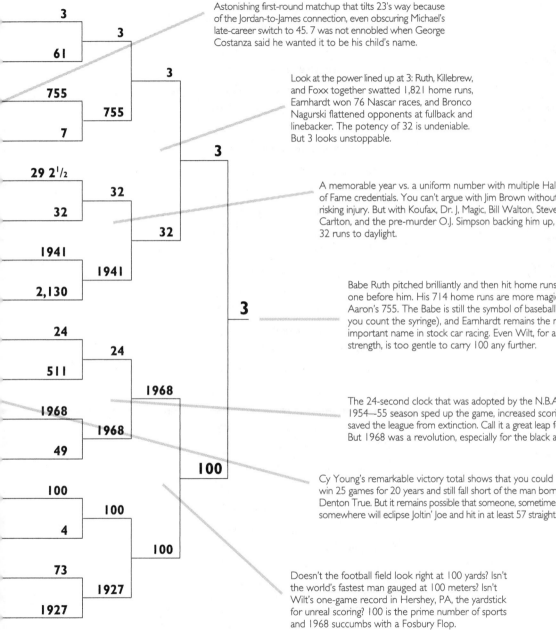

Astonishing first-round matchup that tilts 23's way because of the Jordan-to-James connection, even obscuring Michael's late-career switch to 45. 7 was not ennobled when George Costanza said he wanted it to be his child's name.

Look at the power lined up at 3: Ruth, Killebrew, and Foxx together swatted 1,821 home runs, Earnhardt won 76 Nascar races, and Bronco Nagurski flattened opponents at fullback and linebacker. The potency of 32 is undeniable. But 3 looks unstoppable.

A memorable year vs. a uniform number with multiple Hall of Fame credentials. You can't argue with Jim Brown without risking injury. But with Koufax, Dr. J, Magic, Bill Walton, Steve Carlton, and the pre-murder O.J. Simpson backing him up, 32 runs to daylight.

Babe Ruth pitched brilliantly and then hit home runs like no one before him. His 714 home runs are more magical than Aaron's 755. The Babe is still the symbol of baseball (unless you count the syringe), and Earnhardt remains the most important name in stock car racing. Even Wilt, for all his strength, is too gentle to carry 100 any further.

The 24-second clock that was adopted by the N.B.A. in the 1954—55 season sped up the game, increased scoring, and saved the league from extinction. Call it a great leap forward. But 1968 was a revolution, especially for the black athlete.

Cy Young's remarkable victory total shows that you could win 25 games for 20 years and still fall short of the man born Denton True. But it remains possible that someone, sometime, somewhere will eclipse Joltin' Joe and hit in at least 57 straight.

Doesn't the football field look right at 100 yards? Isn't the world's fastest man gauged at 100 meters? Isn't Wilt's one-game record in Hershey, PA, the yardstick for unreal scoring? 100 is the prime number of sports and 1968 succumbs with a Fosbury Flop.

58

Male Vices
by JOHN ALBERT

I was the child of godless intellectuals. Whatever concept I have of vice came initially from my parents, teachers, and television shows like *Dragnet*. These views then evolved from personal trial and error. I know what society considers acceptable and have strayed well outside these boundaries upon occasion. While I never feared eternal damnation, I feared—and realized—legal, social, and health repercussions, all of which I have experienced. For our purposes here, vice is an enjoyable act with the potential to wreak havoc in one's life. The more you indulge, the more you and the people around you will probably suffer.

JOHN ALBERT grew up in the suburbs of Los Angeles, where he cofounded the cross-dressing "death rock" band Christian Death, then played drums in the low-rent punk band Bad Religion. His memoir *Wrecking Crew* (Scribner), chronicling the adventures of his amateur baseball team comprised of junkies, gambling addicts, transvestites, and washed-up rock stars, is (supposedly) being made into a film by Paramount Pictures.

SEX REGIONAL

- paid S&M sessions
- serial infidelity → infidelity
- polygamy
- transsexual prostitutes → trannies
- Japanese porn
- German porn → German porn
- phone sex
- prostitutes (traditional) → prostitutes

DRUG REGIONAL

- stimulants (cocaine and crystal) → stimulants
- fast food
- BlackBerry scrolling/texting → BlackBerry
- daytime spent at bars
- heroin → heroin
- cigarettes
- designer drugs → weed
- daily weed smoking

SOCIOPATH REGIONAL

- fraudulent handicap parking
- compulsive speeding (vehicular) → speeding
- mean-spirited gossip
- schadenfreude → schadenfreude
- lying to impress naïve relatives
- abuse of irony → irony
- ruthless ambition
- rage addiction → rage

SLOTH & GREED REGIONAL

- bacon → bacon
- Hostess desserts
- Internet gambling
- social gambling (casinos, bookies) → Net gambling
- driving a Hummer
- daytime television viewing (nude or underwear) → daytime TV
- watching *Flavor of Love* (anytime) → *Flavor of Love*
- crass consumerism

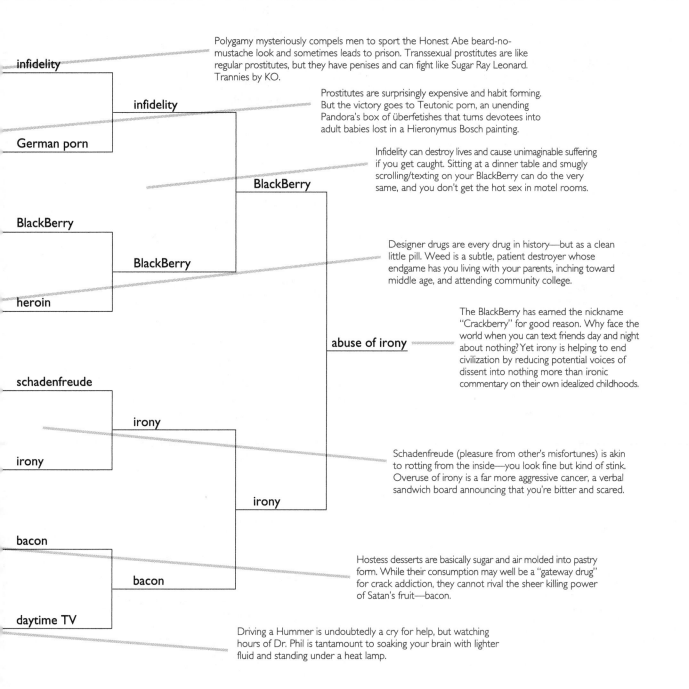

infidelity

infidelity

Polygamy mysteriously compels men to sport the Honest Abe beard-no-mustache look and sometimes leads to prison. Transsexual prostitutes are like regular prostitutes, but they have penises and can fight like Sugar Ray Leonard. Trannies by KO.

German porn

Prostitutes are surprisingly expensive and habit forming. But the victory goes to Teutonic porn, an unending Pandora's box of überfetishes that turns devotees into adult babies lost in a Hieronymus Bosch painting.

BlackBerry

Infidelity can destroy lives and cause unimaginable suffering if you get caught. Sitting at a dinner table and smugly scrolling/texting on your BlackBerry can do the very same, and you don't get the hot sex in motel rooms.

BlackBerry

BlackBerry

Designer drugs are every drug in history—but as a clean little pill. Weed is a subtle, patient destroyer whose endgame has you living with your parents, inching toward middle age, and attending community college.

heroin

abuse of irony

The BlackBerry has earned the nickname "Crackberry" for good reason. Why face the world when you can text friends day and night about nothing? Yet irony is helping to end civilization by reducing potential voices of dissent into nothing more than ironic commentary on their own idealized childhoods.

schadenfreude

irony

irony

Schadenfreude (pleasure from other's misfortunes) is akin to rotting from the inside—you look fine but kind of stink. Overuse of irony is a far more aggressive cancer, a verbal sandwich board announcing that you're bitter and scared.

irony

bacon

Hostess desserts are basically sugar and air molded into pastry form. While their consumption may well be a "gateway drug" for crack addiction, they cannot rival the sheer killing power of Satan's fruit—bacon.

bacon

daytime TV

Driving a Hummer is undoubtedly a cry for help, but watching hours of Dr. Phil is tantamount to soaking your brain with lighter fluid and standing under a heat lamp.

59

Meaningless Sports Statistics

by ALLEN ST. JOHN

When Benjamin Disraeli referred to "lies, damned lies, and statistics" he could have been thinking of sports stats, which have multiplied like players' salaries in the last decade. But this statistical deluge is a classic triumph of quantity over quality. For every illuminating stat splattered across your plasma screen, there are a dozen that are misleading, wrong-headed, or so complex they'd send Stephen Hawking back to the drawing board. I've assembled the worst offenders, the numbers that bear little or no relationship to the bottom line of sports: winning and losing. So if a great sports stat is like a poem, a perfect little window of meaning laid out in elegant shorthand, then these 32 flawed yardsticks must be the mathematical equivalent of *Jonathan Livingston Seagull*.

ALLEN ST. JOHN writes the By the Numbers column for the *Wall Street Journal* and is the coauthor, with Chris Russo, of the *New York Times* bestseller *The Mad Dog 100: The Greatest Sports Arguments of All Time*.

Matchup	Winner
holds (MLB) / penalty yards (NFL)	penalty yards
saves (MLB) / wild pitches (MLB)	baseball saves
three-point shooting percentage (NBA) / fielding percentage (MLB)	fielding percentage
home court advantage (NBA) / win shares (MLB)	win shares
fumble recoveries (NFL) / batter strikeouts (MLB)	fumble recoveries
laps led (NASCAR) / penalty minutes (NHL)	penalty minutes
consecutive games (MLB) / driving accuracy (PGA Tour)	driving accuracy
personal fouls (NBA) / pitching wins (MLB)	pitching wins
batting average (MLB) / penalty killing (NHL)	batting average
triple-doubles (NBA) / punch count (boxing)	triple-doubles
sacrifices (MLB) / scoring average (NBA)	sacrifices
Nextel Cup wins (NASCAR) / penalty yards (NFL)	Nextel Cup wins
putting average (PGA Tour) / runs batted in (MLB)	putting average
BCS ratings (college football) / red zone offense (NFL)	BCS ratings
aces (tennis) / stolen bases (MLB)	stolen bases
outfield assists (MLB) / quarterback rating (NFL)	quarterback rating

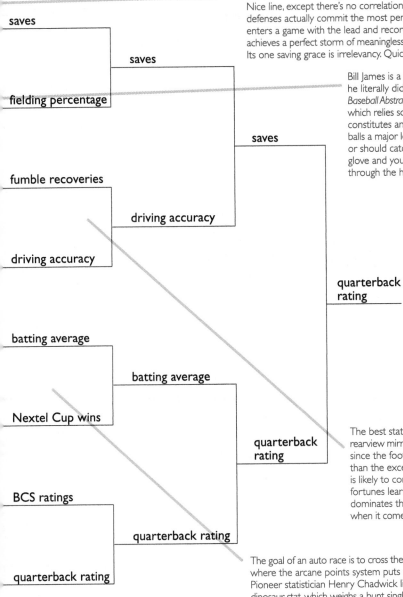

saves

fielding percentage

saves

fumble recoveries

driving accuracy

driving accuracy

saves

batting average

Nextel Cup wins

batting average

BCS ratings

quarterback rating

quarterback rating

quarterback rating

quarterback rating

When refs throw a flag, NFL announcers love to say, "The penalties are killing the team." Nice line, except there's no correlation between total penalties and winning, and the best defenses actually commit the most penalties. The hold, awarded to a relief pitcher who enters a game with the lead and records at least one out without giving up that lead, achieves a perfect storm of meaninglessness, the answer to a question that no one's asking. Its one saving grace is irrelevancy. Quick, who led the majors in holds last season?

Bill James is a genius. But his latest stat, win shares, is so complex that he literally didn't have room to explain it in his 998-page *Historical Baseball Abstract*. Still, win shares has no chance against fielding percentage, which relies solely on some official scorer's uneducated opinion of what constitutes an error. Fielding percentage focuses on the dozen or so balls a major leaguer bungles—rather than the 1,000 that he catches—or should catch—without incident. Let a sinking liner glance off your glove and you're charged with an E. Let a hundred ground balls scoot through the hole untouched, and you're clean.

A stat built by committee versus one man's folly. The preposterously complex NFL quarterback rating takes 630 words to explain—at least twice as long as the Gettysburg Address. Yet this kludgy index still double-counts completion percentage. The baseball save was innocently invented by Chicago sportswriter Jerome Holtzman, who watched Pittsburgh reliever Roy Face compile an 18–1 record in 1959 precisely *because* he allowed the opponents to tie a game late and then got the win when the Pirates hitters saved him. Worthy sentiment, but the save fails to parse excellence (Randy Myers has led the league as often as Mariano Rivera) and it's changed the game for the worse. Managers now hold back their best reliever for a ninth-inning "save situation" even when the game's decisive moment may happen in the seventh or eighth.

The best stats predict the future, but fumble recoveries live in the rearview mirror, where objects are closer than they appear. The problem: since the football isn't round and funny bounces are the rule rather than the exception, the team that falls on the ball five times this week is likely to come up empty-handed next week. Weekend golfers spend fortunes learning to hit the ball straight off the tee, but Tiger Woods dominates the PGA Tour money rankings while missing the top 100 when it comes to the overrated virtue of keeping the ball in the fairway.

The goal of an auto race is to cross the line ahead of all the other cars. But not in NASCAR, where the arcane points system puts an emphasis on finishing rather than finishing first. Pioneer statistician Henry Chadwick lifted batting average from cricket, and today this dinosaur stat, which weighs a bunt single the same as a home run, remains a popular vestige of the days when pitchers threw underhand and nine balls constituted a walk.

60

Most Jersey
by TRIS McCALL

There are 566 municipalities in the Garden State, and in each of them you will encounter young men in curved-bill painter's caps who'll insist that their town is the Most Jersey. They might back this up with a swing at your head. But brute force alone can't settle this: it requires *all* of our Jersey diagnostic tools: snap judgments, resentment, irrational disqualifications, unprovoked defensiveness, and rude commentary. The citizens of North Caldwell will actually tell you that their town is the Most Jersey because Tony Soprano is supposed to live there. Such hero worship—and for a fictional character, no less!—is definitely Not Jersey. The acceptable claim: "My town is the Most Jersey because *I* live there." (By way of reference, Princeton is the Least Jersey, so much so that it would lose to Maspeth, Malibu, Uzbekistan, Alpha Centauri…)

TRIS McCALL used to hang down by Exit 10, but has recently moved up to 14C. He has written for *Jersey Beat* and the *Jersey City Journal*. He's listened to the Jersey Joystick while driving on the Jersey Turnpike. He's ordered a Jersey Ice at the Jersey Gardens and once took Jersey Transit to see the Jersey Generals. He's a Jersey guy.

Camden's got its bridges, its Campbell's Soup factory heritage, and its inferiority complex all damned Jersey. But Eatontown is built around the Monmouth Mall and Highway 35, and its name is the punch line of a *Truly Tasteless Joke*.

Jersey City should consider changing its name. By the last census count, it's got 240,000 people—half of whom are expat New Yorkers praying for Manhattan real estate to collapse. Tavistock, by contrast, has *24* residents and a "No Trespassing" sign on the only road into "town." Eat your heart out, JC condo developers!

Bayonne	Asbury Park
Asbury Park	
New Brunswick	New Brunswick
Perth Amboy	
Woodbridge	Woodbridge
Toms River	
Eatontown	Eatontown
Camden	
Nutley	Trenton
Trenton	
Jersey City	Tavistock
Tavistock	
Moonachie	Seaside Heights
Seaside Heights	
Paramus	Paramus
Red Bank	
Elizabeth	Freehold
Freehold	
Cherry Hill	Cherry Hill
Rahway	
Paterson	Paterson
Atlantic City	
Cape May	Hackensack
Hackensack	
Dunellen	Dunellen
Ho-Ho-Kus	
Secaucus	Hoboken
Hoboken	
Vineland	Newark
Newark	
Swedesboro	Union Township
Union Township	

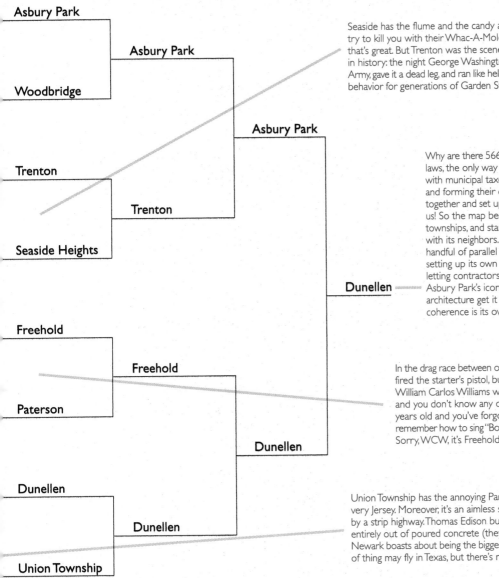

Asbury Park

Asbury Park

Woodbridge

Trenton

Trenton

Seaside Heights

Asbury Park

Seaside has the flume and the candy apples, and mooks who will try to kill you with their Whac-A-Mole mallets for no reason. And that's great. But Trenton was the scene of the Most Jersey moment in history: the night George Washington snuck up on the British Army, gave it a dead leg, and ran like hell, thereby modeling playground behavior for generations of Garden State schoolkids.

Dunellen

Why are there 566 towns in New Jersey? Before zoning laws, the only way that Jerseyans could play dodgeball with municipal taxes was by breaking away from cities and forming their own towns. Let's get our friends together and set up our own borough! They'll never get us! So the map became a jigsaw of municipal shards, townships, and standalone districts, every one at war with its neighbors. Dunellen is just a rail station and a handful of parallel streets, but that didn't stop it from setting up its own school system and government, or letting contractors "redevelop" its tiny town center. Asbury Park's iconography, history, and monumental architecture get it to the finals, but its integrity and coherence is its own undoing. Dunellen wins!

Freehold

Freehold

Paterson

Dunellen

In the drag race between our two great balladeers, Paterson fired the starter's pistol, but it's been all Freehold since. William Carlos Williams wrote five books about Paterson, and you don't know any of them. But when you're ninety years old and you've forgotten your own name, you'll still remember how to sing "Born to Run" and "My Hometown." Sorry, WCW, it's Freehold in a walk.

Dunellen

Dunellen

Union Township

Union Township has the annoying Parkway toll plaza, but that's very Jersey. Moreover, it's an aimless suburban jumble bisected by a strip highway. Thomas Edison built several houses in Union entirely out of poured concrete (they're still there). Meanwhile, Newark boasts about being the biggest city in the state. That sort of thing may fly in Texas, but there's nothing Jersey about it.

61

Mythological Figures

by JAMES C. HOGAN

Connoisseurs of myth may question the absence of some divinities here. Zeus, ever prudent, sends his boys along to do his bidding, watching the combat from above. Poseidon feels out of his element. Ladies like Demeter and Artemis find the rowdy jostling of this knockout format repugnant, preferring to worry over their favorites from the sidelines. Keen-eyed readers will notice that rematches such as Athena vs. Ajax and Achilles vs. Hector have outcomes that are, shall we say, foreordained. More down-to-earth observers may wonder how the gods ever lose to mere heroes. Happily, I am not obliged to moralize or offer allegory. Next time Clytemnestra may not forget her ax, Hector may use more cunning, Orestes may not fall into a raving fit. In the meantime, let us admire the champion's journey to his rightful home.

JAMES C. HOGAN retired as the Frank T. McClure professor of classics at Allegheny College in 1999. He is the author of the commentaries *The Plays of Sophocles* and *The Plays of Aeschylus*.

Pre-tournament favorite Heracles, after an unlucky first draw where his scouting report lets him eke past Hades, meets up with his patroness Athena. Perhaps looking one game ahead to the ferocious Hera, Athena forgets to focus on the muscle-bound lunk—and makes an early departure.

No surprise that Medea caught vain Jason off guard in round 1. But you'd think Oedipus would know how to deal with an angry mother. Even though he has trouble seeing her plots, this is a major upset.

Odysseus cajoles Philoctetes, then impersonates Heracles and moves on for a unique second-round match up against his dad. (Go back to your corner, Oedipus. This fight's not for you.)

Tournament bracket:

- Heracles / Hades → Heracles
- Ajax / Athena → Athena
- Dionysus / Orestes → Dionysus
- Ixion / Hera → Hera
- Apollo / Prometheus → Apollo
- Theseus / Perseus → Perseus
- Jason / Medea → Medea
- Melampus / Oedipus → Oedipus
- Achilles / Hector → Achilles
- Diomedes / Ares → Diomedes
- Adonis / Paris → Paris
- Bellerophon / Hermes → Hermes
- Tantalus / Aeneas → Tantalus
- Orpheus / Orion → Orpheus
- Clytemnestra / Sisyphus → Sisyphus
- Odysseus / Philoctetes → Odysseus

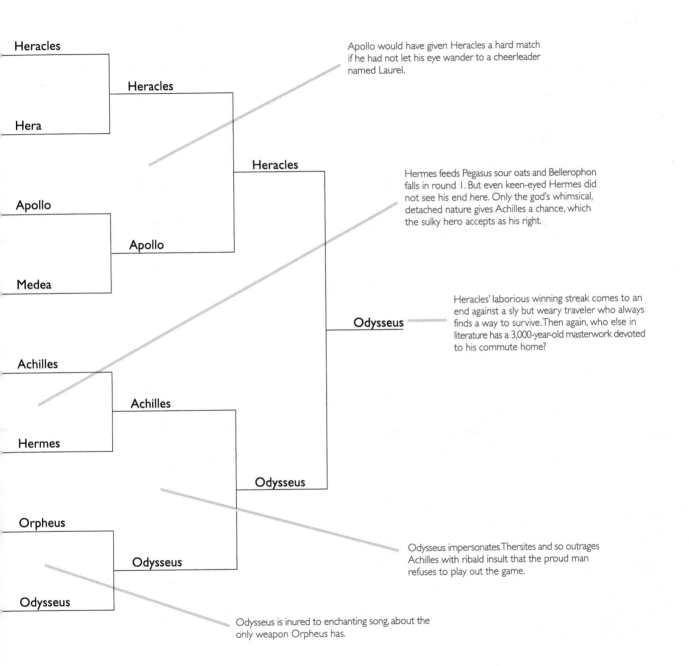

Heracles

Heracles

Hera

Apollo would have given Heracles a hard match
if he had not let his eye wander to a cheerleader
named Laurel.

Heracles

Apollo

Apollo

Medea

Hermes feeds Pegasus sour oats and Bellerophon
falls in round 1. But even keen-eyed Hermes did
not see his end here. Only the god's whimsical,
detached nature gives Achilles a chance, which
the sulky hero accepts as his right.

Odysseus

Heracles' laborious winning streak comes to an
end against a sly but weary traveler who always
finds a way to survive. Then again, who else in
literature has a 3,000-year-old masterwork devoted
to his commute home?

Achilles

Achilles

Hermes

Odysseus

Orpheus

Odysseus

Odysseus

Odysseus impersonates Thersites and so outrages
Achilles with ribald insult that the proud man
refuses to play out the game.

Odysseus is inured to enchanting song, about the
only weapon Orpheus has.

62

NASCAR Phrases
by JEFF MacGREGOR

While NASCAR may or may not be the continent's fastest-rising cultural phenomenon, it is certainly the loudest. And stock car racing, a perfect wedding of mechanical ingenuity and reckless appetite, requires a vernacular all its own. Spoken or shouted from driver to driver, driver to crew chief, car owner to reporter, or race fan to race fan, that language, unleavened by nuance and unconstrained by grammar, is at once as formalized as haiku and as fragmentary as a shattered valve spring.

The phrase "Rubbin' is racin'" is laced with the aggression at the heart of the sport. It's what you say after hammering someone out of the way to win. "One of those racin' deals," on the other hand, is all helpless fatalism, on the order of "Que será, será." What losers say once shunted aside. Drop that last "g" for authenticity.

Shopworn macho punchline, often attributed to bipolar he-man novelist Ernest Hemingway. Mostly found on infield T-shirts. NASCAR fans know by heart the implied setup: "There are only three real sports—boxing, bullfighting, and auto racing." Then why aren't they at a goddamned bullfight? And foxy-boxing doesn't count. Hemingway would weep to see it. Or laugh uncontrollably. Or medicate himself with another mojito. "GSYE!" moves on.

"We run good": beloved postrace catchall of drivers, owners, and crew members when asked about car/driver/weather/strategy. Incorrect tense heightens genial hardscrabble authority of speaker. Save "we ran well" for your next Oxford track meet. Fans only shout "Drive it like you stole it!" to draw attention to matching trucker hat/beer cozy combo stating same.

Most often heard from driver to crew chief on the race radio. When a car won't turn, it's too tight; when a car turns too easily, when it wants to swap ends and spin, it's too loose. But, as in so many areas of human enterprise, a little loose is good. Loose moves through. Because loose is fast.

Core question in the evangelical epistemology of American internal combustion. A real rhetorical puzzler. Ford? Chevy? Which model? What year? So hard to suss out, in fact, let's just set it aside and have another plate of that pork shoulder. Mmmmm. Now what did you want to know?

"Rubbin' is racin'."

"one of those racin' deals"

"Boogity, boogity, boogity!"

"the Big One"

"Gentlemen, start your engines!"

"Everything else is just a game."

"We run good."

"Drive it like you stole it!"

"That was a hard lick!"

"That's racin'!"

"Go, Junior!"

"It's a Bubba thing."

"Car's too tight!"

"Car's too loose!"

"What would Jesus drive?"

"Yeehaw!"

JEFF MacGREGOR is a senior writer at Sports Illustrated and the author of Sunday Money: Speed! Lust! Madness! Death! A Hot Lap Around America with NASCAR (HarperCollins, 2005).

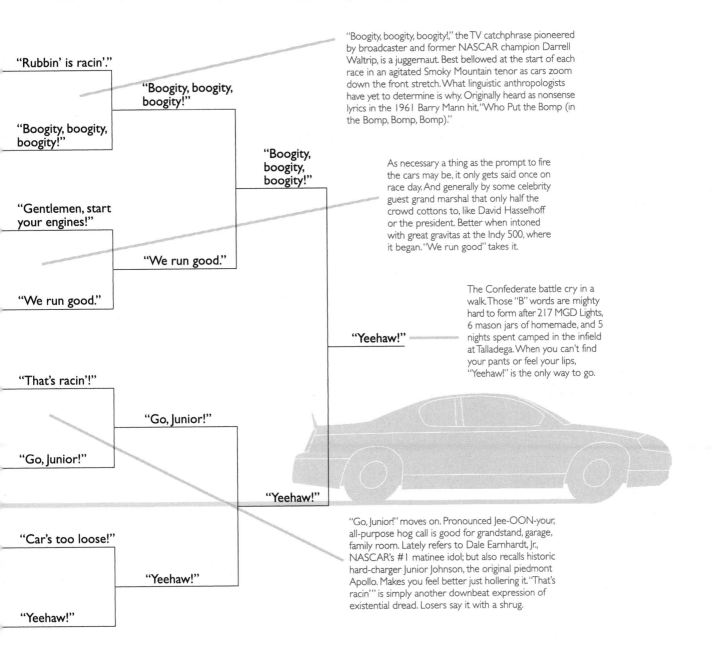

"Rubbin' is racin'."

"Boogity, boogity, boogity!"

"Boogity, boogity, boogity!"

"Boogity, boogity, boogity!"

"Gentlemen, start your engines!"

"We run good."

"We run good."

"That's racin'!"

"Go, Junior!"

"Go, Junior!"

"Yeehaw!"

"Car's too loose!"

"Yeehaw!"

"Yeehaw!"

"Yeehaw!"

"Boogity, boogity, boogity!," the TV catchphrase pioneered by broadcaster and former NASCAR champion Darrell Waltrip, is a juggernaut. Best bellowed at the start of each race in an agitated Smoky Mountain tenor as cars zoom down the front stretch. What linguistic anthropologists have yet to determine is why. Originally heard as nonsense lyrics in the 1961 Barry Mann hit, "Who Put the Bomp (in the Bomp, Bomp, Bomp)."

As necessary a thing as the prompt to fire the cars may be, it only gets said once on race day. And generally by some celebrity guest grand marshal that only half the crowd cottons to, like David Hasselhoff or the president. Better when intoned with great gravitas at the Indy 500, where it began. "We run good" takes it.

The Confederate battle cry in a walk. Those "B" words are mighty hard to form after 217 MGD Lights, 6 mason jars of homemade, and 5 nights spent camped in the infield at Talladega. When you can't find your pants or feel your lips, "Yeehaw!" is the only way to go.

"Go, Junior!" moves on. Pronounced Jee-OON-your, all-purpose hog call is good for grandstand, garage, family room. Lately refers to Dale Earnhardt, Jr., NASCAR's #1 matinee idol; but also recalls historic hard-charger Junior Johnson, the original piedmont Apollo. Makes you feel better just hollering it. "That's racin'" is simply another downbeat expression of existential dread. Losers say it with a shrug.

63

Newspaper Headlines

by JOHN WALTER

Headlines have been with us for about 200 years, since newspaper editors began running summaries atop long columns of type. A great headline does four things: it perfectly captures a moment, with no wasted words; it transcends the merely clever or unfortunate ("Fatal skiing trip gives man new perspective") and reaches the truly appealing or appalling ("Gotcha" made even Rupert Murdoch's editors rethink, given the lives at stake; they yanked it in late editions); it moves the reader (to chortle, weep, gasp in awe) no matter how many times he comes across it; and it sells newspapers (uh, that's why they're there). Should newspapers be overwhelmed by the Web, headlines will suffer, but these artifacts remain.

JOHN WALTER is a longtime newspaper editor (the usual places: Baltimore, Atlanta, Washington. Guam) and currently is co-editor and publisher, with his wife, Jan Pogue, of Vineyard Stories, a bookmaker on Martha's Vineyard (not the Final Four kind of bookmaking.) Full disclosure: As a founding editor of *USA Today*, he wrote a fair number of headlines there — but had no role in crafting the gem included here.

GOTCHA *Sun* (London), 1982, on British sinking of Argentine ship
KOTCHA! *NY Daily News*, 1985, on Koch re-election
— GOTCHA

BASTARDS! *SF Examiner*, Sep. 12, 2001
WE ARE ALL AMERICANS NOW, *Le Monde* (Paris), Sep. 12, 2001
— ALL AMERICANS NOW

AWFUL EVENT; PRESIDENT LINCOLN SHOT BY AN ASSASSIN, *NY Times*, 1865
LINDBERGH DOES IT! TO PARIS IN 33 1/2 HOURS, *NY Times*, 1927
— AWFUL EVENT; LINCOLN SHOT

THE WAR SHIP MAINE WAS SPLIT IN TWO BY AN ENEMY'S SECRET INFERNAL MACHINE, *NY Journal*, 1898
J'ACCUSE! *L'Aurore* (Paris), 1898, the Dreyfus affair
— J'ACCUSE!

DEWEY DEFEATS TRUMAN, *Chicago Tribune*, 1948
CHEER UP, *Chicago Tribune*, 1871, on editorial saying "Chicago shall rise again," in first issue after the Great Fire
— DEWEY DEFEATS TRUMAN

MUSH FROM THE WIMP, *Boston Globe*, 1980
BEST SEX I'VE EVER HAD, *NY Post*, 1990, Marla Maples on Donald Trump
— BEST SEX

STICKS NIX HICK PIX, *Variety*, 1935, on rural taste in movies
HICKS NIX KNICKS IN SIX, *NY Daily News*, 2000, as Indiana wins NBA Eastern Conference Finals
— STICKS NIX HICK PIX

HARVARD BEATS YALE, 29-29, *Harvard Crimson*, 1968, celebrating a come-from-behind tie
WHO'S A BUM! *NY Daily News*, 1955, as Dodgers win Series
— HARVARD BEATS YALE

HEART IS TORN FROM GREAT CITY, *LA Times* on San Francisco quake, 1906
FORD TO CITY: DROP DEAD, *NY Daily News*, 1975
— FORD TO CITY: DROP DEAD

COME HELL AND HIGH WATER, *Grand Forks* (N.D.) *Herald*, 1997, after record flood
CASTRO NARROWLY ESCAPES DROWNING: TOO BAD! TOO BAD! TOO BAD! TOO BAD! *El Paso Times*, date unknown
— COME HELL AND HIGH WATER

WALL ST. LAYS AN EGG, *Variety*, 1929
SICK TRANSIT'S GLORIOUS MONDAY, *NY Daily News*, 1980, on transportation bailout
— WALL ST. EGG

BOBBY DIES, *Chicago Daily News*, 1968
SO LONG, CHICAGO, *Chicago Daily News*, 1978, on closing
— SO LONG, CHICAGO

HEADLESS BODY IN TOPLESS BAR, *NY Post*, 1982
I SLEPT WITH A TRUMPET, *NY Post*, on Pulitzer divorce trial, 1983
— HEADLESS BODY

CLOSE BUT NO CIGAR, *NY Daily News*, on Clinton impeachment vote, 1999
FREDDIE STARR ATE MY HAMSTER, *Sun* (London), 1986
— CLOSE BUT NO CIGAR

MEN, WOMEN: WE'RE STILL DIFFERENT, *USA Today*, 1983
REST OF THE YEAR MAY NOT FOLLOW JANUARY, *Wall Street Journal*, 1989
— MEN, WOMEN: DIFFERENT

RAAF CAPTURES FLYING SAUCER ON RANCH IN ROSWELL REGION, *Roswell* (N.M.) *Daily Record*, 1947
NINTH PLANET DISCOVERED ON EDGE OF SOLAR SYSTEM, *NY Times*, 1930
— FLYING SAUCER

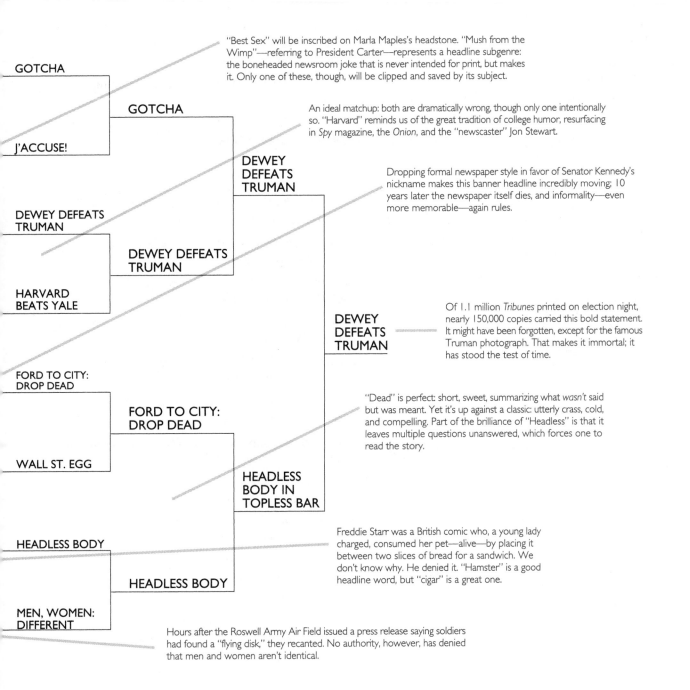

GOTCHA

"Best Sex" will be inscribed on Marla Maples's headstone. "Mush from the Wimp"—referring to President Carter—represents a headline subgenre: the boneheaded newsroom joke that is never intended for print, but makes it. Only one of these, though, will be clipped and saved by its subject.

GOTCHA

J'ACCUSE!

An ideal matchup: both are dramatically wrong, though only one intentionally so. "Harvard" reminds us of the great tradition of college humor, resurfacing in *Spy* magazine, the *Onion*, and the "newscaster" Jon Stewart.

DEWEY DEFEATS TRUMAN

DEWEY DEFEATS TRUMAN

Dropping formal newspaper style in favor of Senator Kennedy's nickname makes this banner headline incredibly moving; 10 years later the newspaper itself dies, and informality—even more memorable—again rules.

DEWEY DEFEATS TRUMAN

HARVARD BEATS YALE

DEWEY DEFEATS TRUMAN

Of 1.1 million *Tribunes* printed on election night, nearly 150,000 copies carried this bold statement. It might have been forgotten, except for the famous Truman photograph. That makes it immortal; it has stood the test of time.

FORD TO CITY: DROP DEAD

FORD TO CITY: DROP DEAD

"Dead" is perfect: short, sweet, summarizing what *wasn't* said but was meant. Yet it's up against a classic: utterly crass, cold, and compelling. Part of the brilliance of "Headless" is that it leaves multiple questions unanswered, which forces one to read the story.

WALL ST. EGG

HEADLESS BODY IN TOPLESS BAR

Freddie Starr was a British comic who, a young lady charged, consumed her pet—alive—by placing it between two slices of bread for a sandwich. We don't know why. He denied it. "Hamster" is a good headline word, but "cigar" is a great one.

HEADLESS BODY

HEADLESS BODY

MEN, WOMEN: DIFFERENT

Hours after the Roswell Army Air Field issued a press release saying soldiers had found a "flying disk," they recanted. No authority, however, has denied that men and women aren't identical.

64

Opera Arias (Male)

by NEIL SHICOFF

I've spent my entire professional life around opera arias, either singing them in the world's major opera houses, or hearing colleagues sing them when I'm onstage, in rehearsal, in the wings, or in the audience. Arias come in many guises: they can be a hit tune ("La donna è mobile") or a tone poem (Wotan's "Farewell") or a comic riff ("Largo al factotum") or a piece of violent oratory (Iago's "Credo"). The only thing they have in common is that they make people feel something—profoundly. They can be technically demanding, sure (and it doesn't hurt if they toss in a ringing high note), but the perfect opera aria is as much a delight for the singer to sing as it is for the audience to hear.

Tenor NEIL SHICOFF has sung at all the world's leading opera houses since his Metropolitan Opera debut in 1976 and has made over two dozen recordings. He lives in Vienna with his wife, the singer Dawn Kotoski, and their son Alexander.

"Vesti la giubba," Leoncavallo, *I Pagliacci*
"In fernem Land," Wagner, *Lohengrin*
→ "Vesti la giubba"

"Flower Song," Bizet, *Carmen*
"Largo al factotum," Rossini, *Il barbiere di Siviglia*
→ "Largo al factotum"

"Salut, demeure," Gounod, *Faust*
"Quando le sere al placido," Verdi, *Luisa Miller*
→ "Quando le sere al placido"

"Spirto gentil," Donizetti, *La Favorita*
"E lucevan le stelle," Puccini, *Tosca*
→ "E lucevan le stelle"

"Che gelida manina," Puccini, *La Bohème*
"Una furtiva lagrima," Donizetti, *L'elisir d'amore*
→ "Che gelida manina"

"Fliedermonolog," Wagner, *Die Meistersinger*
"La donna è mobile," Verdi, *Rigoletto*
→ "Fliedermonolog"

"Prologue," Leoncavallo, *I Pagliacci*
"Ah si, ben mio," Verdi, *Il Trovatore*
→ "Prologue"

"Toreador Song," Bizet, *Carmen*
"En fermant les yeux," Massenet, *Manon*
→ "En fermant les yeux"

"Niun me tema," Verdi, *Otello*
"Amor ti vieta," Giordano, *Fedora*
→ "Niun me tema"

"Cielo e mar," Ponchielli, *La Gioconda*
"Nessun dorma," Puccini, *Turandot*
→ "Nessun dorma"

Wotan's "Farewell," Wagner, *Die Walküre*
"Death of Boris," Mussorgsky, *Boris Godunov*
→ Wotan's "Farewell"

"Di Provenza," Verdi, *La Traviata*
Lensky's aria, Tchaikovsky, *Eugene Onegin*
→ "Di Provenza"

"Eri tu," Verdi, *Un Ballo in Maschera*
"Donna non vidi mai," Puccini, *Manon Lescaut*
→ "Eri tu"

Iago's "Credo," Verdi, *Otello*
"Pourquoi me réveiller," Massenet, *Werther*
→ "Pourquoi me réveiller"

"Asile héréditaire," Rossini, *Guillaume Tell*
"Ella giammai m'amo," Verdi, *Don Carlo*
→ "Ella giammai m'amo"

"Celeste Aida," Verdi, *Aida*
"Il mio tesoro intanto," Mozart, *Don Giovanni*
→ "Celeste Aida"

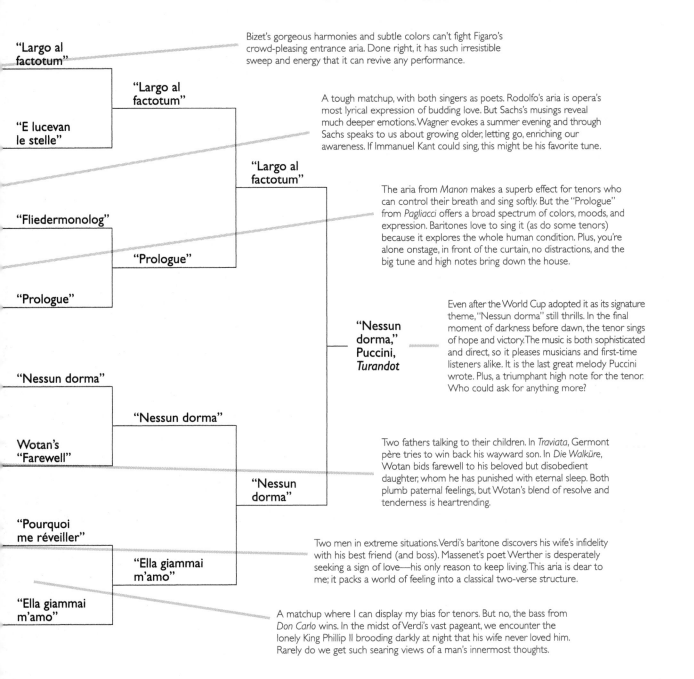

"Largo al factotum"

"E lucevan le stelle"

"Largo al factotum"

"Fliedermonolog"

"Prologue"

"Prologue"

"Largo al factotum"

"Nessun dorma"

"Nessun dorma"

Wotan's "Farewell"

"Nessun dorma"

"Pourquoi me réveiller"

"Ella giammai m'amo"

"Ella giammai m'amo"

"Nessun dorma," Puccini, *Turandot*

Bizet's gorgeous harmonies and subtle colors can't fight Figaro's crowd-pleasing entrance aria. Done right, it has such irresistible sweep and energy that it can revive any performance.

A tough matchup, with both singers as poets. Rodolfo's aria is opera's most lyrical expression of budding love. But Sachs's musings reveal much deeper emotions. Wagner evokes a summer evening and through Sachs speaks to us about growing older, letting go, enriching our awareness. If Immanuel Kant could sing, this might be his favorite tune.

The aria from *Manon* makes a superb effect for tenors who can control their breath and sing softly. But the "Prologue" from *Pagliacci* offers a broad spectrum of colors, moods, and expression. Baritones love to sing it (as do some tenors) because it explores the whole human condition. Plus, you're alone onstage, in front of the curtain, no distractions, and the big tune and high notes bring down the house.

Even after the World Cup adopted it as its signature theme, "Nessun dorma" still thrills. In the final moment of darkness before dawn, the tenor sings of hope and victory. The music is both sophisticated and direct, so it pleases musicians and first-time listeners alike. It is the last great melody Puccini wrote. Plus, a triumphant high note for the tenor. Who could ask for anything more?

Two fathers talking to their children. In *Traviata*, Germont père tries to win back his wayward son. In *Die Walküre*, Wotan bids farewell to his beloved but disobedient daughter, whom he has punished with eternal sleep. Both plumb paternal feelings, but Wotan's blend of resolve and tenderness is heartrending.

Two men in extreme situations. Verdi's baritone discovers his wife's infidelity with his best friend (and boss). Massenet's poet Werther is desperately seeking a sign of love—his only reason to keep living. This aria is dear to me; it packs a world of feeling into a classical two-verse structure.

A matchup where I can display my bias for tenors. But no, the bass from *Don Carlo* wins. In the midst of Verdi's vast pageant, we encounter the lonely King Phillip II brooding darkly at night that his wife never loved him. Rarely do we get such searing views of a man's innermost thoughts.

65

Paul Simon Songs

by LUKE DEMPSEY

He's the greatest living singer-songwriter, period, amen. Unlike the other gods, Dylan and Joni, who mine an esoteric inner landscape, Simon writes for and to all of us. The quintessential Simon song is lyrically astute and streetwise; musically gorgeous (no one modulates through the keys with more felicity); rhythmically complex yet simple sounding (you get the sense he'd rather die than just write in four-four time), and recorded with such care that every disc is a producer's master class (listen for the drum thwack late in "Born at the Right Time," heralding the fade to silence). Add to that his ability to write a state-of-the-nation song for every decade: in the sixties it was "America," in the seventies, "American Tune," in the eighties, "Graceland," in the nineties, "Trailways Bus" (log all those presidential towns), and for the new century, "Wartime Prayers." But he has also written love songs that manage to be personal *and* universal—and often funny ("What—you don't like the way I chew?").

LUKE DEMPSEY is a writer and editor (and a songwriter for the Railbangers). His first book, *A Supremely Bad Idea,* a comic memoir about birds and America, will be published by Bloomsbury in 2008.

STATE-OF-THE-UNION REGIONAL

- "America"
- "American Tune" → "American Tune"
- "Graceland"
- "Trailways Bus" → "Graceland"
- "Wartime Prayers"
- "Cuba Sí, Nixon No" → "Cuba Sí, Nixon No"
- "How Can You Live in the Northeast"
- "Mrs. Robinson" → "Mrs. Robinson"

POOR BOY REGIONAL

- "The Boxer" → "The Boxer"
- "Papa Hobo"
- "Duncan"
- "Jonah" → "Jonah"
- "Darling Lorraine" → "Darling Lorraine"
- "Only Living Boy in New York"
- "Once Upon a Time There Was an Ocean" → "Once Upon a Time"
- "Some Folks' Lives Roll Easy"

HEARTBREAK KID REGIONAL

- "Something So Right"
- "Thelma" → "Thelma"
- "Train in the Distance" → "Train in the Distance"
- "How the Heart Approaches What It Yearns"
- "Kathy's Song"
- "Bernadette" → "Bernadette"
- "Father and Daughter"
- "St. Judy's Comet" → "St. Judy's Comet"

QUIRKY REGIONAL

- "Pigs, Sheep and Wolves" → "Pigs, Sheep and Wolves"
- "At the Zoo"
- "I Know What I Know" → "I Know What I Know"
- "Outrageous"
- "Baby Driver"
- "Me and Julio Down by the Schoolyard" → "Me and Julio"
- "Cecilia"
- "You Can Call Me Al" → "You Can Call Me Al"

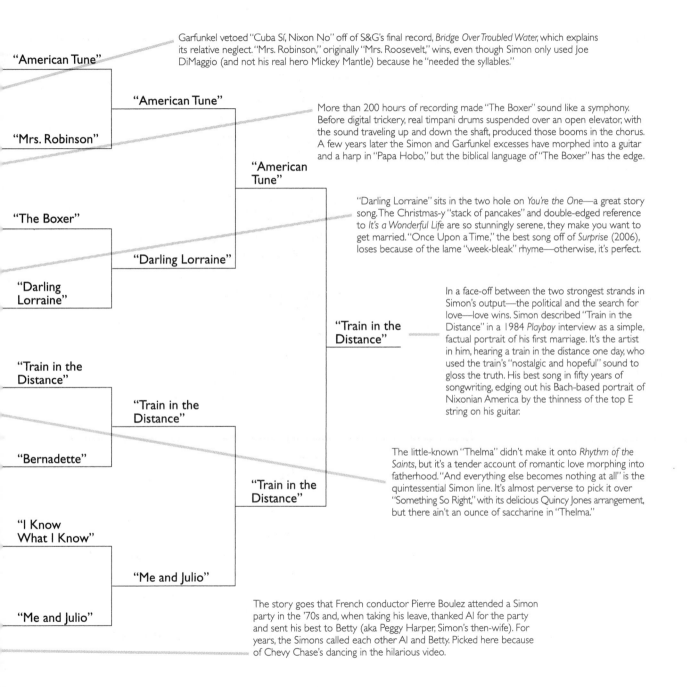

"American Tune"

Garfunkel vetoed "Cuba Sí, Nixon No" off of S&G's final record, *Bridge Over Troubled Water*, which explains its relative neglect. "Mrs. Robinson," originally "Mrs. Roosevelt," wins, even though Simon only used Joe DiMaggio (and not his real hero Mickey Mantle) because he "needed the syllables."

"American Tune"

"Mrs. Robinson"

"American Tune"

More than 200 hours of recording made "The Boxer" sound like a symphony. Before digital trickery, real timpani drums suspended over an open elevator, with the sound traveling up and down the shaft, produced those booms in the chorus. A few years later the Simon and Garfunkel excesses have morphed into a guitar and a harp in "Papa Hobo," but the biblical language of "The Boxer" has the edge.

"The Boxer"

"Darling Lorraine"

"Darling Lorraine"

"Darling Lorraine" sits in the two hole on *You're the One*—a great story song. The Christmas-y "stack of pancakes" and double-edged reference to *It's a Wonderful Life* are so stunningly serene, they make you want to get married. "Once Upon a Time," the best song off of *Surprise* (2006), loses because of the lame "week-bleak" rhyme—otherwise, it's perfect.

"Train in the Distance"

In a face-off between the two strongest strands in Simon's output—the political and the search for love—love wins. Simon described "Train in the Distance" in a 1984 *Playboy* interview as a simple, factual portrait of his first marriage. It's the artist in him, hearing a train in the distance one day, who used the train's "nostalgic and hopeful" sound to gloss the truth. His best song in fifty years of songwriting, edging out his Bach-based portrait of Nixonian America by the thinness of the top E string on his guitar.

"Train in the Distance"

"Train in the Distance"

"Bernadette"

"Train in the Distance"

The little-known "Thelma" didn't make it onto *Rhythm of the Saints*, but it's a tender account of romantic love morphing into fatherhood. "And everything else becomes nothing at all" is the quintessential Simon line. It's almost perverse to pick it over "Something So Right," with its delicious Quincy Jones arrangement, but there ain't an ounce of saccharine in "Thelma."

"I Know What I Know"

"Me and Julio"

"Me and Julio"

The story goes that French conductor Pierre Boulez attended a Simon party in the '70s and, when taking his leave, thanked Al for the party and sent his best to Betty (aka Peggy Harper, Simon's then-wife). For years, the Simons called each other Al and Betty. Picked here because of Chevy Chase's dancing in the hilarious video.

66

Perfect Book Titles

by ROBERT S. MILLER

Publishers used to joke that the perfect book title is *Lincoln's Doctor's Dog*. But that title is merely chasing three avid reader constituencies. It doesn't do what a truly perfect book title does. It doesn't sound like an aphorism or contain a sense of paradox or symmetry. It isn't ironic or euphemistic. It doesn't flatter the reader, or lie to him, or offer to cure the impossible. Nor does it employ a magical number or invoke the promise of eternal life. The perfect book title does at least one of these, often more, which is why we've segregated these 32 snappy titles into eight regionals. As a publisher, I am biased toward titles that grab attention when they are first published but keep finding new readers for years to come.

ROBERT S. MILLER is the president of Hyperion Books, which he started up for Disney 15 years ago. In the interest of full disclosure, three of the titles included here are from the Hyperion list…

FAMILIAR APHORISMS REGIONAL
- Don't Know Much About History
- Don't Sweat the Small Stuff
- Wherever You Go, There You Are
- Life Is Uncertain…Eat Dessert First

→ Don't Sweat the Small Stuff
→ Wherever You Go

SATISFYING SYMMETRY REGIONAL
- When Bad Things Happen to Good People
- What to Expect When You're Expecting
- How to Talk So Kids Will Listen & Listen So Kids Will Talk
- Good to Great

→ When Bad Things Happen
→ How to Talk So Kids Will Listen

EUPHEMISTIC OXYMORONS REGIONAL
- The Dance of Anger
- The Year of Magical Thinking
- Siblings Without Rivalry
- Wealth Without Risk

→ The Dance of Anger
→ Wealth Without Risk

IMPOSSIBLE PROMISES REGIONAL
- Nothing Down
- Eat More, Weigh Less
- Spontaneous Healing
- No More Menstrual Cramps

→ Eat More, Weigh Less
→ Spontaneous Healing

ETERNAL LIFE REGIONAL
- Live Longer Now
- Fit for Life
- Life Extension
- Ageless

→ Fit for Life
→ Life Extension

CURES AND MIRACLES REGIONAL
- Natural Cures "They" Don't Want You to Know About
- Love, Medicine & Miracles
- The Eight-Week Cholesterol Cure
- Miracle Cures

→ Love, Medicine & Miracles
→ Miracle Cures

MAGIC NUMBERS REGIONAL
- 1000 Places to See Before You Die
- The 7 Habits of Highly Effective People
- 10 Stupid Things Women Do to Mess Up Their Lives
- The Five People You Meet in Heaven

→ The 7 Habits
→ The Five People You Meet

FLATTERY REGIONAL
- Women Who Love Too Much
- Smart Women, Foolish Choices
- Meditations for Women Who Do Too Much
- How the Irish Saved Civilization

→ Women Who Love Too Much
→ Meditations for Women

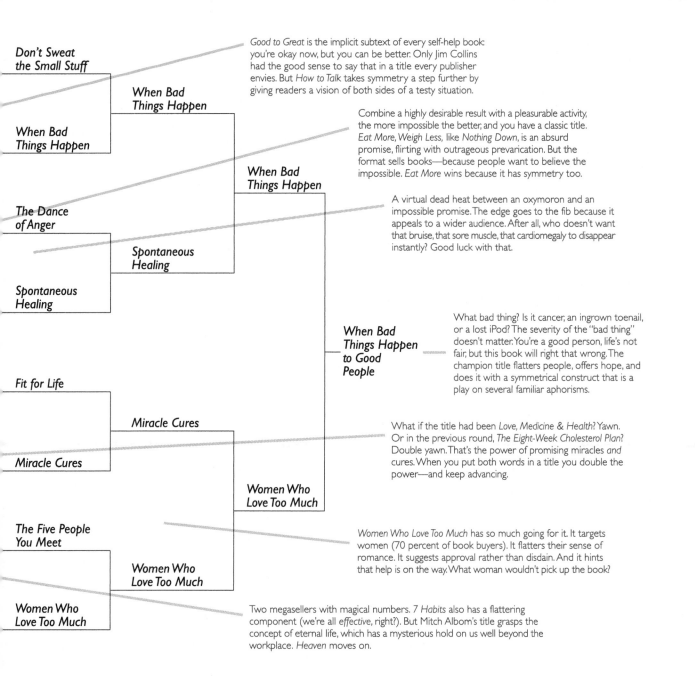

Don't Sweat
the Small Stuff

When Bad
Things Happen

When Bad
Things Happen

When Bad
Things Happen

The Dance
of Anger

Spontaneous
Healing

Spontaneous
Healing

Fit for Life

Miracle Cures

Miracle Cures

Women Who
Love Too Much

The Five People
You Meet

Women Who
Love Too Much

Women Who
Love Too Much

When Bad
Things Happen
to Good
People

Good to Great is the implicit subtext of every self-help book: you're okay now, but you can be better. Only Jim Collins had the good sense to say that in a title every publisher envies. But *How to Talk* takes symmetry a step further by giving readers a vision of both sides of a testy situation.

Combine a highly desirable result with a pleasurable activity, the more impossible the better, and you have a classic title. *Eat More, Weigh Less*, like *Nothing Down*, is an absurd promise, flirting with outrageous prevarication. But the format sells books—because people want to believe the impossible. *Eat More* wins because it has symmetry too.

A virtual dead heat between an oxymoron and an impossible promise. The edge goes to the fib because it appeals to a wider audience. After all, who doesn't want that bruise, that sore muscle, that cardiomegaly to disappear instantly? Good luck with that.

What bad thing? Is it cancer, an ingrown toenail, or a lost iPod? The severity of the "bad thing" doesn't matter. You're a good person, life's not fair, but this book will right that wrong. The champion title flatters people, offers hope, and does it with a symmetrical construct that is a play on several familiar aphorisms.

What if the title had been *Love, Medicine & Health*? Yawn. Or in the previous round, *The Eight-Week Cholesterol Plan*? Double yawn. That's the power of promising miracles *and* cures. When you put both words in a title you double the power—and keep advancing.

Women Who Love Too Much has so much going for it. It targets women (70 percent of book buyers). It flatters their sense of romance. It suggests approval rather than disdain. And it hints that help is on the way. What woman wouldn't pick up the book?

Two megasellers with magical numbers. *7 Habits* also has a flattering component (we're all *effective*, right?). But Mitch Albom's title grasps the concept of eternal life, which has a mysterious hold on us well beyond the workplace. *Heaven* moves on.

67

Pickup Lines
by EM & LO

People—to be specific, *straight men*—expect too much from a pickup line. A truly effective line, the thinking goes, should convince a woman to go home with you on the spot. Not so fast, cowboy! The most effective pickup line is simply one that gets your foot in the door: It's not a closer, it's an opener. It makes a lady laugh, elicits a *multi-word* response from her, intrigues her enough to keep listening. But after that, it's up to you to keep the conversation going and turn it into something like seduction. The following are some of the best gambits designed to help break the ice with a stranger at a bar—all of them guaranteed to be more successful than "Does this look infected?"

EMMA TAYLOR and LORELEI SHARKEY are the authors of *Em & Lo's Rec Sex: An A–Z Guide to Hooking Up* and *Em & Lo's Sex Toy: An A-Z Guide to Bedside Accessories.* As a sex and relationship writing duo, they contribute regularly to *New York* magazine, *Glamour,* and *Men's Health.* They can be found dishing about all things love- and lust-related on their Web site, EMandLO.com.

So, what haven't you been told tonight?
Who's your friend?

So, what haven't

I'm sorry, were you talking to me? No? Then could you please start?
Where are you going? You're not going to leave me here, are you?

Where are you going

See my friend over there? He wants to know if you think I'm cute.
Wanna go halvsies on a bastard?

See my friend

Excuse me, does this tequila taste funny to you?
I know it sounds cheesy, but you're the most beautiful woman I've ever seen. I just had to tell you.

most beautiful

If I were to ask you out, would your answer be the same as the answer to this question?
You know, you might be asked to leave soon. You're making the other women here look bad.

If I were to ask you

Inheriting 80 million doesn't mean much when you only have 3 weeks to live.
My friends and I are having a debate. Paper or plastic?

Paper or plastic

Excuse me, did you just touch my ass? No? Damn, do you want to?
Excuse me, can I borrow your towel? My car just hit a water buffalo.

touch my ass

Mind if I stand here for a second? My friend just farted over there.
You're so pretty you made me forget my pickup line.

You're so pretty

So, I heard you wanted to fight me.
Hi, my name's _____. How do you like me so far?

fight me

Have you always been this cute, or did you have to work at it?
So, do you like fat guys with no money?

fat guys with no money

That looks good. Can I have a sip?
Well, here I am. What were your other two wishes?

Can I have a sip

Nice shoes. Wanna fuck?
I'm the one responsible for all those crop circles in England.

circles in England

Buy me a beer, will ya?
Fat penguin. I just thought I'd say something to break the ice.

Buy me a beer

You should stop drinking—I don't want you to take me home just cause you're drunk.
I'm going outside to make out. Care to join me?

I'm going outside

Can you give me three good reasons why I shouldn't buy you a drink.
I'm not actually this tall. I'm just sitting on my wallet.

three good reasons

I just learned today that you can't catch a cold from going out with wet hair.
Hi, do you speak English? No way, me too.

wet hair

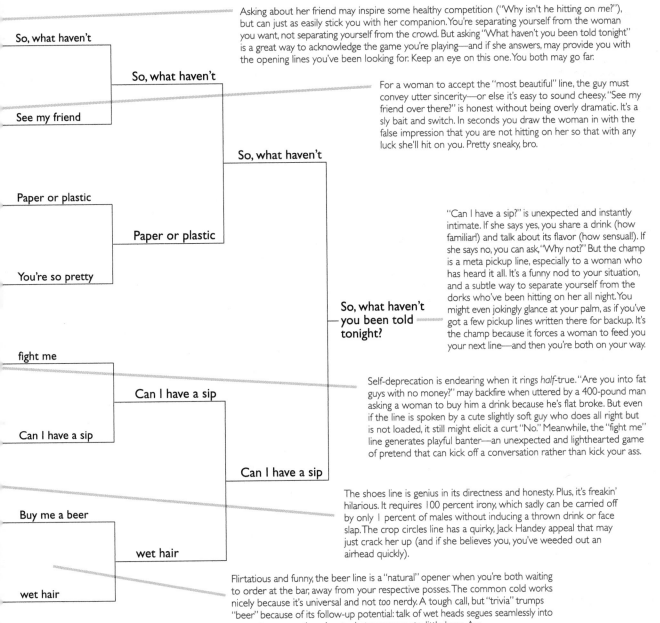

So, what haven't

See my friend

So, what haven't

So, what haven't

Paper or plastic

Paper or plastic

You're so pretty

So, what haven't
you been told
tonight?

fight me

Can I have a sip

Can I have a sip

Can I have a sip

Buy me a beer

wet hair

wet hair

Asking about her friend may inspire some healthy competition ("Why isn't he hitting on *me*?"), but can just as easily stick you with her companion. You're separating yourself from the woman you want, not separating yourself from the crowd. But asking "What haven't you been told tonight" is a great way to acknowledge the game you're playing—and if she answers, may provide you with the opening lines you've been looking for. Keep an eye on this one. You both may go far.

For a woman to accept the "most beautiful" line, the guy must convey utter sincerity—or else it's easy to sound cheesy. "See my friend over there?" is honest without being overly dramatic. It's a sly bait and switch. In seconds you draw the woman in with the false impression that you are not hitting on her so that with any luck she'll hit on you. Pretty sneaky, bro.

"Can I have a sip?" is unexpected and instantly intimate. If she says yes, you share a drink (how familiar!) and talk about its flavor (how sensual!). If she says no, you can ask, "Why not?" But the champ is a meta pickup line, especially to a woman who has heard it all. It's a funny nod to your situation, and a subtle way to separate yourself from the dorks who've been hitting on her all night. You might even jokingly glance at your palm, as if you've got a few pickup lines written there for backup. It's the champ because it forces a woman to feed you your next line—and then you're both on your way.

Self-deprecation is endearing when it rings *half*-true. "Are you into fat guys with no money?" may backfire when uttered by a 400-pound man asking a woman to buy him a drink because he's flat broke. But even if the line is spoken by a cute slightly soft guy who does all right but is not loaded, it still might elicit a curt "No." Meanwhile, the "fight me" line generates playful banter—an unexpected and lighthearted game of pretend that can kick off a conversation rather than kick your ass.

The shoes line is genius in its directness and honesty. Plus, it's freakin' hilarious. It requires 100 percent irony, which sadly can be carried off by only 1 percent of males without inducing a thrown drink or face slap. The crop circles line has a quirky, Jack Handey appeal that may just crack her up (and if she believes you, you've weeded out an airhead quickly).

Flirtatious and funny, the beer line is a "natural" opener when you're both waiting to order at the bar, away from your respective posses. The common cold works nicely because it's universal and not *too* nerdy. A tough call, but "trivia" trumps "beer" because of its follow-up potential: talk of wet heads segues seamlessly into a sweet conversation about what moms say to little boys. Aw.

68

Punctuation

by JESSE SHEIDLOWER

Punctuation is a system of marks used to clarify the meaning of written language by showing how words and clauses relate to each other. We can make do without much punctuation—the principal marks in modern use arose only in the fifteenth and sixteenth centuries. But punctuation is so useful that we now have a vast array of marks for various purposes, especially when the category includes other written symbols such as diacritical marks and printer's marks. Which are the ones we really need?

JESSE SHEIDLOWER is editor at large of the *Oxford English Dictionary*. He managed to write an entire book, *The F-Word*, about one word (yes, that one), and has written about language for such publications as the *New York Times*, *Slate*, *Harper's*, the *Atlantic Monthly*, and *Esquire*.

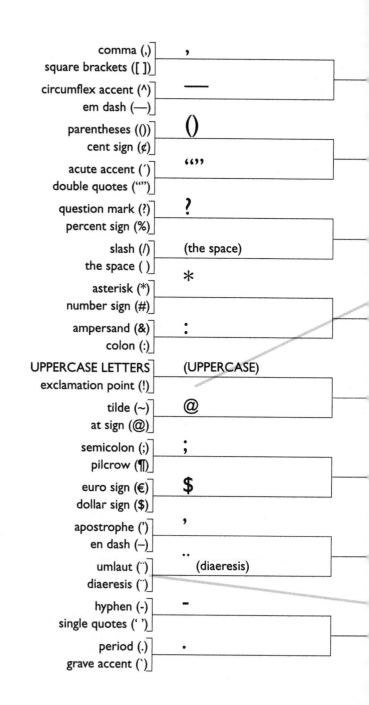

comma (,)
square brackets ([ ])
circumflex accent (^)
em dash (—)
parentheses (())
cent sign (¢)
acute accent (´)
double quotes ("")
question mark (?)
percent sign (%)
slash (/)
the space ( )
asterisk (*)
number sign (#)
ampersand (&)
colon (:)
UPPERCASE LETTERS
exclamation point (!)
tilde (~)
at sign (@)
semicolon (;)
pilcrow (¶)
euro sign (€)
dollar sign ($)
apostrophe (')
en dash (–)
umlaut (¨)
diaeresis (¨)
hyphen (-)
single quotes (' ')
period (.)
grave accent (`)

,
—
()
""
?
(the space)
*
:
(UPPERCASE)
@
;
$
,
.. (diaeresis)
-
•

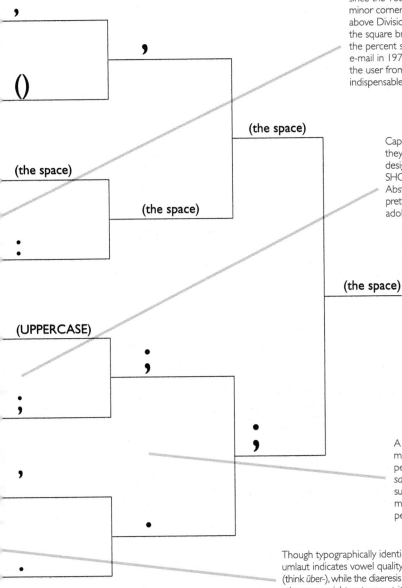

,

( )

,

(the space)

•

(the space)

(the space)

(UPPERCASE)

;

;

,

•

•

;

;

(the space)

•

•

The at sign, used in European mercantile records since the 16th century, seemed destined for a minor corner of the punctuation hierarchy—well above Division III marks like the triple prime or the square bracket with quill, but far below even the percent sign—until Ray Tomlinson invented e-mail in 1971 and chose the at sign to separate the user from the domain name. Now it's indispensable, but can't quite reach the top 8.

Capital letters hardly even seem like punctuation, but they do so much: begin sentences or lines of poetry, designate proper nouns and the pronoun "I," emphasize SHOUTS, allow David Foster Wallace to denote Important Abstract Concepts. In the end, though, we can make do pretty well without them, as a generation of text-messaging adolescents is proving quite handily.

We need art in our writing, but we can't get past the basic need to communicate. The space is absolutely crucial—special characters used to separate words have been around since Linear B—and ever since the regular word divisions became standard around the fifteenth century, it's impossible to imagine a world without it.

A tough battle indeed. While the period is objectively more important, in the end it has no soul. You master the period when you learn to write. The semicolon actually *says* something. What Nicholson Baker has called "that supremely self-possessed valet of phraseology" is a relatively modern mark, yet skilled use of it is what separates the pedestrian from the elegant.

Though typographically identical, these serve different functions: the umlaut indicates vowel quality in certain languages, especially German (think *über-*), while the diaeresis shows that a vowel should be pronounced when you might not expect it (*coöperate, naïve, Brontë*). Becoming old-fashioned, but where would the *New Yorker* be without it?

69

Short Books
by SARA NELSON

"Write it till it's done," the workshop gurus say. But why are some books done at 100 or 150 pages while others are still half-baked at 500? There's nothing lesser about short books, except maybe their price. The cutoff here was no more than 150 pages (my copies). The criterion was bang for the word, or literary fuel mileage: how much satisfying territory did the author cover employing the least amount of ink? All of these short books can share shelf space with the classics. The best of them say more, in less space, than the longest of the long. At the very least, they're the books that, once you finish them, you might even wish you had more of to read.

SARA NELSON is the editor in chief of *Publishers Weekly* and the author of *So Many Books, So Little Time*, the bestselling memoir/reading guide that at 242 pages never had a chance here.

The Death of Ivan Ilych by Leo Tolstoy
The Communist Manifesto by Karl Marx
— Communist Manifesto

Jonathan Livingston Seagull by Richard Bach
On Bullshit by Harry G. Frankfurt
— On Bullshit

Of Mice and Men by John Steinbeck
Desperate Characters by Paula Fox
— Of Mice and Men

Getting Over John Doe by Suzanne Yalof
The Stranger by Albert Camus
— The Stranger

The Writing Life by Annie Dillard
The Old Man and the Sea by Ernest Hemingway
— The Writing Life

Nine and a Half Weeks by Elizabeth McNeill
Horse's Neck by Pete Townshend
— Horse's Neck

Heart of Darkness by Joseph Conrad
Animal Farm by George Orwell
— Heart of Darkness

Legends of the Fall by Jim Harrison
A Room of One's Own by Virginia Woolf
— A Room of One's Own

Darkness Visible by William Styron
One Writer's Beginnings by Eudora Welty
— Darkness Visible

Fahrenheit 451 by Ray Bradbury
Einstein's Dreams by Alan Lightman
— Einstein's Dreams

Night by Elie Wiesel
Walkabout by James Vance Marshall
— Night

Death in Venice by Thomas Mann
Illness as Metaphor by Susan Sontag
— Illness as Metaphor

Hiroshima by John Hersey
The Diving Bell and the Butterfly by Jean-Dominique Bauby
— Hiroshima

Giovanni's Room by James Baldwin
The House on Mango Street by Sandra Cisneros
— House on Mango Street

A Christmas Carol by Charles Dickens
Balzac and the Little Chinese Seamstress by Dai Sijie
— A Christmas Carol

Here Is New York by E. B. White
Why I Don't Write Like Franz Kafka by William S. Wilson
— Here Is New York

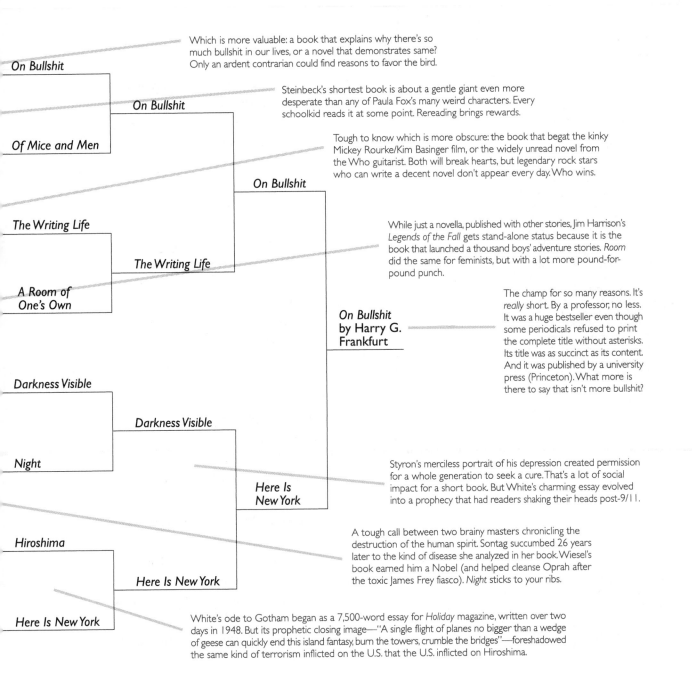

On Bullshit

On Bullshit

Of Mice and Men

Which is more valuable: a book that explains why there's so much bullshit in our lives, or a novel that demonstrates same? Only an ardent contrarian could find reasons to favor the bird.

Steinbeck's shortest book is about a gentle giant even more desperate than any of Paula Fox's many weird characters. Every schoolkid reads it at some point. Rereading brings rewards.

On Bullshit

The Writing Life

The Writing Life

A Room of One's Own

Tough to know which is more obscure: the book that begat the kinky Mickey Rourke/Kim Basinger film, or the widely unread novel from the Who guitarist. Both will break hearts, but legendary rock stars who can write a decent novel don't appear every day. Who wins.

While just a novella, published with other stories, Jim Harrison's *Legends of the Fall* gets stand-alone status because it is the book that launched a thousand boys' adventure stories. *Room* did the same for feminists, but with a lot more pound-for-pound punch.

On Bullshit
by Harry G.
Frankfurt

The champ for so many reasons. It's *really* short. By a professor, no less. It was a huge bestseller even though some periodicals refused to print the complete title without asterisks. Its title was as succinct as its content. And it was published by a university press (Princeton). What more is there to say that isn't more bullshit?

Darkness Visible

Darkness Visible

Night

Styron's merciless portrait of his depression created permission for a whole generation to seek a cure. That's a lot of social impact for a short book. But White's charming essay evolved into a prophecy that had readers shaking their heads post-9/11.

Here Is
New York

Hiroshima

Here Is New York

A tough call between two brainy masters chronicling the destruction of the human spirit. Sontag succumbed 26 years later to the kind of disease she analyzed in her book. Wiesel's book earned him a Nobel (and helped cleanse Oprah after the toxic James Frey fiasco). *Night* sticks to your ribs.

Here Is New York

White's ode to Gotham began as a 7,500-word essay for *Holiday* magazine, written over two days in 1948. But its prophetic closing image—"A single flight of planes no bigger than a wedge of geese can quickly end this island fantasy, burn the towers, crumble the bridges"—foreshadowed the same kind of terrorism inflicted on the U.S. that the U.S. inflicted on Hiroshima.

70

Plastic Surgery Disasters

by MICHAEL MUSTO

To go far in this bracket, the cosmetic changes not only have to be obvious and hideously misguided, they have to derail your career. That knocks out politicians like Hillary Clinton (whose subtle renovation work is the gold standard for public figures) in round 1. Same with Bob Dole, whose wax-museum look came after he left office and had nowhere left to fall. As a general rule, winners advance based on an algebraic formula that is the sum of the immense efforts they have made to alter their looks multiplied by the distance their careers have tumbled. The irony, of course, is that all the competitors, craving attention like heat-seeking missiles, exist to make us look at them but end up making us look away in horror.

MICHAEL MUSTO writes the weekly "La Dolce Musto" gossip and entertainment column for the *Village Voice*. He appears frequently on VH1, E!, and *Countdown with Keith Olbermann*. His columns have been collected in *La Dolce Musto* (Carroll & Graf, 2007).

A matchup of skeletal beauties. But Boyle acquired her bee-stung lips when she was young and beautiful—and did not need it. Makes you wonder who punched her in the mouth.

Kenny Rogers played "the gambler" with his face and now he looks like Will Ferrell meets Colonel Sanders. When he was on *American Idol*, even Paula Abdul opened her eyes for a second—and screamed.

Barbara's lips enter a room 5 minutes before she does. Melanie's enter 5 minutes before Barbara's.

Bob Dole
Michael Jackson — Michael Jackson

Meg Ryan
Marg Helgenberger — Meg Ryan

La Toya Jackson
Hillary Clinton — La Toya Jackson

Lil' Kim
Bruce Jenner — Lil' Kim

Joan Rivers
Michael Douglas — Joan Rivers

Faye Dunaway
Marie Osmond — Faye Dunaway

Mary Tyler Moore
Lara Flynn Boyle — Lara Flynn Boyle

Jennifer Grey
Rupert Everett — Jennifer Grey

Ozzy Osbourne
Cher — Cher

Janice Dickinson
Kenny Rogers — Kenny Rogers

Mickey Rourke
Ivana Trump — Mickey Rourke

Courtney Love
Vivica A. Fox — Courtney Love

Barbara Walters
Victoria Principal — Barbara Walters

Ashlee Simpson
Star Jones — Star Jones

Joan Van Ark
Burt Reynolds — Burt Reynolds

Melanie Griffith
Barbara Hershey — Melanie Griffith

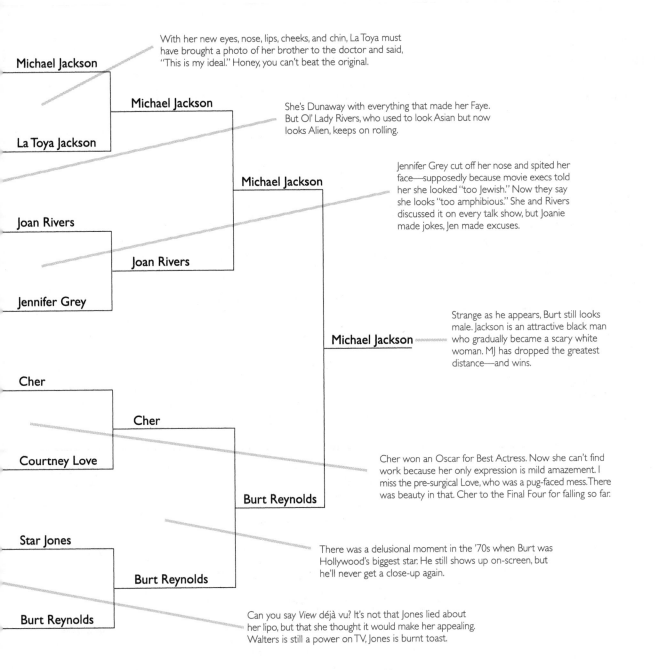

Michael Jackson

With her new eyes, nose, lips, cheeks, and chin, La Toya must have brought a photo of her brother to the doctor and said, "This is my ideal." Honey, you can't beat the original.

Michael Jackson

La Toya Jackson

She's Dunaway with everything that made her Faye. But Ol' Lady Rivers, who used to look Asian but now looks Alien, keeps on rolling.

Michael Jackson

Joan Rivers

Jennifer Grey cut off her nose and spited her face—supposedly because movie execs told her she looked "too Jewish." Now they say she looks "too amphibious." She and Rivers discussed it on every talk show, but Joanie made jokes, Jen made excuses.

Joan Rivers

Jennifer Grey

Michael Jackson

Strange as he appears, Burt still looks male. Jackson is an attractive black man who gradually became a scary white woman. MJ has dropped the greatest distance—and wins.

Cher

Cher

Courtney Love

Cher won an Oscar for Best Actress. Now she can't find work because her only expression is mild amazement. I miss the pre-surgical Love, who was a pug-faced mess. There was beauty in that. Cher to the Final Four for falling so far.

Burt Reynolds

Star Jones

There was a delusional moment in the '70s when Burt was Hollywood's biggest star. He still shows up on-screen, but he'll never get a close-up again.

Burt Reynolds

Burt Reynolds

Can you say *View* déjà vu? It's not that Jones lied about her lipo, but that she thought it would make her appealing. Walters is still a power on TV, Jones is burnt toast.

71

Greatest Political Blunders of the Past 50 Years

by PAUL SLANSKY

Two factors determine the greatness of a political blunder: the damage done to the community and the political cost for the blunderer. A blunder that damages the country and the world is greater than one that only damages the country. A blunder that damages the country is greater than one that only humiliates the blunderer. A blunder that causes one to lose the presidency, or even the chance to run for it, is greater than one that only costs a Senate seat or mayoralty. A blunder that costs lives is bigger than one that only hurts feelings or offends sensibilities. Hence, great political blunders tend to be presidential blunders. Each blunder is judged by these standards, regardless of how much coverage it received in the tabloids or, in recent years, on cable TV.

PAUL SLANSKY, a frequent contributor to the New Yorker, is the author of The Clothes Have No Emperor and The George W. Bush Quiz Book, and the coauthor of Dan Quayle: Airhead Apparent and My Bad: 25 Years of Public Apologies and the Appalling Behavior That Inspired Them.

GEORGE W. BUSH ignores warnings about 9/11 [2001]
GEORGE BUSH pledges not to raise taxes [1988]

→ GEORGE W. BUSH ignores warnings about 9/11

GERALD FORD pardons disgraced ex-president [1974]
JIMMY CARTER diagnoses America's ills with "malaise speech" [1979]

→ FORD pardons disgraced ex-president

GEORGE BUSH picks idiot running mate [1988]
GEORGE McGOVERN picks electroshocked running mate [1972]

→ GEORGE BUSH picks idiot running mate

GEORGE BUSH looks at watch during debate [1992]
GEORGE W. BUSH ignores hurricane warnings [2005]

→ GEORGE W. BUSH ignores hurricane warnings

SPIRO AGNEW becomes vice president, still takes bribes [1969–73]
RICHARD NIXON installs White House taping system [1971]

→ NIXON installs White House taping system

GERALD FORD seems ignorant about Eastern Europe in debate [1976]
DAN QUAYLE compares self to JFK in debate [1988]

→ QUAYLE compares self to JFK in debate

MICHAEL DUKAKIS robotically discusses wife's hypothetical rape/murder in debate [1988]
MICHAEL DUKAKIS poses for pictures in tank [1988]

→ DUKAKIS poses for pictures in tank

DONALD REGAN pisses off quick-to-anger first lady [1987]
RONALD REAGAN trades arms for hostages [1986]

→ REAGAN trades arms for hostages

LYNDON JOHNSON escalates Vietnam war [1963–68]
DICK CHENEY shoots fellow hunter in face [2006]

→ JOHNSON escalates Vietnam war

RICHARD NIXON gets drunk and tells off reporters [1962]
TED KENNEDY gets drunk and drives off bridge [1969]

→ TED KENNEDY gets drunk and drives off bridge

NEWT GINGRICH shuts down government after perceived presidential snub [1995]
JOHN KERRY allows character to be assassinated [2004]

→ KERRY allows character to be assassinated

TRENT LOTT sucks up to ancient colleague known for racist past [2002]
AL GORE distances self from most popular Democrat in decades [2000]

→ GORE distances self from most popular Democrat in decades

BILL CLINTON gets serviced by White House intern [1995]
MARION BARRY smokes crack in videotaped sting [1990]

→ CLINTON gets serviced by White House intern

GARY HART challenges reporters to catch him cheating [1987]
ROBERT PACKWOOD forces self on many women [1980s–1990s]

→ HART challenges reporters to catch him cheating

DAN QUAYLE corrects student about spelling of "potato" [1992]
GEORGE BUSH throws up on Japanese head of state [1992]

→ QUAYLE corrects student about spelling of "potato"

JOHN F. KENNEDY authorizes failed effort to invade Cuba [1961]
GEORGE W. BUSH ignores warnings against invading Iraq [2003]

→ GEORGE W. BUSH ignores warnings against invading Iraq

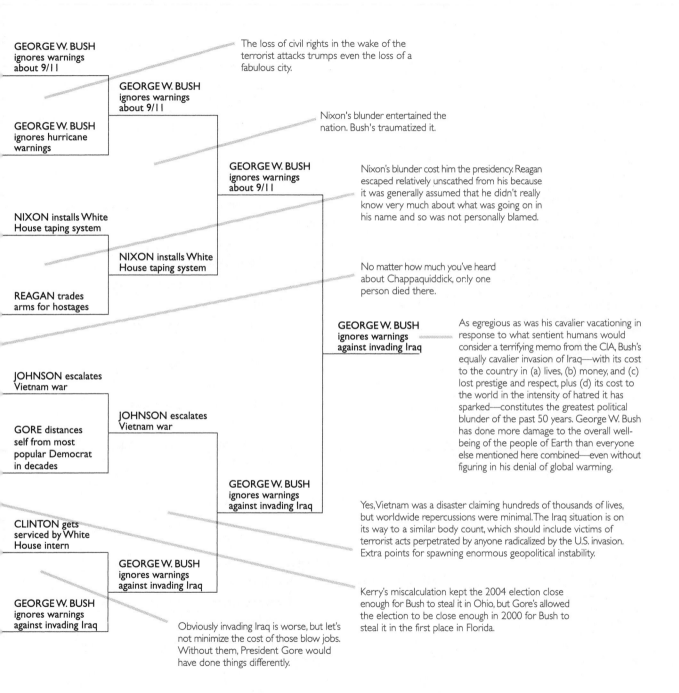

GEORGE W. BUSH ignores warnings about 9/11

The loss of civil rights in the wake of the terrorist attacks trumps even the loss of a fabulous city.

GEORGE W. BUSH ignores warnings about 9/11

GEORGE W. BUSH ignores hurricane warnings

Nixon's blunder entertained the nation. Bush's traumatized it.

GEORGE W. BUSH ignores warnings about 9/11

Nixon's blunder cost him the presidency. Reagan escaped relatively unscathed from his because it was generally assumed that he didn't really know very much about what was going on in his name and so was not personally blamed.

NIXON installs White House taping system

NIXON installs White House taping system

No matter how much you've heard about Chappaquiddick, only one person died there.

REAGAN trades arms for hostages

GEORGE W. BUSH ignores warnings against invading Iraq

As egregious as was his cavalier vacationing in response to what sentient humans would consider a terrifying memo from the CIA, Bush's equally cavalier invasion of Iraq—with its cost to the country in (a) lives, (b) money, and (c) lost prestige and respect, plus (d) its cost to the world in the intensity of hatred it has sparked—constitutes the greatest political blunder of the past 50 years. George W. Bush has done more damage to the overall well-being of the people of Earth than everyone else mentioned here combined—even without figuring in his denial of global warming.

JOHNSON escalates Vietnam war

JOHNSON escalates Vietnam war

GORE distances self from most popular Democrat in decades

GEORGE W. BUSH ignores warnings against invading Iraq

Yes, Vietnam was a disaster claiming hundreds of thousands of lives, but worldwide repercussions were minimal. The Iraq situation is on its way to a similar body count, which should include victims of terrorist acts perpetrated by anyone radicalized by the U.S. invasion. Extra points for spawning enormous geopolitical instability.

CLINTON gets serviced by White House intern

GEORGE W. BUSH ignores warnings against invading Iraq

Kerry's miscalculation kept the 2004 election close enough for Bush to steal it in Ohio, but Gore's allowed the election to be close enough in 2000 for Bush to steal it in the first place in Florida.

GEORGE W. BUSH ignores warnings against invading Iraq

Obviously invading Iraq is worse, but let's not minimize the cost of those blow jobs. Without them, President Gore would have done things differently.

72

Political Hot Buttons

by MO ROCCA

If American political campaigns were about wonky issues like social security reform or deficit reduction, few of us would vote. Thank goodness for hot-button issues. Gas prices, prayer in school, same-sex marriage: these are the topics that can make even the staunchest opponents of the death penalty go postal. And go to the voting booth. Early on in our republic these issues included whiskey taxes and the gold standard, but they seem quaint now—much ado about nothing. (Slavery is the exception; that really was a big deal.) Exit polls, controversial in their own right, will rank the importance of these controversial issues after the fact. But how seriously can we take them? "Poll-tested politics" didn't even qualify to play.

MO ROCCA is a contributor to *The Tonight Show with Jay Leno* and *CBS Sunday Morning*. He's a regular panelist with NPR's *Wait Wait…Don't Tell Me!* and a former correspondent for *The Daily Show with Jon Stewart*. His exposé *All the Presidents' Pets: The Story of One Reporter Who Refused to Roll Over* (Crown) is available in paperback.

Polygamy hasn't been a contender since Utah outlawed it in 1890 as a condition for statehood. Since then it's been the subject of a lackluster HBO show and a bogeyman for opponents of same-sex marriage. ("What's next? Legalizing polygamy?!") It falls to the marriage penalty, the supposed tax burden placed on married couples.

You'd think that the Nazis would goose-step all over the Confederate flag. But flying the Dixie colors is about more than freedom of speech. It's about the costliest war in U.S. history, states' rights vs. federal government, North vs. South, and our permanent hot button—race. By the way, the Nazis never ended up marching in Skokie.

Matchup	Winner
gay marriage / gay adoption	gay marriage
polygamy / marriage penalty	marriage penalty
death penalty / death tax	death penalty
flag burning / global warming	global warming
medical marijuana / steroids in pro sports	medical marijuana
e-mail sex with pages / e-mail surveillance and wiretaps (privacy)	privacy
preemptive action / affirmative action	affirmative action
gun control / troop safety	gun control
abortion / cloning	abortion
minimum wage / gas prices	gas prices
the Clintons / the Bushes	the Clintons
Nazis marching in Skokie / flying of Confederate flag	Confederate flag
levees / levies	levees
drilling for oil in Alaska / Alaska's bridge to nowhere (and other pork)	drilling in Alaska
border security / outsourcing	border security
prayer in schools / evolution in schools	evolution in schools

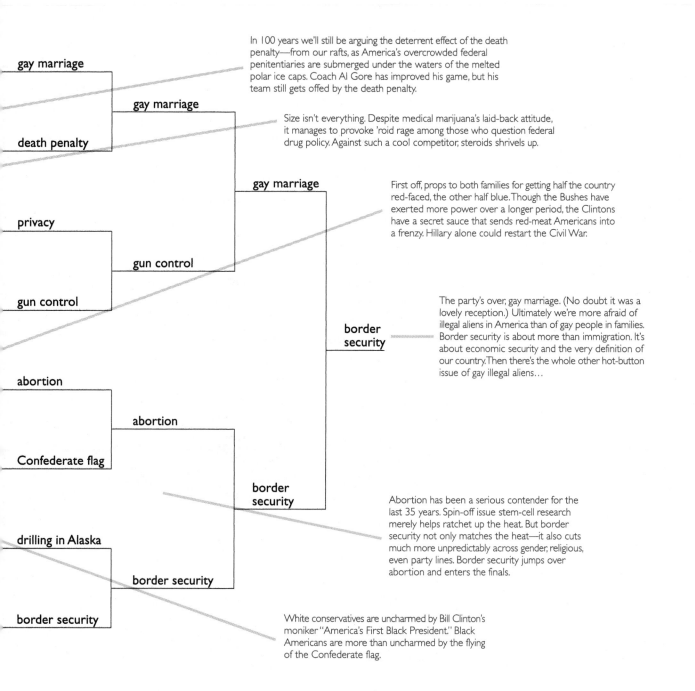

gay marriage

death penalty

gay marriage

In 100 years we'll still be arguing the deterrent effect of the death penalty—from our rafts, as America's overcrowded federal penitentiaries are submerged under the waters of the melted polar ice caps. Coach Al Gore has improved his game, but his team still gets offed by the death penalty.

Size isn't everything. Despite medical marijuana's laid-back attitude, it manages to provoke 'roid rage among those who question federal drug policy. Against such a cool competitor, steroids shrivels up.

gay marriage

privacy

gun control

gun control

First off, props to both families for getting half the country red-faced, the other half blue. Though the Bushes have exerted more power over a longer period, the Clintons have a secret sauce that sends red-meat Americans into a frenzy. Hillary alone could restart the Civil War.

border security

The party's over, gay marriage. (No doubt it was a lovely reception.) Ultimately we're more afraid of illegal aliens in America than of gay people in families. Border security is about more than immigration. It's about economic security and the very definition of our country. Then there's the whole other hot-button issue of gay illegal aliens…

abortion

abortion

Confederate flag

border security

drilling in Alaska

border security

border security

Abortion has been a serious contender for the last 35 years. Spin-off issue stem-cell research merely helps ratchet up the heat. But border security not only matches the heat—it also cuts much more unpredictably across gender, religious, even party lines. Border security jumps over abortion and enters the finals.

White conservatives are uncharmed by Bill Clinton's moniker "America's First Black President." Black Americans are more than uncharmed by the flying of the Confederate flag.

73

Presidential Speeches

by CURT SMITH

Since George Washington's first inaugural in 1789, the most successful presidents have employed what Teddy Roosevelt labeled the "bully pulpit": the office's power to persuade. Their best speeches are remembered for social impact, political consequence, and/or rhetorical artistry, which create a unique form of oral history that is passed from one generation to another. Some of the speeches need contain only two of the criteria, while others, like Abraham Lincoln's second inaugural and Franklin Delano Roosevelt's first, contain all three. Pre-presidential speeches, however great, such as Lincoln's 1858 "house divided" speech, did not qualify.

CURT SMITH wrote more speeches than anyone for President George H.W. Bush. The author of 12 books, he has been named to the prestigious Judson Welliver Society of former presidential speechwriters and teaches presidential rhetoric and public speaking at the University of Rochester.

George Washington First Inaugural (1789)
Abraham Lincoln, First Inaugural (1861) — **Lincoln, First Inaugural**

George Washington, Farewell Address (1796)
Thomas Jefferson, First Inaugural (1801) — **Jefferson, First Inaugural**

Abraham Lincoln, Gettysburg Address (1863)
Theodore Roosevelt, "Man with the Muck-rake" (1906) — **Lincoln, Gettysburg**

Abraham Lincoln, Second Inaugural (1865)
Woodrow Wilson, World War I Message (1917) — **Lincoln, Second Inaugural**

Franklin Roosevelt, Acceptance Speech (1936)
Harry Truman, "Truman Doctrine" (1947) — **FDR, Acceptance**

Franklin Roosevelt, World War II Message (1941)
Dwight Eisenhower, Farewell Address (1961) — **FDR, WW II**

Franklin Roosevelt, "Arsenal of Democracy" (1940)
John F. Kennedy, Cuban Missile Crisis (1962) — **FDR, Arsenal**

Franklin Roosevelt, "Four Freedoms" (1941)
John F. Kennedy, Inaugural Address (1961) — **JFK, Inaugural**

Franklin Roosevelt, First Inaugural (1933)
John F. Kennedy, "Ich Bin Ein Berliner" (1963) — **FDR, First Inaugural**

Lyndon Johnson, Post-JFK-Assassination Speech (1963)
Richard Nixon, "Silent Majority" Speech (1969) — **Nixon, Silent Majority**

Richard Nixon, Leningrad Address on Soviet TV (1972)
Ronald Reagan, "Evil Empire" Speech (1983) — **Nixon, Leningrad**

Richard Nixon, White House Farewell (1974)
Gerald Ford, Swearing-In Speech (1974) — **Nixon, Farewell**

Ronald Reagan, *Challenger* Explosion (1986)
George H.W. Bush, Pearl Harbor (1991) — **Reagan, *Challenger***

Lyndon Johnson, Voting Rights Act (1965)
Ronald Reagan, D-Day Speech (1984) — **Reagan, D-Day**

Jimmy Carter, "Malaise" Speech (1979)
Ronald Reagan, Brandenburg Gate (1987) — **Reagan, Brandenburg**

Bill Clinton, Martin Luther King Jr. Speech (1993)
George W. Bush, National Cathedral (2001) — **Clinton, King**

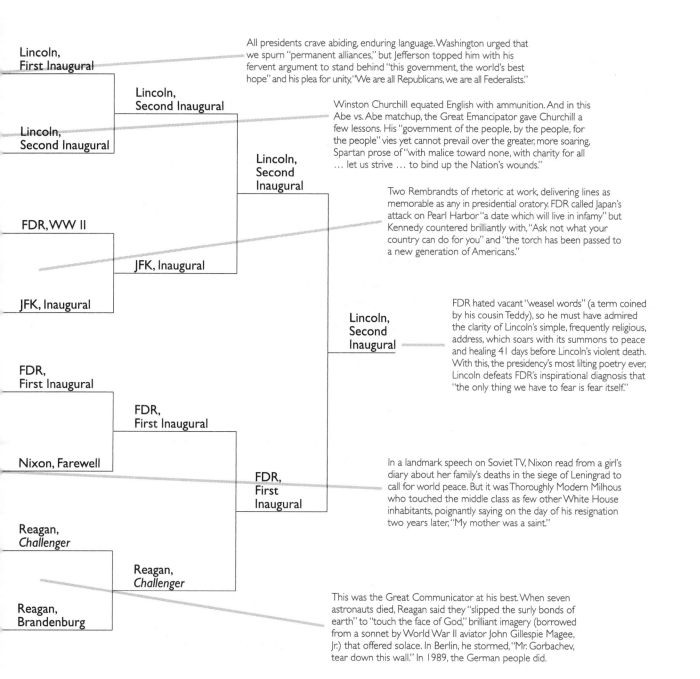

Lincoln,
First Inaugural

Lincoln,
Second Inaugural

Lincoln,
Second Inaugural

Lincoln,
Second
Inaugural

FDR, WW II

JFK, Inaugural

JFK, Inaugural

Lincoln,
Second
Inaugural

FDR,
First Inaugural

FDR,
First Inaugural

Nixon, Farewell

FDR,
First
Inaugural

Reagan,
Challenger

Reagan,
Challenger

Reagan,
Brandenburg

All presidents crave abiding, enduring language. Washington urged that we spurn "permanent alliances," but Jefferson topped him with his fervent argument to stand behind "this government, the world's best hope" and his plea for unity, "We are all Republicans, we are all Federalists."

Winston Churchill equated English with ammunition. And in this Abe vs. Abe matchup, the Great Emancipator gave Churchill a few lessons. His "government of the people, by the people, for the people" vies yet cannot prevail over the greater, more soaring, Spartan prose of "with malice toward none, with charity for all … let us strive … to bind up the Nation's wounds."

Two Rembrandts of rhetoric at work, delivering lines as memorable as any in presidential oratory. FDR called Japan's attack on Pearl Harbor "a date which will live in infamy" but Kennedy countered brilliantly with, "Ask not what your country can do for you" and "the torch has been passed to a new generation of Americans."

FDR hated vacant "weasel words" (a term coined by his cousin Teddy), so he must have admired the clarity of Lincoln's simple, frequently religious, address, which soars with its summons to peace and healing 41 days before Lincoln's violent death. With this, the presidency's most lilting poetry ever, Lincoln defeats FDR's inspirational diagnosis that "the only thing we have to fear is fear itself."

In a landmark speech on Soviet TV, Nixon read from a girl's diary about her family's deaths in the siege of Leningrad to call for world peace. But it was Thoroughly Modern Milhous who touched the middle class as few other White House inhabitants, poignantly saying on the day of his resignation two years later, "My mother was a saint."

This was the Great Communicator at his best. When seven astronauts died, Reagan said they "slipped the surly bonds of earth" to "touch the face of God," brilliant imagery (borrowed from a sonnet by World War II aviator John Gillespie Magee, Jr.) that offered solace. In Berlin, he stormed, "Mr. Gorbachev, tear down this wall." In 1989, the German people did.

74

Priceless Things

by LEILA DUNBAR and Colleagues at Sotheby's

Priceless things are tangible objects that have never been sold. The buildings, landmarks, artwork, sculpture, and important documents here were all chosen for their impact on history, their longevity, their iconic standing, their sheer enormity, and their symbolism. The criterion: which is the least likely to ever come up for sale, privately or at an auction house? Most are owned by governments or the public, which suggests but doesn't guarantee that they'll never go on the block. Is there such a thing as the most priceless? According to our bracket, the answer is yes!

LEILA "LEE" DUNBAR is senior vice president of Sotheby's Collectibles in New York. In her seven years, the Collectibles Department has been responsible for more than $60 million in sales of sports and entertainment memorabilia, including the estates of Katharine Hepburn and Johnny Cash and the bat Babe Ruth used to hit the first home run ever in Yankee Stadium. Thanks to colleagues Lisa Ladish, Hugh Hildesley, Mary Bartow, Charles Moffett, Richard Keresey, Christopher Gaillard, and the Chinese Works of Art Department.

Statue of Liberty	Statue of Liberty
Eiffel Tower	
Parthenon	Parthenon
Stonehenge	
Taj Mahal	Pyramids/Sphinx
the Pyramids of Giza/Sphinx	
Ka'ba in Mecca	Sistine Chapel
Sistine Chapel Ceiling by Michelangelo	
Mona Lisa (La Gioconda) by Leonardo da Vinci	Mona Lisa
Birth of Venus by Sandro Botticelli	
Guernica by Pablo Picasso	Guernica
The Night Watch by Rembrandt van Rijn	
Impression: Sunrise by Claude Monet	Impression: Sunrise
Head of a Young Woman by Johannes Vermeer	
Venus de Milo, attributed to Alexandros of Antioch	Venus de Milo
Winged Victory of Samothrace by unknown artist	
Crown Jewels of Great Britain	Crown Jewels
Pope's ring	
Rosetta Stone	Rosetta Stone
Code of Hammurabi	
David by Michelangelo	David
The Thinker by Auguste Rodin	
King Tutankhamun artifacts	King Tut artifacts
Queen Nefertiti's bust	
buried city of Pompeii	Terracotta Army
Terracotta Army	
Great Wall of China	Great Wall of China
Forbidden City	
Magna Carta	Magna Carta
United States Constitution	
Blarney Stone	Blarney Stone
Book of Kells	

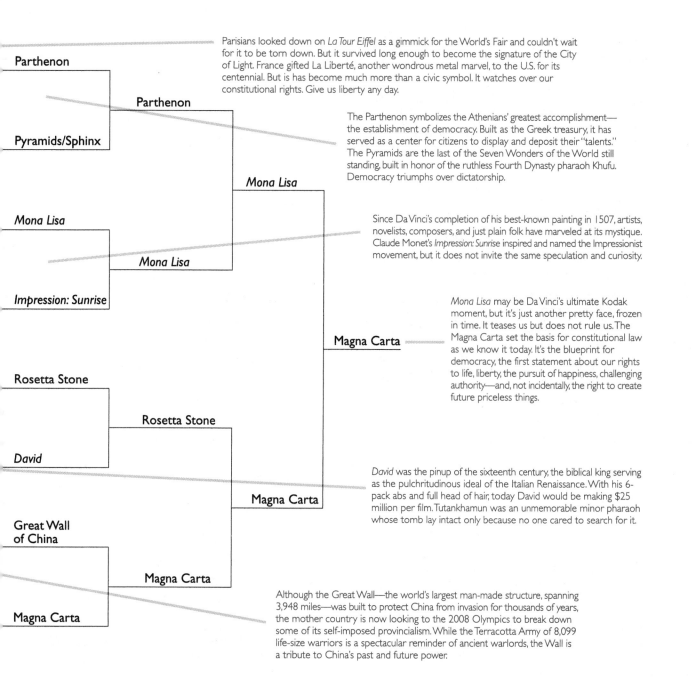

Parthenon

Pyramids/Sphinx

Parthenon

Mona Lisa

Mona Lisa

Impression: Sunrise

Mona Lisa

Magna Carta

Rosetta Stone

David

Rosetta Stone

Magna Carta

Great Wall
of China

Magna Carta

Magna Carta

Parisians looked down on *La Tour Eiffel* as a gimmick for the World's Fair and couldn't wait for it to be torn down. But it survived long enough to become the signature of the City of Light. France gifted La Liberté, another wondrous metal marvel, to the U.S. for its centennial. But is has become much more than a civic symbol. It watches over our constitutional rights. Give us liberty any day.

The Parthenon symbolizes the Athenians' greatest accomplishment— the establishment of democracy. Built as the Greek treasury, it has served as a center for citizens to display and deposit their "talents." The Pyramids are the last of the Seven Wonders of the World still standing, built in honor of the ruthless Fourth Dynasty pharaoh Khufu. Democracy triumphs over dictatorship.

Since Da Vinci's completion of his best-known painting in 1507, artists, novelists, composers, and just plain folk have marveled at its mystique. Claude Monet's *Impression: Sunrise* inspired and named the Impressionist movement, but it does not invite the same speculation and curiosity.

Mona Lisa may be Da Vinci's ultimate Kodak moment, but it's just another pretty face, frozen in time. It teases us but does not rule us. The Magna Carta set the basis for constitutional law as we know it today. It's the blueprint for democracy, the first statement about our rights to life, liberty, the pursuit of happiness, challenging authority—and, not incidentally, the right to create future priceless things.

David was the pinup of the sixteenth century, the biblical king serving as the pulchritudinous ideal of the Italian Renaissance. With his 6-pack abs and full head of hair, today David would be making $25 million per film. Tutankhamun was an unmemorable minor pharaoh whose tomb lay intact only because no one cared to search for it.

Although the Great Wall—the world's largest man-made structure, spanning 3,948 miles—was built to protect China from invasion for thousands of years, the mother country is now looking to the 2008 Olympics to break down some of its self-imposed provincialism. While the Terracotta Army of 8,099 life-size warriors is a spectacular reminder of ancient warlords, the Wall is a tribute to China's past and future power.

75

Rednecks
by ALLISON GLOCK

Know this: rednecks are happy to be red. Unlike crackers and poor white trash, rednecks make no apologies for their chosen status, nor do they endeavor to improve it. To be a redneck is to bask in the glory of underachievement. Appalachian in root, belligerent by breeding, the redneck descends from the Scots who fled English rule, hard-bitten men and women who made a lifestyle out of giving the finger to whomever they chose. Even now, centuries later, rednecks do not conform. They do not shirk. They make no apologies. They take little seriously, not even God. Rednecks prefer to find their own religion, often in a bottle. Rednecks need not be southern, though it helps. More important is an innate sense of entitlement, regardless of actual social status, and a healthy disregard for airs. And if you've got a problem with that, then to hell with y'all.

ALLISON GLOCK is the author of the southern memoir *Beauty Before Comfort*. Having been reared in West Virginia, North Florida, Georgia, and Tennessee, she considers herself a gumbo of redneck, cracker, and white trash. She is inexplicably proud of being all three.

Royals can be rednecks too. Stephanie drinks, breeds impulsively, snarls at decorum, has blink-and-you-miss-it marriages with her bodyguards. She's just like Britney, only with shoes. And until you walk barefoot in a public restroom, you're not beating Brit.

The McCoys may have started the legendary, deadly Appalachian feud over the ownership of a hog. But no family, not even the intermarrying, moonshining kind, beats Lynyrd Skynyrd, suppliers of the redneck national anthem, "Free Bird."

The R&B jailbird is a prime example of how, black or white, you can still be red all over. And really, it's his prerogative. Shockey may be a homophobic tight end, but I'd like to see him tackle life with Whitney "show-me-the-receipts" Houston.

Cain is the original redneck. Bullying, skilled at hand-to-hand combat. But still, no match against the Nuge and his crossbow.

The former slow-witted pitcher slurred "kids with purple hair … queer[s] with AIDS … 20-year-old mom[s] with four kids," among others. But once you marry your 13-year-old cousin, who also happens to be your *third* wife, when you are only 23, your redneck cred is incontestable. Add that Lewis is a cousin to Jimmy Swaggart and Mickey Gilley, and you've got an embarrassment of nouveau riches.

Round 1	Round 2
Bocephus	Bocephus
John Daly	
Junior Johnson	Jimmy Johnson
Jimmy Johnson	
Han Solo	Han Solo
Huck Finn	
Terry Bradshaw	Terry Bradshaw
Ted Turner	
Princess Stephanie of Monaco	Britney Spears
Britney Spears	
Elvis	Johnny Cash
Johnny Cash	
The McCoys	Lynyrd Skynyrd
Lynyrd Skynyrd	
Billy Carter	Billy Carter
Roger Clinton	
Bobby Brown	Bobby Brown
Jeremy Shockey	
Andrew Jackson	LBJ
LBJ	
W.	W.
Larry Flynt	
Matthew McConaughey	Matthew McConaughey
Johnny Knoxville	
Ted Nugent	Ted Nugent
Cain	
Burt Reynolds	Burt Reynolds
Eminem	
John Rocker	Jerry Lee Lewis
Jerry Lee Lewis	
James Carville	Any tow truck driver
Any tow truck driver	

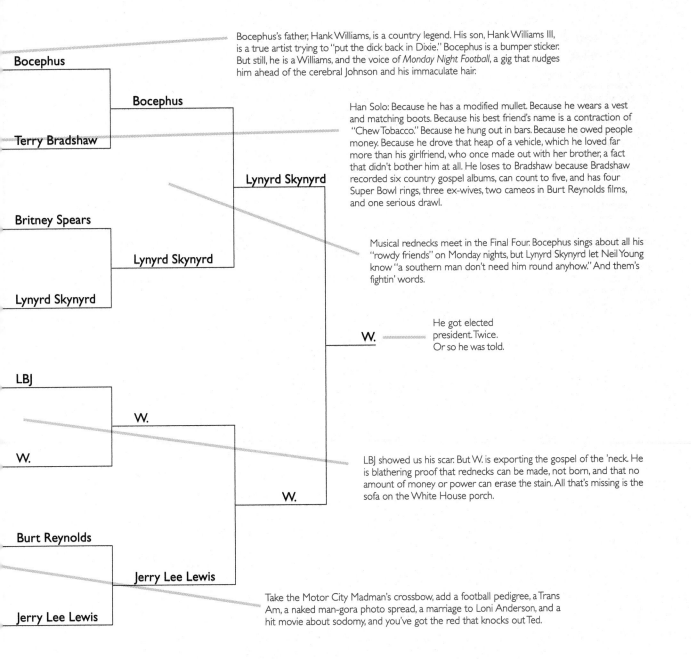

Bocephus's father, Hank Williams, is a country legend. His son, Hank Williams III, is a true artist trying to "put the dick back in Dixie." Bocephus is a bumper sticker. But still, he is a Williams, and the voice of *Monday Night Football*, a gig that nudges him ahead of the cerebral Johnson and his immaculate hair.

Han Solo: Because he has a modified mullet. Because he wears a vest and matching boots. Because his best friend's name is a contraction of "Chew Tobacco." Because he hung out in bars. Because he owed people money. Because he drove that heap of a vehicle, which he loved far more than his girlfriend, who once made out with her brother, a fact that didn't bother him at all. He loses to Bradshaw because Bradshaw recorded six country gospel albums, can count to five, and has four Super Bowl rings, three ex-wives, two cameos in Burt Reynolds films, and one serious drawl.

Musical rednecks meet in the Final Four. Bocephus sings about all his "rowdy friends" on Monday nights, but Lynyrd Skynyrd let Neil Young know "a southern man don't need him round anyhow." And them's fightin' words.

He got elected president. Twice. Or so he was told.

LBJ showed us his scar. But W. is exporting the gospel of the 'neck. He is blathering proof that rednecks can be made, not born, and that no amount of money or power can erase the stain. All that's missing is the sofa on the White House porch.

Take the Motor City Madman's crossbow, add a football pedigree, a Trans Am, a naked man-gora photo spread, a marriage to Loni Anderson, and a hit movie about sodomy, and you've got the red that knocks out Ted.

76

Great Red Wines

by JOSEPH WARD

Virtually 32 number-one seeds, these wines represent the best of both Europe's historic regions and New World challengers from California and Australia. What separates the great in the opening rounds from the even greater in the Final Four are (1) a track record of consistent excellence; (2) the ability to evolve interestingly over a long life span; and (3) how much pleasure a wine has given me. It is objectively impossible to say that La Tâche is greater than Château Ausone. I simply prefer La Tâche.

JOSEPH WARD is the wine editor of *Condé Nast Traveler* and the coauthor (with Steven Spurrier) of *How to Buy Fine Wines: Practical Advice for the Investor and Connoisseur.*

Grange Penfolds — Grange
Viña Tondonia Gran Reserva López de Heredia

Sori Tildin Gaja — Sori Tildin
Château Montelena

Musigny Vielles Vignes Comte de Vogüé — Musigny
Clos des Papes

Cabernet Sauvignon Special Selection Caymus — Côte-Rôtie
Côte-Rôtie La Landonne Guigal

La Tâche DRC — La Tâche
Sassicaia

Pingus — Hill of Grace
Hill of Grace Henschke

Brumello di Montalcino Riserva Soldera — Château Ausone
Château Ausone

Chambertin Clos de Beze Rousseau — Chambertin Clos de Beze
Harlan Estate

Astralis Clarendon Hills — Château Margaux
Château Margaux

Château Latour — Château Latour
Bonnes Mares Roumier

Barolo Monfortino Riserva Giacomo Conterno — Barolo Monfortino
Hillside Select Shafer

Château Pétrus — Château Pétrus
Château Rayas

Barbaresco Santo Stefano Riserva Giacosa — Château Haut-Brion
Château Haut-Brion

Dominus — Vega Sicilia
Vega Sicilia

Château Lafleur — Château Lafleur
Barolo Gran Bussia Riserva Aldo Conterno

Hermitage J.L. Chave — Hermitage
Château Cheval-Blanc

Grange

Grange

Musigny

La Tâche

La Tâche

Château Ausone

La Tâche

Château Latour

Château Latour

Château Pétrus

Hermitage

Hermitage J.L. Chave

Vega Sicilia

Hermitage

Hermitage

Many enthusiasts consider de Vogüé's Musigny to be the greatest wine of Burgundy.
Marcel Guigal's single-vineyard Côte-Rôties have come to define the appellation. Both legitimate
Final Four contenders, but I'm a Burgundy man at heart. Musigny to the quarters—in overtime.

One of the best of California's
cult Cabernets versus a
benchmark expression of Côte
de Nuits Grand Cru. Harlan is
power; the Chambertin power
and grace. Chambertin moves on.

The Chaves have been
winegrowers in the northern
Rhône for over five hundred
years. This wine, assembled
from a number of choice parcels
on the steep slopes of Hermitage,
has the depth, concentration,
balance, length, and long-term
aging potential found only in the
rarest wines. Like Penfolds Grange,
it is made from syrah (or shiraz),
and the presence of two syrahs in
the Final Four suggests a minor
upset. Anyone with experience of
these wines knows otherwise.
How can a self-confessed Burgundy
man choose any wine over La
Tâche? Not easily, believe me,
and there is only one.

The ultimate expression of
Cabernet Sauvignon and
Merlot, respectively, both
wines would be in every
critic's top ten in the world.
This could easily have been a
championship matchup, and
while I can't say one is better,
the Cab is more to my liking.
Latour in the Final Four.

This early-round matchup shows the quality of the field. The
Langhe in Piedmont is the greatest red wine region outside
France, and Bruno Giacosa is an acknowledged master with
the Nebbiolo grape. For decades Haut-Brion has been among
the most consistent of Bordeaux's legendary first growths.
The Bordeaux gets the nod.

77

Rivalries

by WILL BLYTHE

Who needs wars of religion and culture to decide issues of virtue? That's the purpose of sports rivalries. The best of them pit good against evil and somebody wins within hours (except for the interminable longueurs of cricket, which may require days). That race between the tortoise and the hare was an early clash between blue-collar virtue and glitz, better known in our time as the Celtics versus the Lakers. Likewise, David and Goliath foreshadow such asymmetrical agonies as the Boston Red Sox' eternal pursuit of the New York Yankees. The rivalries that triumphed here did so because of the vehement passions they've aroused in their partisans over the decades. Extra points were allotted for proximity. The final criterion: the degree to which the rivalries embody conflict beyond sport.

WILL BLYTHE is the author of *To Hate Like This Is to Be Happy Forever* (HarperCollins, 2006), a personal memoir of the basketball rivalry between Duke and the University of North Carolina.

This rivalry began in 1888, when a faction broke away from the Ottawa club to form the Rideau in an unfriendly dispute about whether to become a drinking establishment. The clubs still battle, with Rideau dominating recent play, but the acrimony is mostly gone, as is the temperance.

Real Madrid vs. Barcelona / Glasgow Celtic vs. Glasgow Rangers	Celtic vs. Rangers
Jack Nicklaus vs. Arnold Palmer / Ben Hogan vs. Sam Snead	Nicklaus vs. Palmer
Texas vs. Oklahoma (football) / Ohio State vs. Michigan (football)	Ohio State vs. Michigan
Björn Borg vs. John McEnroe / Tiger Woods vs. Phil Mickelson	Borg vs. McEnroe
Affirmed vs. Alydar / Muhammad Ali vs. Joe Frazier	Ali vs. Frazier
Tonya Harding vs. Nancy Kerrigan / Sandy Koufax vs. Juan Marichal	Harding vs. Kerrigan
Ottawa Curling Club vs. Rideau Curling Club / Toronto Maple Leafs vs. Montreal Canadiens	Ottawa vs. Rideau
Chicago Bears vs. Green Bay Packers / Washington Redskins vs. Dallas Cowboys	Redskins vs. Cowboys
Boston Celtics vs. Los Angeles Lakers / Wilt Chamberlain vs. Bill Russell	Celtics vs. Lakers
India vs. Pakistan (cricket) / New Zealand All Blacks vs. Australia Wallabies (rugby)	India vs. Pakistan
Richard Petty vs. Cale Yarborough / Harvard vs. Yale	Petty vs. Yarborough
North Carolina vs. Duke (basketball) / Calvin vs. Hope (basketball)	UNC vs. Duke
USSR vs. Canada (ice hockey) / USA vs. USSR (everything)	USSR vs. Canada
Auburn vs. Alabama / Notre Dame vs. USC (football)	Auburn vs. Alabama
Chris Evert vs. Martina Navratilova / Larry Bird vs. Magic Johnson	Evert vs. Navratilova
Boston Red Sox vs. New York Yankees / Giants vs. Dodgers	Red Sox vs. Yankees

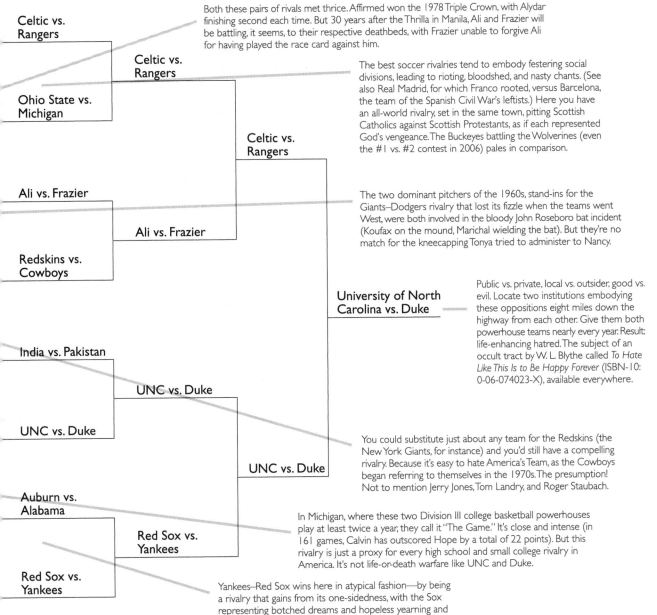

Celtic vs.
Rangers

Ohio State vs.
Michigan

Celtic vs.
Rangers

Celtic vs.
Rangers

Ali vs. Frazier

Redskins vs.
Cowboys

Ali vs. Frazier

India vs. Pakistan

UNC vs. Duke

UNC vs. Duke

Auburn vs.
Alabama

Red Sox vs.
Yankees

Red Sox vs.
Yankees

University of North
Carolina vs. Duke

UNC vs. Duke

Both these pairs of rivals met thrice. Affirmed won the 1978 Triple Crown, with Alydar finishing second each time. But 30 years after the Thrilla in Manila, Ali and Frazier will be battling, it seems, to their respective deathbeds, with Frazier unable to forgive Ali for having played the race card against him.

The best soccer rivalries tend to embody festering social divisions, leading to rioting, bloodshed, and nasty chants. (See also Real Madrid, for which Franco rooted, versus Barcelona, the team of the Spanish Civil War's leftists.) Here you have an all-world rivalry, set in the same town, pitting Scottish Catholics against Scottish Protestants, as if each represented God's vengeance. The Buckeyes battling the Wolverines (even the #1 vs. #2 contest in 2006) pales in comparison.

The two dominant pitchers of the 1960s, stand-ins for the Giants–Dodgers rivalry that lost its fizzle when the teams went West, were both involved in the bloody John Roseboro bat incident (Koufax on the mound, Marichal wielding the bat). But they're no match for the kneecapping Tonya tried to administer to Nancy.

Public vs. private, local vs. outsider, good vs. evil. Locate two institutions embodying these oppositions eight miles down the highway from each other. Give them both powerhouse teams nearly every year. Result: life-enhancing hatred. The subject of an occult tract by W. L. Blythe called *To Hate Like This Is to Be Happy Forever* (ISBN-10: 0-06-074023-X), available everywhere.

You could substitute just about any team for the Redskins (the New York Giants, for instance) and you'd still have a compelling rivalry. Because it's easy to hate America's Team, as the Cowboys began referring to themselves in the 1970s. The presumption! Not to mention Jerry Jones, Tom Landry, and Roger Staubach.

In Michigan, where these two Division III college basketball powerhouses play at least twice a year, they call it "The Game." It's close and intense (in 161 games, Calvin has outscored Hope by a total of 22 points). But this rivalry is just a proxy for every high school and small college rivalry in America. It's not life-or-death warfare like UNC and Duke.

Yankees–Red Sox wins here in atypical fashion—by being a rivalry that gains from its one-sidedness, with the Sox representing botched dreams and hopeless yearning and the Yankees standing for success at all costs.

78

Samuel L. Jackson Films

by RICK STAEHLING

Samuel Leroy Jackson is a very busy man who never seems to be working hard on-screen. Like cool-cat pioneer Robert Mitchum, he takes small parts and big ones, plays good guys and bad. He's worked with top-rung directors, including Scorsese, Spielberg, Tarantino, and Shyamalan, appeared in uninspired programmers *Amos & Andrew* and *Snakes on a Plane*, and found time for voice work on animated films and video games. Jackson is a talented actor, but more than that he has the on-screen muscle to ensure that his scenes will be remembered and admired even if the film he's in fades. He goes where the work is—over 70 movies in the last 20 years—and always delivers the Jackson-branded voice, attitude, and gravitas like a true pro.

RICK STAEHLING is the Canadian Broadcasting Corporation's film critic in British Columbia. His long-standing theory that Jackson is better in films when his head is shaved was disproved by research for this project.

SMALL PARTS REGIONAL

Out of Sight / Sea of Love → Out of Sight
Goodfellas / Coming to America → Goodfellas
White Sands / Do the Right Thing → White Sands
True Romance / Kill Bill: Vol. 2 → True Romance

BIG PARTS REGIONAL

The Negotiator / 187 → The Negotiator
Pulp Fiction / Basic → Pulp Fiction
Jackie Brown / Shaft → Jackie Brown
Unbreakable / Coach Carter → Unbreakable

LIGHTWEIGHT REGIONAL

The Long Kiss Goodnight / Deep Blue Sea → The Long Kiss Goodnight
Star Wars Episode III: Revenge of the Sith / XXX → XXX
The Man / The Great White Hype → The Great White Hype
Jurassic Park / Snakes on a Plane → Jurassic Park

HEAVYWEIGHT REGIONAL

Hard Eight / A Time to Kill → Hard Eight
Jungle Fever / In My Country → Jungle Fever
Changing Lanes / The Red Violin → Changing Lanes
Eve's Bayou / Losing Isaiah → Eve's Bayou

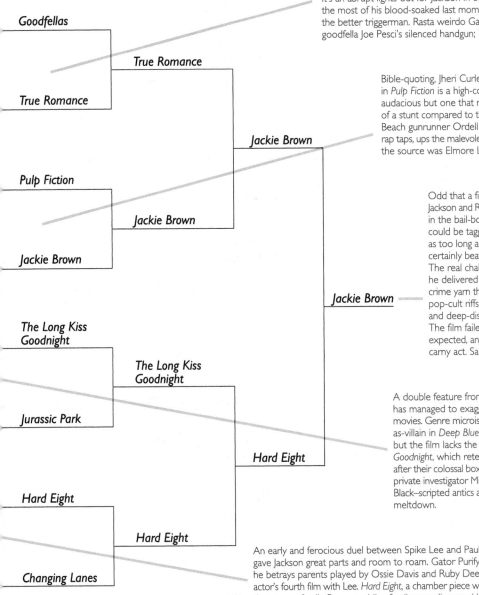

Goodfellas

True Romance

True Romance

Pulp Fiction

Jackie Brown

Jackie Brown

Jackie Brown

Jackie Brown

The Long Kiss Goodnight

The Long Kiss Goodnight

Jurassic Park

Hard Eight

Hard Eight

Hard Eight

Changing Lanes

It's an abrupt lights-out for Jackson in these violent contenders, but he makes the most of his blood-soaked last moments in both. The tie must be broken by the better triggerman. Rasta weirdo Gary Oldman and his shotgun trumps goodfella Joe Pesci's silenced handgun; *True Romance* wins.

Bible-quoting, Jheri Curled, Academy Award–nominated Jackson in *Pulp Fiction* is a high-concept character in a film considered audacious but one that remains schematic and synthetic—a bit of a stunt compared to the underrated *Jackie Brown*. As Hermosa Beach gunrunner Ordell Robbie in *Brown*, Jackson turns on the rap taps, ups the malevolence, and makes it totally real. No wonder: the source was Elmore Leonard's novel *Rum Punch*.

Odd that a film so well written, so well acted—check Jackson and Robert Forster's first culture-clash exchange in the bail-bond office—and so confidently directed could be tagged on release, and hounded to this day, as too long and boring. After *Reservoir Dogs*, Tarantino certainly beat the sophomore jinx with *Pulp Fiction*. The real challenge was his third film, and with *Brown* he delivered a beauty: an understated, pitch-perfect crime yarn that dropped the grindhouse gore and the pop-cult riffs and took its time celebrating character and deep-dish adult concerns like trust and honor. The film failed to generate the heat that Tarantino expected, and he has since become a bit of a film-buff carny act. Samuel Leroy Jackson endures.

A double feature from Renny Harlin, the Finnish director who has managed to exaggerate and coarsen American action movies. Genre microists rightfully celebrated the return of shark-as-villain in *Deep Blue Sea*, 24 years after the release of *Jaws*, but the film lacks the hysterical flop-sweat energy of *Kiss Goodnight*, which reteamed Harlin and then-wife Geena Davis after their colossal box-office bust in *Cutthroat Island*. As skeptical private investigator Mitch Henessey, Jackson anchors the Shane Black–scripted antics and saves the third act from melodramatic meltdown.

An early and ferocious duel between Spike Lee and Paul Thomas Anderson, two auteurs who gave Jackson great parts and room to roam. Gator Purify (the *Fever* crackhead so debauched that he betrays parents played by Ossie Davis and Ruby Dee!) was a career breakthrough and the actor's fourth film with Lee. *Hard Eight*, a chamber piece with Jackson as a sleazeball who memorably threatens a fragile Reno gambling family, was disowned by Anderson, then resurrected on DVD. Edge to *Eight* for the most sinister performance to date from Jackson.

79

Scrabble Words

by STEFAN FATSIS

A mind-numbing 178,691 words of two to fifteen letters are acceptable in competitive Scrabble in North America. Though culled from several standard college dictionaries, Scrabble's lexicographic expanse is still hard for nonplayers to accept. ("That's not a word!") So is the idea of memorizing, as I have, tens of thousands of weird letter strings just to play a game. How then to narrow Scrabble to 0.0179 percent of its possibilities? Pick the strategically important, the historically significant, the linguistically unusual, the creatively brilliant, the mathematically improbable (and probable), and the shots heard round the Scrabble world.

The first of six straight rack-clearing "bingos" by former national and world champion Brian Cappelletto to start a 1990 game can't hold off a single-turn record 365 points by relative novice Michael Cresta in his record 830-point game at a Scrabble club in Lexington, Mass., in 2006. (Cresta also scored 239 points with FLATFISH.) The previous single-game high, and still the tournament standard: 770 points, by Mark Landsberg in 1993.

Outraged that *The Official Scrabble Players Dictionary* included JEW—defined as "to bargain with"—a Virginia woman in 1994 helped persuade Scrabble's owner, Hasbro, to purge the OSPD of "offensive" words. (TUP, "to copulate with a ewe," was spared after executives were told it referred to the ram.) Competitive players, to whom meanings are meaningless, revolted. The result: an expurgated over-the-counter dictionary, a definition-free list for sanctioned play, and an infamous word.

STEFAN FATSIS is the author of *Word Freak: Heartbreak, Triumph, Genius, and Obsession in the World of Competitive Scrabble Players.* He has scored 603 points in a game. He is proudest of playing OQUASSA and SWITCHEROO.

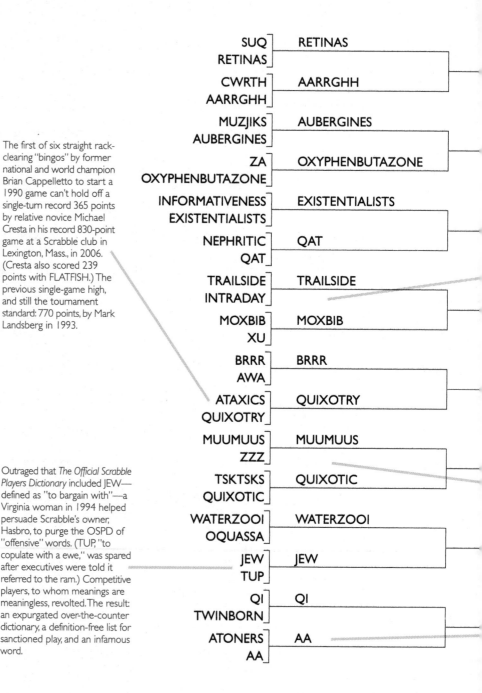

SUQ
RETINAS — RETINAS

CWRTH
AARRGHH — AARRGHH

MUZJIKS
AUBERGINES — AUBERGINES

ZA
OXYPHENBUTAZONE — OXYPHENBUTAZONE

INFORMATIVENESS
EXISTENTIALISTS — EXISTENTIALISTS

NEPHRITIC
QAT — QAT

TRAILSIDE — TRAILSIDE
INTRADAY

MOXBIB — MOXBIB
XU

BRRR — BRRR
AWA

ATAXICS
QUIXOTRY — QUIXOTRY

MUUMUUS — MUUMUUS
ZZZ

TSKTSKS
QUIXOTIC — QUIXOTIC

WATERZOOI — WATERZOOI
OQUASSA

JEW — JEW
TUP

QI — QI
TWINBORN

ATONERS
AA — AA

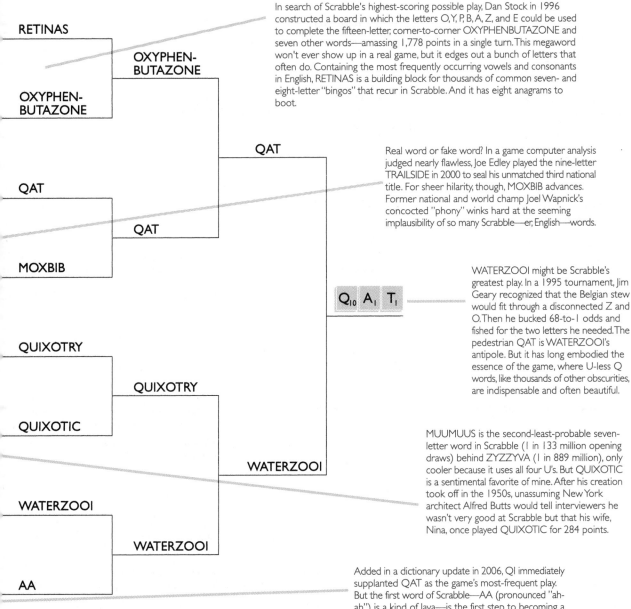

RETINAS

OXYPHEN-
BUTAZONE

OXYPHEN-
BUTAZONE

OXYPHEN-
BUTAZONE

In search of Scrabble's highest-scoring possible play, Dan Stock in 1996 constructed a board in which the letters O, Y, P, B, A, Z, and E could be used to complete the fifteen-letter, corner-to-corner OXYPHENBUTAZONE and seven other words—amassing 1,778 points in a single turn. This megaword won't ever show up in a real game, but it edges out a bunch of letters that often do. Containing the most frequently occurring vowels and consonants in English, RETINAS is a building block for thousands of common seven- and eight-letter "bingos" that recur in Scrabble. And it has eight anagrams to boot.

QAT

QAT

QAT

QAT

MOXBIB

Real word or fake word? In a game computer analysis judged nearly flawless, Joe Edley played the nine-letter TRAILSIDE in 2000 to seal his unmatched third national title. For sheer hilarity, though, MOXBIB advances. Former national and world champ Joel Wapnick's concocted "phony" winks hard at the seeming implausibility of so many Scrabble—er, English—words.

Q_{10} A_1 T_1

WATERZOOI might be Scrabble's greatest play. In a 1995 tournament, Jim Geary recognized that the Belgian stew would fit through a disconnected Z and O. Then he bucked 68-to-1 odds and fished for the two letters he needed. The pedestrian QAT is WATERZOOI's antipole. But it has long embodied the essence of the game, where U-less Q words, like thousands of other obscurities, are indispensable and often beautiful.

QUIXOTRY

QUIXOTRY

QUIXOTIC

WATERZOOI

MUUMUUS is the second-least-probable seven-letter word in Scrabble (1 in 133 million opening draws) behind ZYZZYVA (1 in 889 million), only cooler because it uses all four U's. But QUIXOTIC is a sentimental favorite of mine. After his creation took off in the 1950s, unassuming New York architect Alfred Butts would tell interviewers he wasn't very good at Scrabble but that his wife, Nina, once played QUIXOTIC for 284 points.

WATERZOOI

WATERZOOI

AA

Added in a dictionary update in 2006, QI immediately supplanted QAT as the game's most-frequent play. But the first word of Scrabble—AA (pronounced "ah-ah")—is a kind of lava—is the first step to becoming a real player: learning the 101 two-letter words.

80

Sex and the City Wisdom
by SHERRI RIFKIN

People watched *Sex and the City* for the fabulous clothes, the sassy women, the knotty (and naughty) relationships, the sexual frankness, the comic mishaps, and the New York glitter, not its worldly wisdom. But there were pearls among the diamonds and gold. Buried amid the witty repartee, the bitchy one-liners, and the sometimes cloying Carrie voice-overs are life lessons that are universal and enduring. As the show's runway-ready clothes show their age, the characters' commentary about dating, sex, and moving forward takes on the sound of (how does one say this?) philosophy. Self-help philosophy, to be sure, but profound and still relevant to women seeking men, and vice versa.

SHERRI RIFKIN is a former cable television marketing executive who lives in New York City and has written "Carrie-esque" Web columns relating to *Sex and the City*. She is completing her first novel.

"After a while, you just want to be with the one who makes you laugh." *Mr. Big*

"Marriage doesn't guarantee a happy ending. Just an ending." *Samantha*

"People go to casinos for the same reason they go on blind dates: hoping to hit the jackpot. But mostly, you just wind up broke or alone in a bar." *Carrie*

"Men cheat for the same reason dogs lick their balls: because they can." *Samantha*

"I like my money right where I can see it: hanging in my closet." *Carrie*

"It takes half the total time you went out with someone to get over them." *Charlotte*

"Men who have had a lot of sexual partners are not called sluts. They're called very good kissers. A few are even called romantics." *Carrie*

"From my experience, honey, if he seems too good to be true—he probably is." *Samantha*

"Absofuckinglutely." *Mr. Big*

"Men in their forties are like the *New York Times* Sunday crossword puzzle: tricky, complicated, and you're never really sure you got the right answer." *Carrie*

"That's the thing about needs. Sometimes when you get them met, you don't need them anymore." *Carrie*

"My Zen teacher also said: the only way to true happiness is to live in the moment and not worry about the future. Of course, he died penniless and single." *Carrie*

"In a city of infinite options, sometimes there's no better feeling than you only have one." *Carrie*

"I admit it's tempting to wish for the perfect boss, the perfect parent, or the perfect outfit. But maybe the best any of us can do is not quit, play the hand we've been dealt, and accessorize what we've got." *Carrie*

"That's the key to having it all: stop expecting it to look like what you thought it was going to look like. It's true of the fall lines, and it's true of relationships." *Enid*

"No matter who broke your heart, or how long it takes to heal, you'll never get through it without your friends." *Carrie*

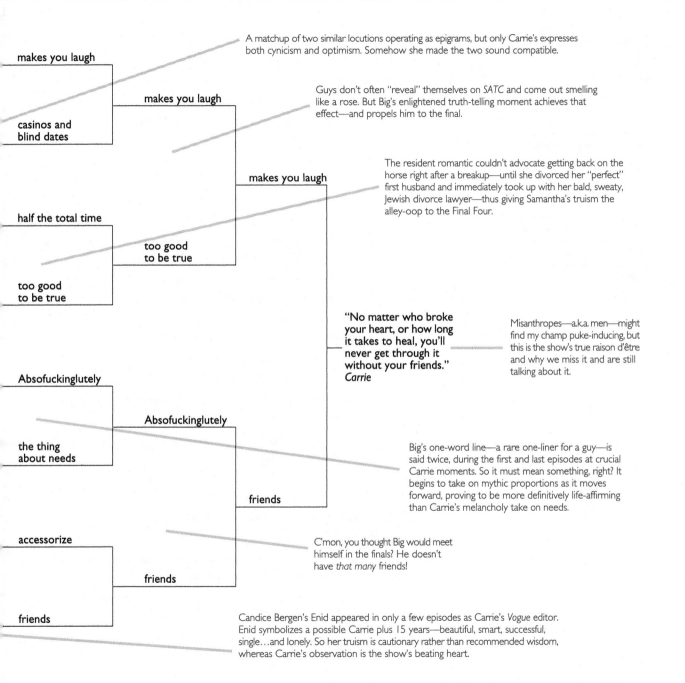

makes you laugh

casinos and
blind dates

makes you laugh

A matchup of two similar locutions operating as epigrams, but only Carrie's expresses both cynicism and optimism. Somehow she made the two sound compatible.

Guys don't often "reveal" themselves on *SATC* and come out smelling like a rose. But Big's enlightened truth-telling moment achieves that effect—and propels him to the final.

makes you laugh

The resident romantic couldn't advocate getting back on the horse right after a breakup—until she divorced her "perfect" first husband and immediately took up with her bald, sweaty, Jewish divorce lawyer—thus giving Samantha's truism the alley-oop to the Final Four.

half the total time

too good
to be true

too good
to be true

"No matter who broke your heart, or how long it takes to heal, you'll never get through it without your friends."
Carrie

Misanthropes—a.k.a. men—might find my champ puke-inducing, but this is the show's true raison d'être and why we miss it and are still talking about it.

Absofuckinglutely

Absofuckinglutely

the thing
about needs

Big's one-word line—a rare one-liner for a guy—is said twice, during the first and last episodes at crucial Carrie moments. So it must mean something, right? It begins to take on mythic proportions as it moves forward, proving to be more definitively life-affirming than Carrie's melancholy take on needs.

friends

accessorize

C'mon, you thought Big would meet himself in the finals? He doesn't have *that many* friends!

friends

friends

Candice Bergen's Enid appeared in only a few episodes as Carrie's *Vogue* editor. Enid symbolizes a possible Carrie plus 15 years—beautiful, smart, successful, single…and lonely. So her truism is cautionary rather than recommended wisdom, whereas Carrie's observation is the show's beating heart.

81

Shakespeare in Film

by TOM AKSTENS

Filmmakers have struggled with Shakespeare. The richness and abundance of his language challenge a medium that's at its best when it tells a story with images more than with words. Nevertheless, filmmakers keep turning out screen adaptations of the plays, as well as other films that explore why Shakespeare matters. The irony, of course, is that if Shakespeare were alive today, he'd be writing for films himself. He'd find the prospect of reaching an audience in the millions irresistible.

TOM AKSTENS holds a doctorate in English literature from the University of Pennsylvania. He's taught Shakespeare in Film at Siena College and SUNY/ Empire State College. He lives in the Adirondacks, where he writes, fishes, gardens, and shoots photographs

For pure shock value, not much beats the beheading scene at the end of *Ran*. *Ran*'s epic scope is dazzling, but *Throne of Blood* captures the restraint and tension of Noh theater and is a more satisfying film. Asaji (the counterpart to Lady Macbeth) is supercreepy.

Titus (Julie Taymor) — *Titus*
The Merchant of Venice (Michael Radford)

Rosencrantz & Guildenstern Are Dead (Tom Stoppard) — *A Midwinter's Tale*
A Midwinter's Tale (Kenneth Branagh)

Hamlet (Franco Zeffirelli) — *Hamlet* (Zeffirelli)
Hamlet (Kenneth Branagh)

Hamlet (Grigori Kozintsev) — *Hamlet* (Kozintsev)
Hamlet (Michael Almereyda)

Henry V (Kenneth Branagh) — *Henry V* (Kenneth Branagh)
Henry V (Laurence Olivier)

The Dresser (Peter Yates) — *King Lear*
King Lear (Peter Brook)

Richard III (Laurence Olivier) — *Richard III* (Olivier)
Richard III (Richard Loncraine)

Ran (Akira Kurosawa) — *Throne of Blood*
Throne of Blood (Akira Kurosawa)

Looking for Richard (Al Pacino) — *Looking for Richard*
Macbeth (Orson Welles)

Romeo and Juliet (Franco Zeffirelli) — *Romeo + Juliet* (Luhrmann)
Romeo + Juliet (Baz Luhrmann)

Twelfth Night (Trevor Nunn) — *Twelfth Night*
Prospero's Books (Peter Greenaway)

O (Tim Blake Nelson) — *Othello*
Othello (Oliver Parker)

The Taming of the Shrew (Franco Zeffirelli) — *Shrew*
10 Things I Hate About You (Gil Junger)

A Midsummer Night's Dream (Max Reinhardt/William Dieterle) — *Dream* (Reinhardt/Dieterle)
A Midsummer Night's Dream (Michael Hoffman)

My Own Private Idaho (Gus Van Sant) — *Private Idaho*
Forbidden Planet (Fred M. Wilcox)

Shakespeare Behind Bars (Hank Rogerson) — *Shakespeare Behind Bars*
West Side Story (Jerome Robbins/Robert Wise)

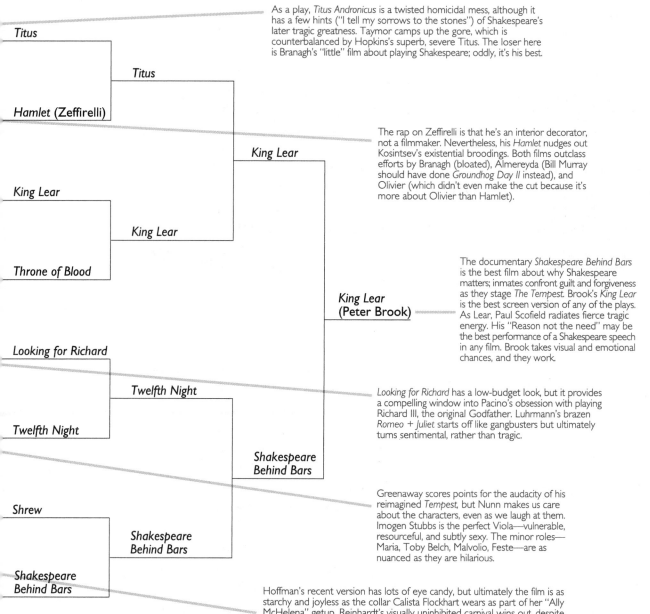

Titus

Titus

Hamlet (Zeffirelli)

As a play, *Titus Andronicus* is a twisted homicidal mess, although it has a few hints ("I tell my sorrows to the stones") of Shakespeare's later tragic greatness. Taymor camps up the gore, which is counterbalanced by Hopkins's superb, severe Titus. The loser here is Branagh's "little" film about playing Shakespeare; oddly, it's his best.

King Lear

The rap on Zeffirelli is that he's an interior decorator, not a filmmaker. Nevertheless, his *Hamlet* nudges out Kosintsev's existential broodings. Both films outclass efforts by Branagh (bloated), Almereyda (Bill Murray should have done *Groundhog Day II* instead), and Olivier (which didn't even make the cut because it's more about Olivier than Hamlet).

King Lear

King Lear

Throne of Blood

King Lear
(Peter Brook)

The documentary *Shakespeare Behind Bars* is the best film about why Shakespeare matters; inmates confront guilt and forgiveness as they stage *The Tempest*. Brook's *King Lear* is the best screen version of any of the plays. As Lear, Paul Scofield radiates fierce tragic energy. His "Reason not the need" may be the best performance of a Shakespeare speech in any film. Brook takes visual and emotional chances, and they work.

Looking for Richard

Twelfth Night

Twelfth Night

Shakespeare
Behind Bars

Looking for Richard has a low-budget look, but it provides a compelling window into Pacino's obsession with playing Richard III, the original Godfather. Luhrmann's brazen *Romeo + Juliet* starts off like gangbusters but ultimately turns sentimental, rather than tragic.

Shrew

Shakespeare
Behind Bars

Greenaway scores points for the audacity of his reimagined *Tempest,* but Nunn makes us care about the characters, even as we laugh at them. Imogen Stubbs is the perfect Viola—vulnerable, resourceful, and subtly sexy. The minor roles— Maria, Toby Belch, Malvolio, Feste—are as nuanced as they are hilarious.

Shakespeare
Behind Bars

Hoffman's recent version has lots of eye candy, but ultimately the film is as starchy and joyless as the collar Calista Flockhart wears as part of her "Ally McHelena" getup. Reinhardt's visually uninhibited carnival wins out, despite a supremely irritating performance by Mickey Rooney as Puck.

82

Sidekicks
by STEVEN REDDICLIFFE

Partners and pairs are glamorous: Butch and Sundance, Astaire and Rogers, Lennon and McCartney, Romeo and Juliet, Heckle and Jeckle. Sidekicks are another story. They are essential to satisfying storytelling, sure, but also somewhat unnerving. Everyone wants a sidekick, but no one actually wants to be one (something about subservience, even in its most subtle form, troubles us). Which is the dynamic that informs our anxious enjoyment of the most entertaining sidekicks, of whom 32 face off here. As the tournament plays out, a corollary truth becomes apparent: sad sidekicks rarely win. Garth Algar of *Wayne's World*, sure; Steinbeck's Lenny, nah. Who would want to hear the whole rabbit deal again? There's got to be some kick in a sidekick, after all.

STEVEN REDDICLIFFE is the television editor of the *New York Times*. Before that he was editor in chief of *TV Guide* and a television critic at the *Miami Herald, Dallas Times Herald,* and *Baltimore News-American,* two of which are no longer in the newspaper bracket. Assistance provided by James Reddicliffe, a student, but not a sidekick, at Mamaroneck High School in New York.

Barney Fife (*The Andy Griffith Show*) — Fife
Ed Norton (*The Honeymooners*)

Wilson the Volleyball (*Cast Away*) — Brick
Brick Tamland (*Anchorman*)

George Costanza (*Seinfeld*) — Costanza
Piglet (*Winnie-the-Pooh*)

Lenny (*Of Mice and Men*) — Bush
George W. Bush (The White House)

Hank Kingsley (*The Larry Sanders Show*) — Kingsley
Ed McMahon (*The Tonight Show with Johnny Carson*)

Milhouse Van Houten (*The Simpsons*) — Borden
Howard Borden (*The Bob Newhart Show*)

Boo Boo (Yogi Bear) — Boo Boo
Jelly (Peanut Butter)

Nicole Richie (Paris Hilton) — Rhoda
Rhoda Morgenstern (*The Mary Tyler Moore Show*)

Garth Algar (*Wayne's World*) — Garth
Dr. Watson (Sherlock Holmes)

The Seven Dwarfs (Snow White) — Tinker Bell
Tinker Bell (Peter Pan)

Robin (Batman) — Robin
Gilligan (*Gilligan's Island*)

Sherman (Mr. Peabody) — Timmy
Timmy (Lassie)

Gabrielle (*Xena: Warrior Princess*) — Gabrielle
Lenny and Squiggy (*Laverne & Shirley*)

Mr. Spock (Star Trek) — Marcie
Marcie (Peppermint Patty)

Ron Weasley (Harry Potter) — Weasley
Andy Richter (Conan O'Brien)

Jimmy Olsen (Superman) — Olsen
Scottie Pippen (Michael Jordan)

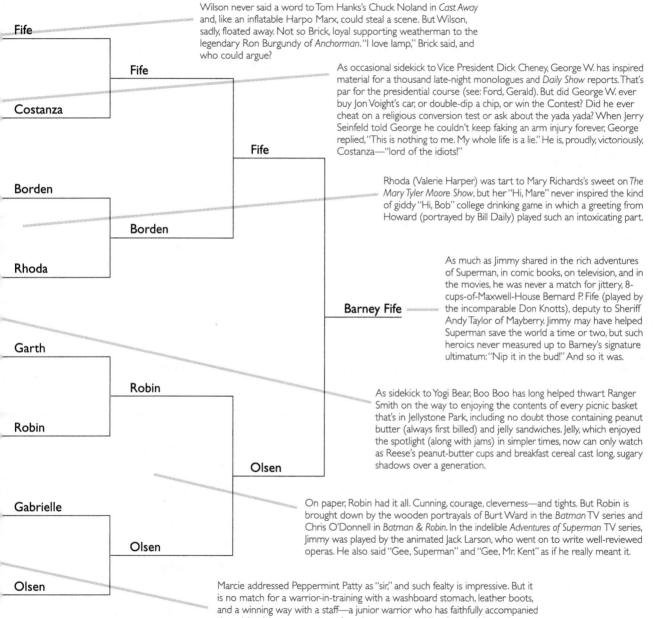

Fife

Fife

Costanza

Fife

Borden

Borden

Rhoda

Barney Fife

Garth

Robin

Robin

Olsen

Gabrielle

Olsen

Olsen

Wilson never said a word to Tom Hanks's Chuck Noland in *Cast Away* and, like an inflatable Harpo Marx, could steal a scene. But Wilson, sadly, floated away. Not so Brick, loyal supporting weatherman to the legendary Ron Burgundy of *Anchorman*. "I love lamp," Brick said, and who could argue?

As occasional sidekick to Vice President Dick Cheney, George W. has inspired material for a thousand late-night monologues and *Daily Show* reports. That's par for the presidential course (see: Ford, Gerald). But did George W. ever buy Jon Voight's car, or double-dip a chip, or win the Contest? Did he ever cheat on a religious conversion test or ask about the yada yada? When Jerry Seinfeld told George he couldn't keep faking an arm injury forever, George replied, "This is nothing to me. My whole life is a lie." He is, proudly, victoriously, Costanza—"lord of the idiots!"

Rhoda (Valerie Harper) was tart to Mary Richards's sweet on *The Mary Tyler Moore Show*, but her "Hi, Mare" never inspired the kind of giddy "Hi, Bob" college drinking game in which a greeting from Howard (portrayed by Bill Daily) played such an intoxicating part.

As much as Jimmy shared in the rich adventures of Superman, in comic books, on television, and in the movies, he was never a match for jittery, 8-cups-of-Maxwell-House Bernard P. Fife (played by the incomparable Don Knotts), deputy to Sheriff Andy Taylor of Mayberry. Jimmy may have helped Superman save the world a time or two, but such heroics never measured up to Barney's signature ultimatum: "Nip it in the bud!" And so it was.

As sidekick to Yogi Bear, Boo Boo has long helped thwart Ranger Smith on the way to enjoying the contents of every picnic basket that's in Jellystone Park, including no doubt those containing peanut butter (always first billed) and jelly sandwiches. Jelly, which enjoyed the spotlight (along with jams) in simpler times, now can only watch as Reese's peanut-butter cups and breakfast cereal cast long, sugary shadows over a generation.

On paper, Robin had it all. Cunning, courage, cleverness—and tights. But Robin is brought down by the wooden portrayals of Burt Ward in the *Batman* TV series and Chris O'Donnell in *Batman & Robin*. In the indelible *Adventures of Superman* TV series, Jimmy was played by the animated Jack Larson, who went on to write well-reviewed operas. He also said "Gee, Superman" and "Gee, Mr. Kent" as if he really meant it.

Marcie addressed Peppermint Patty as "sir," and such fealty is impressive. But it is no match for a warrior-in-training with a washboard stomach, leather boots, and a winning way with a staff—a junior warrior who has faithfully accompanied the mighty Xena everywhere from ice cave to bubbling (ancient) hot tub.

83

Simple Things
by HENRY PETROSKI

For an everyday object to get an invite to the tournament, it must have as few parts and as many uses as possible. Simple things should also be elegant in form and straightforward in function. They should have classic lines and timeless purpose. They should be so highly evolved as to be considered "perfected." The best have reached iconic status. When simple things are paired off against one another, the advantage goes to the one with fewer parts and greater versatility. For those matchups between simple things that each have but one part and countless applications, victory goes to the object that is considered more organic in its construction and commonly thought of as a masterpiece of invention and design. Upsets are predictable. The winner here surprised me—even though it is the subject of my next book.

HENRY PETROSKI is the Aleksandar S. Vesic professor of civil engineering and a professor of history at Duke University. He is the author of a dozen books on engineering and design, including *The Evolution of Useful Things*, *Small Things Considered*, and *Success Through Failure: The Paradox of Design*. Among the simple things he has written about are pencils, paper clips, and pizza savers—those little plastic tripods that keep the top of the pizza box from touching the cheese. For 25 seasons, he has watched ACC basketball from seat 9 in row C of section 2 in Cameron Indoor Stadium.

Though Pencil was the odds-on favorite because of its height advantage, Eraser in its Pink Pearl uniform was able to get better traction on the floor and wiped out every point advantage that Pencil racked up on the scoreboard.

Lanky Q played above the basket for most of the game, using its height advantage for tip-ins after soft shots. Cotton Ball, who did not dribble well, was slow getting down the court. A very quiet game—and a mismatch.

Tiddlywink looked good from the moment it came out for pre-game practice, sinking snap shots from outside the three-point line; Button, constantly victimized by traps, had multiple holes in its flat-footed defense.

A battle of opposites. Paperweight was lead-footed, lazily setting picks and relying on its wide body to block moves to the basket. Pizza Saver was nimble, a crowd-pleasing three-prong scoring machine that raised the roof in what could have been a boring game.

Round 1	Round 2
pencil / eraser	eraser
marble / ball bearing	ball bearing
key ring / brass ring	key ring
Band-Aid / paper clip	paper clip
rubber band / earplug	rubber band
Q-tip / cotton ball	cotton ball
checker / tiddlywink	tiddlywink
button / collar stay	button
pushpin / thumbtack	thumbtack
toothpick / Post-it note	toothpick
shoelace / dental floss	dental floss
pipe cleaner / drinking straw	pipe cleaner
straight pin / safety pin	straight pin
needle / thimble	needle
coaster / paperweight	paperweight
staple / pizza saver	pizza saver

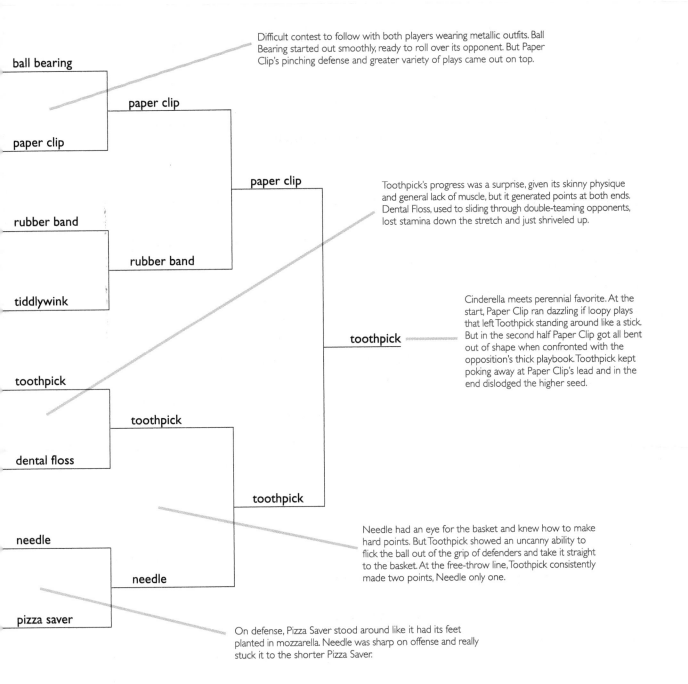

ball bearing

paper clip

Difficult contest to follow with both players wearing metallic outfits. Ball Bearing started out smoothly, ready to roll over its opponent. But Paper Clip's pinching defense and greater variety of plays came out on top.

paper clip

paper clip

rubber band

rubber band

tiddlywink

Toothpick's progress was a surprise, given its skinny physique and general lack of muscle, but it generated points at both ends. Dental Floss, used to sliding through double-teaming opponents, lost stamina down the stretch and just shriveled up.

toothpick

Cinderella meets perennial favorite. At the start, Paper Clip ran dazzling if loopy plays that left Toothpick standing around like a stick. But in the second half Paper Clip got all bent out of shape when confronted with the opposition's thick playbook. Toothpick kept poking away at Paper Clip's lead and in the end dislodged the higher seed.

toothpick

toothpick

dental floss

toothpick

needle

Needle had an eye for the basket and knew how to make hard points. But Toothpick showed an uncanny ability to flick the ball out of the grip of defenders and take it straight to the basket. At the free-throw line, Toothpick consistently made two points, Needle only one.

needle

pizza saver

On defense, Pizza Saver stood around like it had its feet planted in mozzarella. Needle was sharp on offense and really stuck it to the shorter Pizza Saver.

84

Sins Against the Language
by BEN YAGODA

Tsk-tsking about declining grammatical standards has been a popular pastime since the early seventeenth century and shows no sign of going away. Much of the hand-wringing can be chalked up to retrograde nostalgia and an insufficient recognition that the protocol of the language is continuously changing. (Not very long ago, we were taught that the first-person future tense is *shall*, remember?) On the other hand, the use of language is a good representation—maybe the best—of the condition of a speaker's or writer's thought. Judging from what I read in the papers (my students', and the ones published on newsprint and online), that condition is currently serious but could swerve toward critical at any moment.

BEN YAGODA directs the journalism program at the University of Delaware and is the author of *About Town: The New Yorker and the World It Made*, *The Sound on the Page: Style and Voice in Writing*, and, most recently, *When You Catch an Adjective, Kill It: The Parts of Speech, for Better and/or Worse*.

First round	Second round
mixed metaphors / wordiness	wordiness
clichés / bogus apostrophes, as in "Apple's—$1.19 lb"	clichés
journalese / it's/its, who's/whose, you're/your confusion	it's/its
dangling modifiers / double negatives	dangling modifiers
no comma after parenthetical phrase / commas or periods outside quotation marks	no comma
verbing nouns / nouning verbs	nouning verbs
"that"/"which" confusion / vagueness and abstraction	vagueness
"less" instead of "fewer" / antecedent-pronoun disagreement	disagreement
"of" in clauses like "I didn't have that good of a time" / hypercorrection, e.g., "between you and I"	hypercorrection
sesquipedality / "presently" to mean "currently"	sesquipedality
spellcheck errors like "pour over" to mean "pore over" / faux ebonic diction, e.g., "My bad"	spellcheck errors
semicolon abuse / elegant variation	semicolon abuse
comma splices / subjunctive errors, such as "If I was rich"	comma splices
incorrect or imprecise word choice / using "who" instead of "whom"	poor word choice
"myself" to mean "me" or "I" / e-mail abuse like emoticons and acronyms (LOL)	"myself"
vocalisms like "um," "uh," "er," and "ew" in print / faulty parallelism	vocalisms

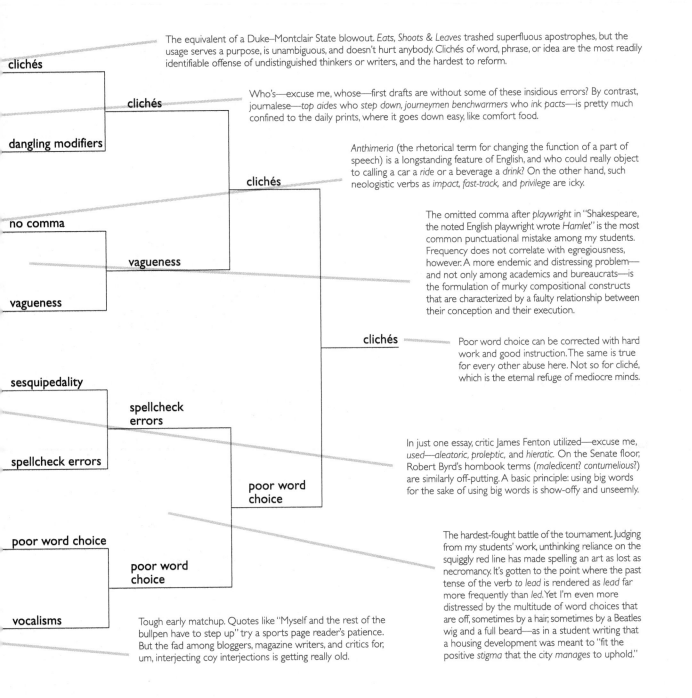

cliché

clichés

dangling modifiers

The equivalent of a Duke–Montclair State blowout. *Eats, Shoots & Leaves* trashed superfluous apostrophes, but the usage serves a purpose, is unambiguous, and doesn't hurt anybody. Clichés of word, phrase, or idea are the most readily identifiable offense of undistinguished thinkers or writers, and the hardest to reform.

clichés

Who's—excuse me, whose—first drafts are without some of these insidious errors? By contrast, journalese—*top aides* who *step down, journeymen benchwarmers* who *ink pacts*—is pretty much confined to the daily prints, where it goes down easy, like comfort food.

clichés

Anthimeria (the rhetorical term for changing the function of a part of speech) is a longstanding feature of English, and who could really object to calling a car a *ride* or a beverage a *drink*? On the other hand, such neologistic verbs as *impact, fast-track,* and *privilege* are icky.

no comma

vagueness

The omitted comma after *playwright* in "Shakespeare, the noted English playwright wrote *Hamlet*" is the most common punctuational mistake among my students. Frequency does not correlate with egregiousness, however. A more endemic and distressing problem—and not only among academics and bureaucrats—is the formulation of murky compositional constructs that are characterized by a faulty relationship between their conception and their execution.

vagueness

clichés

Poor word choice can be corrected with hard work and good instruction. The same is true for every other abuse here. Not so for cliché, which is the eternal refuge of mediocre minds.

sesquipedality

spellcheck errors

In just one essay, critic James Fenton utilized—excuse me, *used*—*aleatoric, proleptic,* and *hieratic.* On the Senate floor, Robert Byrd's hornbook terms (*maledicent? contumelious?*) are similarly off-putting. A basic principle: using big words for the sake of using big words is show-offy and unseemly.

spellcheck errors

poor word choice

The hardest-fought battle of the tournament. Judging from my students' work, unthinking reliance on the squiggly red line has made spelling an art as lost as necromancy. It's gotten to the point where the past tense of the verb *to lead* is rendered as *lead* far more frequently than *led*. Yet I'm even more distressed by the multitude of word choices that are off, sometimes by a hair, sometimes by a Beatles wig and a full beard—as in a student writing that a housing development was meant to "fit the positive *stigma* that the city *manages* to uphold."

poor word choice

poor word choice

vocalisms

Tough early matchup. Quotes like "Myself and the rest of the bullpen have to step up" try a sports page reader's patience. But the fad among bloggers, magazine writers, and critics for, um, interjecting coy interjections is getting really old.

85

Sport/Not a Sport

by BILL SCHEFT

A free-for-all only slightly less chaotic or emotionally satisfying than reading your dad's will at Applebee's. The entries needed to meet criteria based on a complex formula involving tradition, popularity, and cultural impact, divided by percentage of participants who could do a sit-up. (As opposed to merely sitting up.) In other words, how much skill is required? Is there more sweating during the actual event or waiting for the beer guy to return? Can the scoring system be explained only by a degenerate gambler or one of Liza Minnelli's ex-husbands? It is my fervent wish that this chart will end rather than prolong the spirited argument of what is a sport and what is not. But I am not hopeful—not as long as men hold up couch springs and cash disability checks for remote-induced carpal tunnel syndrome.

BILL SCHEFT, a longtime writer for David Letterman, is the author of two novels, *The Ringer* and *Time Won't Let Me*. For three years he wrote a weekly humor column, "The Show," in *Sports Illustrated*. He lives in Manhattan with his wife and the voices in his head.

OLYMPIAN REGIONAL

- rhythmic gymnastics
- synchronized swimming → rhythmic gymnastics
- archery
- snowboarding → snowboarding
- ice dancing
- javelin → ice dancing
- curling
- dressage → curling

YARD, DEN, PUB REGIONAL

- ice fishing
- badminton → ice fishing
- croquet
- skeet shooting → croquet
- billiards
- darts → billiards
- paintball
- quail hunting → quail hunting

GAS- OR FIXED-POWER REGIONAL

- pro wrestling
- jai-alai → pro wrestling
- greyhound racing
- harness racing → greyhound racing
- roller derby
- soapbox derby → roller derby
- NASCAR
- drag racing → NASCAR

OIL, ROSIN, BEER REGIONAL

- golf
- frolf → golf
- bodybuilding
- sumo wrestling → bodybuilding
- skydiving
- poker → poker
- bowling
- slo-pitch softball → bowling

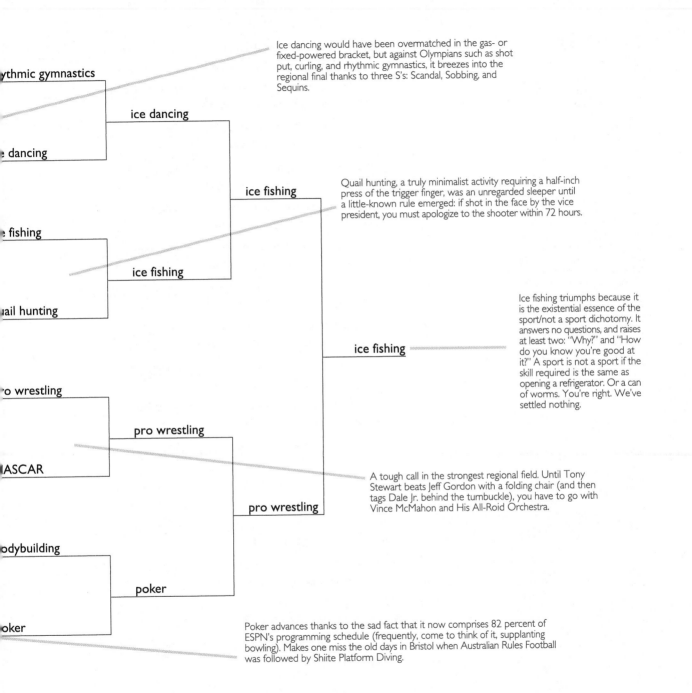

ythmic gymnastics

ice dancing

e dancing

Ice dancing would have been overmatched in the gas- or fixed-powered bracket, but against Olympians such as shot put, curling, and rhythmic gymnastics, it breezes into the regional final thanks to three S's: Scandal, Sobbing, and Sequins.

ice fishing

e fishing

ice fishing

Quail hunting, a truly minimalist activity requiring a half-inch press of the trigger finger, was an unregarded sleeper until a little-known rule emerged: if shot in the face by the vice president, you must apologize to the shooter within 72 hours.

uail hunting

ice fishing

Ice fishing triumphs because it is the existential essence of the sport/not a sport dichotomy. It answers no questions, and raises at least two: "Why?" and "How do you know you're good at it?" A sport is not a sport if the skill required is the same as opening a refrigerator. Or a can of worms. You're right. We've settled nothing.

o wrestling

pro wrestling

ASCAR

pro wrestling

A tough call in the strongest regional field. Until Tony Stewart beats Jeff Gordon with a folding chair (and then tags Dale Jr. behind the turnbuckle), you have to go with Vince McMahon and His All-Roid Orchestra.

odybuilding

poker

oker

Poker advances thanks to the sad fact that it now comprises 82 percent of ESPN's programming schedule (frequently, come to think of it, supplanting bowling). Makes one miss the old days in Bristol when Australian Rules Football was followed by Shiite Platform Diving.

86

Sports Books
by DICK FRIEDMAN

Although sports deals with fun and games, what distinguishes these books is their close, painful, and evocative examinations of defeat and despair. The very best, in presenting fully rounded portraits of our icons, often leave the reader with a lingering sadness, along with an enhanced awareness of our inevitable decline. There is so much depth in this field that many reserves missed the cut. Where have you gone, Richard Ben Cramer's *Joe DiMaggio: The Hero's Life*? Or *The Bill James Historical Baseball Abstract*? Or Pete Axthelm's *The City Game*, or even the Chip Hilton series? And the peerless David Halberstam can't make it out of round 1?

DICK FRIEDMAN is a senior editor at *Sports Illustrated* who has reviewed books for si.com. At the magazine, he has supervised coverage of pro and college basketball, baseball, golf, sports media, and fantasy football. He grew up in the Boston area, where he spent his weekends watching such heroes as Bob Cousy, Bill Russell, Bobby Orr, and Carl Yastrzemski. The Red Sox' win in the 2004 World Series relegated his daughter's birth to the second-greatest event in his life. His daughter understood.

The Sweet Science, by A.J. Liebling — Sweet Science
Sunday Money, by Jeff MacGregor

Instant Replay, by Jerry Kramer — Instant Replay
Eight Men Out, by Eliot Asinof

A Season on the Brink, by John Feinstein — Brink
The Natural, by Bernard Malamud

Paper Lion, by George Plimpton — Paper Lion
The Gilded Age of Sport, by Herbert Warren Wind

The Game, by Ken Dryden — Game
North Dallas Forty, by Peter Gent

Ball Four, by Jim Bouton — Ball Four
The Junction Boys, by Jim Dent

The Summer Game, by Roger Angell — Summer Game
The Long Season, by Jim Brosnan

When Pride Still Mattered, by David Maraniss — Pride
Loose Balls, by Terry Pluto

Moneyball, by Michael Lewis — Moneyball
Babe, by Robert Creamer

Fever Pitch, by Nick Hornby — Fever Pitch
Levels of the Game, by John McPhee

Seabiscuit, by Laura Hillenbrand — Seabiscuit
You Know Me Al, by Ring Lardner

Semi-Tough, by Dan Jenkins — Semi-Tough
Heaven Is a Playground, by Rick Telander

Friday Night Lights, by H.G. Bissinger — Friday Night Lights
Summer of '49, by David Halberstam

The Golf Omnibus, by P. G. Wodehouse — Golf Omnibus
Everybody's All-American, by Frank Deford

A River Runs Through It, by Norman Maclean — River
Bang the Drum Slowly, by Mark Harris

The Boys of Summer, by Roger Kahn — Boys of Summer
My Losing Season, by Pat Conroy

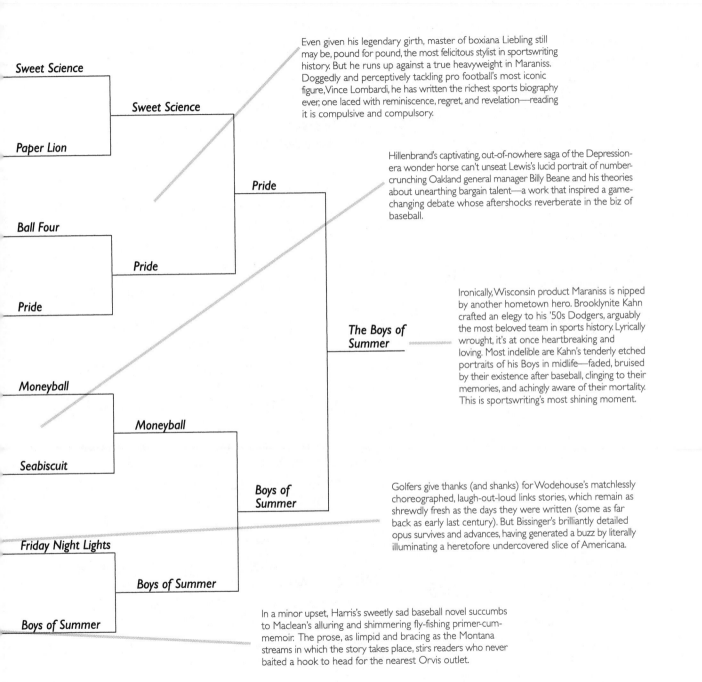

Sweet Science

Paper Lion

Sweet Science

Pride

Ball Four

Pride

Pride

Moneyball

Moneyball

Seabiscuit

Boys of
Summer

Friday Night Lights

Boys of Summer

Boys of Summer

The Boys of
Summer

Even given his legendary girth, master of boxiana Liebling still may be, pound for pound, the most felicitous stylist in sportswriting history. But he runs up against a true heavyweight in Maraniss. Doggedly and perceptively tackling pro football's most iconic figure, Vince Lombardi, he has written the richest sports biography ever, one laced with reminiscence, regret, and revelation—reading it is compulsive and compulsory.

Hillenbrand's captivating, out-of-nowhere saga of the Depression-era wonder horse can't unseat Lewis's lucid portrait of number-crunching Oakland general manager Billy Beane and his theories about unearthing bargain talent—a work that inspired a game-changing debate whose aftershocks reverberate in the biz of baseball.

Ironically, Wisconsin product Maraniss is nipped by another hometown hero. Brooklynite Kahn crafted an elegy to his '50s Dodgers, arguably the most beloved team in sports history. Lyrically wrought, it's at once heartbreaking and loving. Most indelible are Kahn's tenderly etched portraits of his Boys in midlife—faded, bruised by their existence after baseball, clinging to their memories, and achingly aware of their mortality. This is sportswriting's most shining moment.

Golfers give thanks (and shanks) for Wodehouse's matchlessly choreographed, laugh-out-loud links stories, which remain as shrewdly fresh as the days they were written (some as far back as early last century). But Bissinger's brilliantly detailed opus survives and advances, having generated a buzz by literally illuminating a heretofore undercovered slice of Americana.

In a minor upset, Harris's sweetly sad baseball novel succumbs to Maclean's alluring and shimmering fly-fishing primer-cum-memoir. The prose, as limpid and bracing as the Montana streams in which the story takes place, stirs readers who never baited a hook to head for the nearest Orvis outlet.

87

Sucker Bets
by RICHARD HOFFER

There are wagers and then there are foolish wagers. The latter is one where wishful thinking not only trumps rational cognition, but we accept the egregious imbalance of risk and reward even as we place our bets. Of course, it's one thing to book passage on a hydrogen-filled dirigible named *Hindenburg* and something else to plunk down a dollar on the Pick 6. In between is a vast program of propositions that, taken together, amounts to everyday life. Everything's a gamble, right? Still, when the chance of a reward becomes dangerously remote or the possible outcome just too calamitous (is the discount received at Ned's Near-Perfect Sky Diving really worth the disappointment of a frayed rip cord?), we are all advised to lock the doors and retreat into the safety of basic cable.

RICHARD HOFFER spent two years and roughly 125 percent of his publisher's advance researching *Jackpot Nation: Rambling and Gambling Across Our Landscape of Luck*, a book that became disastrously interactive when, for the sake of "color," he split four nines against the dealer's six and lost $14,000 in 30 seconds. When he isn't watching cable TV in his suburban ranch house, Hoffer writes for *Sports Illustrated*.

LAS VEGAS REGIONAL

- keno — keno
- video poker
- splitting 10s — splitting 10s
- insuring blackjack
- playing cards with a man named Doc — WSOP buy-in
- World Series of Poker buy-in
- all-in on 2-7 — all-in on 2-7
- big 6 or 8

FAITH-BASED REGIONAL

- extended warranty — extended warranty
- rustproofing
- on-time departure — on-time departure
- New York Jets cover
- gas station next exit — Pascal's wager
- Pascal's wager
- GM pension — GM pension
- Social Security

SPORTS REGIONAL

- boxing draw — Super Bowl OT
- Super Bowl OT
- three-parlay — three-parlay
- teaser
- Tiger Woods vs. the field — Rose inducted
- Pete Rose inducted into Hall of Fame
- NCAA Final Four office pool — Bonds clears name
- Barry Bonds clears name

BUSINESS AND CULTURE REGIONAL

- Powerball — Powerball
- Pamela Anderson, Kid Rock celebrate 50th anniversary
- progressive slots — AOL Time Warner
- AOL Time Warner merger pays off
- around the world in 80 days — around the world
- dropped putt in *Caddyshack*
- Mel Gibson arrested again for DUI — Mel/Woody
- Mel Gibson stars in Woody Allen film

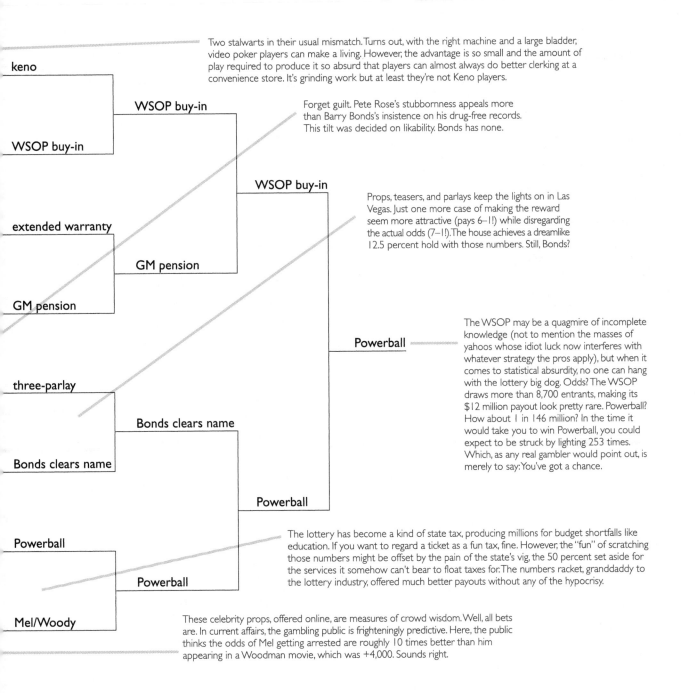

keno

WSOP buy-in

Two stalwarts in their usual mismatch. Turns out, with the right machine and a large bladder, video poker players can make a living. However, the advantage is so small and the amount of play required to produce it so absurd that players can almost always do better clerking at a convenience store. It's grinding work but at least they're not Keno players.

WSOP buy-in

WSOP buy-in

Forget guilt. Pete Rose's stubbornness appeals more than Barry Bonds's insistence on his drug-free records. This tilt was decided on likability. Bonds has none.

extended warranty

GM pension

GM pension

WSOP buy-in

Props, teasers, and parlays keep the lights on in Las Vegas. Just one more case of making the reward seem more attractive (pays 6–1!) while disregarding the actual odds (7–1!). The house achieves a dreamlike 12.5 percent hold with those numbers. Still, Bonds?

Powerball

The WSOP may be a quagmire of incomplete knowledge (not to mention the masses of yahoos whose idiot luck now interferes with whatever strategy the pros apply), but when it comes to statistical absurdity, no one can hang with the lottery big dog. Odds? The WSOP draws more than 8,700 entrants, making its $12 million payout look pretty rare. Powerball? How about 1 in 146 million? In the time it would take you to win Powerball, you could expect to be struck by lighting 253 times. Which, as any real gambler would point out, is merely to say: You've got a chance.

three-parlay

Bonds clears name

Bonds clears name

Powerball

Powerball

Powerball

Powerball

Mel/Woody

The lottery has become a kind of state tax, producing millions for budget shortfalls like education. If you want to regard a ticket as a fun tax, fine. However, the "fun" of scratching those numbers might be offset by the pain of the state's vig, the 50 percent set aside for the services it somehow can't bear to float taxes for. The numbers racket, granddaddy to the lottery industry, offered much better payouts without any of the hypocrisy.

These celebrity props, offered online, are measures of crowd wisdom. Well, all bets are. In current affairs, the gambling public is frighteningly predictive. Here, the public thinks the odds of Mel getting arrested are roughly 10 times better than him appearing in a Woodman movie, which was +4,000. Sounds right.

88

Talk Show Hosts

by BILL CARTER

In television, chat has always been phat. From morning through the wee hours, television has always been filled with talk, and the wallets of networks and syndicators have always been filled with the money generated by all that chatter. The format, which includes variations from comedy to news to celebrity interviews, has created a long roster of superstars enriched by rivalries that produce truly intense competition. My criteria here: (a) impact, (b) durability, and (c) the elusive ability to wear well on your audience, which the best do by magically reinventing themselves while appearing unchanged. The champion here, defeating a most formidable opponent in the finals, never outstayed his welcome.

BILL CARTER, the television industry correspondent for the *New York Times,* has covered the business for 30 years. He is also the author of three books on television: *Monday Night Mayhem* (coauthored with Marc Gunther), *The Late Shift,* and *Desperate Networks.* He also wrote the scripts for the film adaptations of the first two books.

LATE-NIGHT REGIONAL

Johnny Carson	Carson
Dick Cavett	
David Letterman	Letterman
Jack Paar	
Conan O'Brien	O'Brien
Jon Stewart	
Jay Leno	Leno
Steve Allen	

MORNING REGIONAL

Dave Garroway	Garroway
Joan Lunden	
Diane Sawyer	Lauer
Matt Lauer	
Bryant Gumbel	Gumbel
Barbara Walters	
Katie Couric	Couric
David Hartman	

DAYTIME REGIONAL

Oprah Winfrey	Winfrey
Rosie O'Donnell	
Merv Griffin	Griffin
Art Linkletter	
Mike Douglas	Philbin
Regis Philbin	
Phil Donahue	Donahue
Dr. Phil	

HARD-NEWS REGIONAL

Ted Koppel	Koppel
David Susskind	
Bill O'Reilly	O'Reilly
David Frost	
Larry King	Rose
Charlie Rose	
Mike Wallace	Wallace
Anderson Cooper	

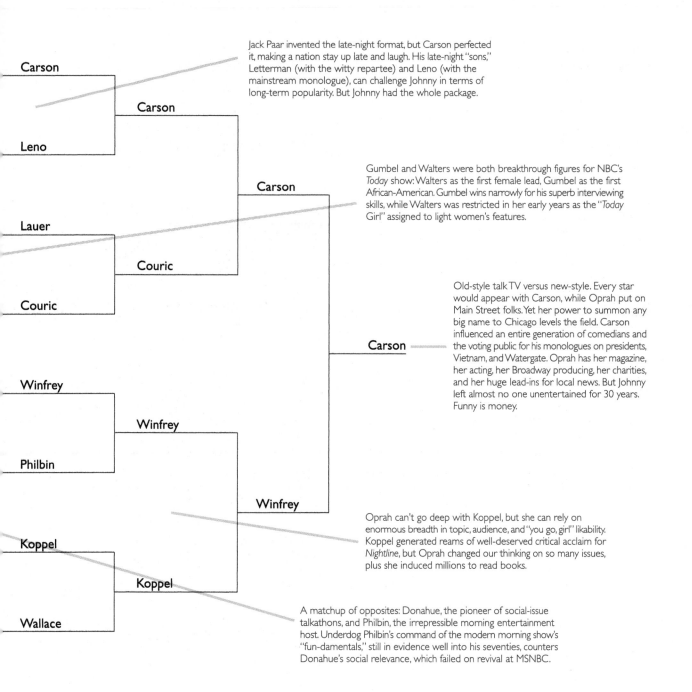

Carson

Leno

Carson

Lauer

Couric

Couric

Carson

Carson

Winfrey

Philbin

Winfrey

Koppel

Wallace

Winfrey

Koppel

Carson

Jack Paar invented the late-night format, but Carson perfected it, making a nation stay up late and laugh. His late-night "sons," Letterman (with the witty repartee) and Leno (with the mainstream monologue), can challenge Johnny in terms of long-term popularity. But Johnny had the whole package.

Gumbel and Walters were both breakthrough figures for NBC's *Today* show: Walters as the first female lead, Gumbel as the first African-American. Gumbel wins narrowly for his superb interviewing skills, while Walters was restricted in her early years as the "*Today* Girl" assigned to light women's features.

Old-style talk TV versus new-style. Every star would appear with Carson, while Oprah put on Main Street folks. Yet her power to summon any big name to Chicago levels the field. Carson influenced an entire generation of comedians and the voting public for his monologues on presidents, Vietnam, and Watergate. Oprah has her magazine, her acting, her Broadway producing, her charities, and her huge lead-ins for local news. But Johnny left almost no one unentertained for 30 years. Funny is money.

Oprah can't go deep with Koppel, but she can rely on enormous breadth in topic, audience, and "you go, girl" likability. Koppel generated reams of well-deserved critical acclaim for *Nightline*, but Oprah changed our thinking on so many issues, plus she induced millions to read books.

A matchup of opposites: Donahue, the pioneer of social-issue talkathons, and Philbin, the irrepressible morning entertainment host. Underdog Philbin's command of the modern morning show's "fun-damentals," still in evidence well into his seventies, counters Donahue's social relevance, which failed on revival at MSNBC.

89

Tell Me Again Why They're Famous

by LARRY AMOROS

It all started when I first saw Zsa Zsa Gabor on *The Merv Griffin Show*. She was of indeterminate age and even more indeterminate talent. That's when I realized that the tides of celebrity were turning. No longer did someone need talent or achievement to get on TV, just a pulse, some good fortune, and chutzpah. Fast-forward to now. Our TV screens and magazine covers are filled with people who have undeservedly become celebrities—usually for the four reasons highlighted in our regionals. The least deserving wins.

LARRY AMOROS is a writer who bitterly resents the undeserved notoriety the people in this bracket have attained.

NO REASON/WRONG REASON REGIONAL

Paris Hilton | Paris Hilton
Regis Philbin
Stephen Hawking | Andy Dick
Andy Dick
Vanna White | Vanna White
Monica Lewinsky
Nicole Richie | Nicole Richie
Baby Jessica

GENETIC LINK REGIONAL

Jim Belushi | Jim Belushi
any Baldwin brother other than Alec
Ashlee Simpson | Ashlee Simpson
the Bush twins
Victoria Gotti | Soon-Yi
Soon-Yi Previn Allen
Melissa Rivers | Melissa Rivers
Cody, Cassidy

CRIMINAL REGIONAL

Jeffrey Dahmer | Jeffrey Dahmer
John Hinkley, Jr.
Lorena Bobbitt | Lorena Bobbitt
the Menendez brothers
Amy Fisher | Amy Fisher
Kenneth Lay
"Son of Sam" dog | "Son of Sam" dog
Sammy the Bull Gravano

MARRIED REGIONAL

Ivana Trump | Ivana Trump
Camilla Parker Bowles
Yoko Ono | Yoko Ono
Heather Mills
David Gest | David Gest
Roy (but not Siegfried)
Bianca Jagger | Bianca Jagger
Guy Ritchie

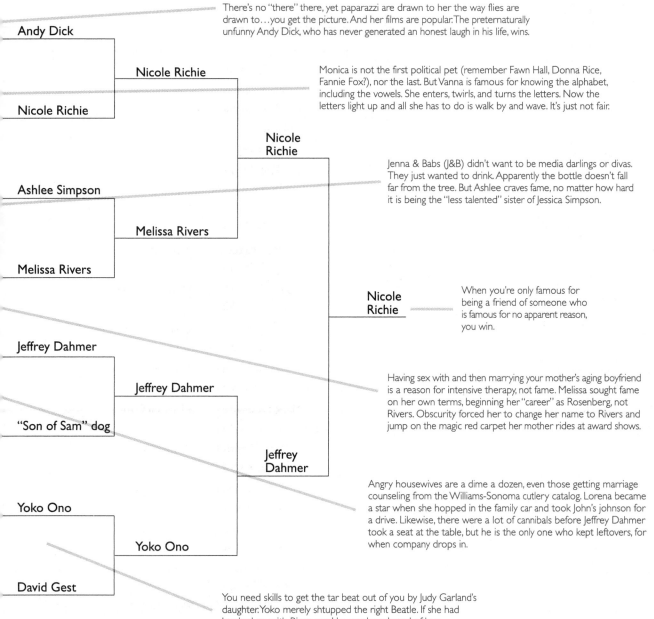

There's no "there" there, yet paparazzi are drawn to her the way flies are drawn to…you get the picture. And her films are popular. The preternaturally unfunny Andy Dick, who has never generated an honest laugh in his life, wins.

Andy Dick

Nicole Richie

Nicole Richie

Monica is not the first political pet (remember Fawn Hall, Donna Rice, Fannie Fox?), nor the last. But Vanna is famous for knowing the alphabet, including the vowels. She enters, twirls, and turns the letters. Now the letters light up and all she has to do is walk by and wave. It's just not fair.

Nicole Richie

Jenna & Babs (J&B) didn't want to be media darlings or divas. They just wanted to drink. Apparently the bottle doesn't fall far from the tree. But Ashlee craves fame, no matter how hard it is being the "less talented" sister of Jessica Simpson.

Ashlee Simpson

Melissa Rivers

Melissa Rivers

Nicole Richie

When you're only famous for being a friend of someone who is famous for no apparent reason, you win.

Jeffrey Dahmer

Jeffrey Dahmer

Having sex with and then marrying your mother's aging boyfriend is a reason for intensive therapy, not fame. Melissa sought fame on her own terms, beginning her "career" as Rosenberg, not Rivers. Obscurity forced her to change her name to Rivers and jump on the magic red carpet her mother rides at award shows.

"Son of Sam" dog

Jeffrey Dahmer

Angry housewives are a dime a dozen, even those getting marriage counseling from the Williams-Sonoma cutlery catalog. Lorena became a star when she hopped in the family car and took John's johnson for a drive. Likewise, there were a lot of cannibals before Jeffrey Dahmer took a seat at the table, but he is the only one who kept leftovers, for when company drops in.

Yoko Ono

Yoko Ono

David Gest

You need skills to get the tar beat out of you by Judy Garland's daughter. Yoko merely shtupped the right Beatle. If she had hooked up with Ringo, you'd never have heard of her.

90

Troll Models
by ROBERT LIPSYTE

We've been so conditioned to view sports figures as role models that when they fall short (i.e., are human) we feel betrayed and quickly make them troll models, examples of arrogance, greed, even criminality. Maybe there's something passive-aggressive going on here; we're in denial about a star's thuggishness until he either hurts somebody off the field or loses his tools and the power to thrill us (Mike Tyson did both.). There's also something schizzie in fandom. Half the NASCAR crowd turned on a dazzling champion, Jeff Gordon (with some using the lame acronym of Fans Against Gordon), because he was replacing Dale Earnhardt. And two of the greatest role models, Muhammad Ali and Howard Cosell, were both beloved and despised not only for their political stances but because their overwhelming talents turned sports upside down. Could the fault be in us, not in our stars?

ROBERT LIPSYTE avoided hating even the athletes who gave him a hard time as a sports journalist at the New York Times, CBS, and NBC, and as writer of the TBS documentary miniseries Idols of the Game, until forced to confront this bracket. Lipsyte is also the author of the young adult novels Raiders Night and the upcoming Yellow Flag, among others. His Web site is www.robertlipsyte.com.

Cobb, petty and violent, channeled his rage into brilliant play. His mom killed his dad and then Babe Ruth eclipsed his acclaim. What excuse is there for Rose, who broke Cobb's career hits record while blatantly cheating on his wife and our pastime?

The San Diego Chicken was the most famous of the despicable ballpark mascots, ushering in an era of participatory rude behavior on the scoreboard and in the stands. But the Chicken was merely foul, while Olympic leader Avery Brundage, a Nazi-sympathizing hypocrite, was evil.

Bracket:

- Floyd Landis / Kenesaw Mountain Landis → K.M. Landis
- Jimmy the Greek Snyder / Latrell Sprewell → Latrell Sprewell
- Hootie Johnson / Zinedine Zidane → Hootie Johnson
- Marge Schott / Tony Stewart → Marge Schott
- Phil Knight / Bob Knight → Phil Knight
- Pete Rose / Ty Cobb → Pete Rose
- Ron Artest / Jack Tatum → Jack Tatum
- Howard Cosell / Muhammad Ali → Muhammad Ali
- George Steinbrenner / Charles Comiskey → Charles Comiskey
- Mike Tyson / O.J. Simpson → O.J. Simpson
- Mark McGwire / Shoeless Joe Jackson → Mark McGwire
- Barry Bonds / Kobe Bryant → Kobe Bryant
- Jeff Gordon / Margo Adams → Margo Adams
- Billy Martin / Tonya Harding → Billy Martin
- Avery Brundage / San Diego Chicken → Avery Brundage
- Don King / John McEnroe → Don King

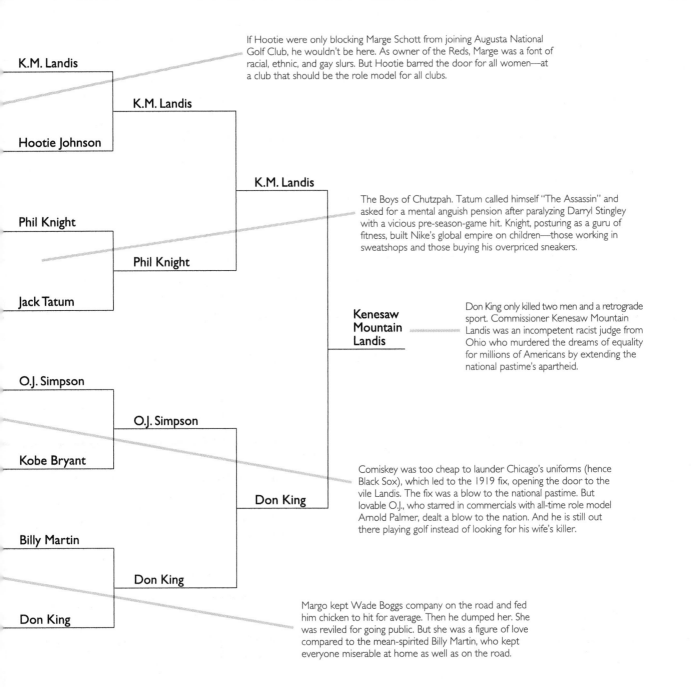

K.M. Landis

K.M. Landis

Hootie Johnson

K.M. Landis

If Hootie were only blocking Marge Schott from joining Augusta National Golf Club, he wouldn't be here. As owner of the Reds, Marge was a font of racial, ethnic, and gay slurs. But Hootie barred the door for all women—at a club that should be the role model for all clubs.

Phil Knight

Phil Knight

Jack Tatum

The Boys of Chutzpah. Tatum called himself "The Assassin" and asked for a mental anguish pension after paralyzing Darryl Stingley with a vicious pre-season-game hit. Knight, posturing as a guru of fitness, built Nike's global empire on children—those working in sweatshops and those buying his overpriced sneakers.

Kenesaw Mountain Landis

Don King only killed two men and a retrograde sport. Commissioner Kenesaw Mountain Landis was an incompetent racist judge from Ohio who murdered the dreams of equality for millions of Americans by extending the national pastime's apartheid.

O.J. Simpson

O.J. Simpson

Kobe Bryant

Don King

Comiskey was too cheap to launder Chicago's uniforms (hence Black Sox), which led to the 1919 fix, opening the door to the vile Landis. The fix was a blow to the national pastime. But lovable O.J., who starred in commercials with all-time role model Arnold Palmer, dealt a blow to the nation. And he is still out there playing golf instead of looking for his wife's killer.

Billy Martin

Don King

Don King

Margo kept Wade Boggs company on the road and fed him chicken to hit for average. Then he dumped her. She was reviled for going public. But she was a figure of love compared to the mean-spirited Billy Martin, who kept everyone miserable at home as well as on the road.

91

TV One-Liners
by MICHAEL DAVIS

I'm not a brain surgeon. I just play one when I'm watching TV. As a result, I have a bulging mass of TV memories in my head. Occupying a special crevice between my ears are the signature lines and phrases that I've accumulated from 50 years of uncritical TV watching. When I shake my head reflecting on all that couch time, these 32 phrases fall out. The best ones are not only vivid and memorable, but they easily roll off the tongue in all sorts of situations. That's the main criterion here: how frequently do we use them in real life? If my arrangement of this bracket displeases you, you can kiss my grits.

MICHAEL DAVIS is a senior editor at *TV Guide*. *Street Gang*, his history of *Sesame Street*, will be published by Viking in 2008.

You're fired. (*The Apprentice*) — Eat my shorts.
Eat my shorts. (*The Simpsons*)

Hi-Ho, Steverino. (*The Steve Allen Show*) — Not that there's
Not that there's anything wrong with that. (*Seinfeld*)

Tell me what you don't like about yourself. (*Nip/Tuck*) — Come on down!
Come on down! (*The Price Is Right*)

What you talkin' 'bout, Willis? (*Diff'rent Strokes*) — What you talkin' 'bout
Is that your final answer? (*Who Wants to Be a Millionaire*)

Say goodnight, Gracie. (*The George Burns and Gracie Allen Show*) — Stifle yourself
Stifle yourself, Edith. (*All in the Family*)

This is *Today* on NBC. (*Today*) — that's the way it is
And that's the way it is. (*CBS Evening News with Walter Cronkite*)

We are two wild and crazy guys. (*Saturday Night Live*) — Sock it to me!
Sock it to me! (*Rowan & Martin's Laugh-In*)

Jeepers, Mr. Kent! (*Adventures of Superman*) — Holy crap!
Holy crap! (*Everybody Loves Raymond*)

Good night, and good luck. (*Person to Person*) — Lucy
Lucy, you've got some 'splainin' to do. (*I Love Lucy*)

Yabba-dabba do! (*The Flintstones*) — Norm!
Norm! (*Cheers*)

D'oh! (*The Simpsons*) — D'oh!
Me love cookie. (*Sesame Street*)

Nanu Nanu. (*Mork & Mindy*) — one more question
Just one more question. (*Columbo*)

How you doin'? (*Friends*) — Book 'em, Dano.
Book 'em, Dano. (*Hawaii Five-0*)

Danger, Will Robinson. Danger. (*Lost in Space*) — One of these days
One of these days, Alice. Pow! Right in the kisser. (*The Honeymooners*)

I like you just the way you are. (*Mister Rogers' Neighborhood*) — you're the greatest
Baby, you're the greatest. (*The Honeymooners*)

Here's Johnny! (*The Tonight Show Starring Johnny Carson*) — Here's Johnny!
This tape will self-destruct in 5 seconds. (*Mission: Impossible*)

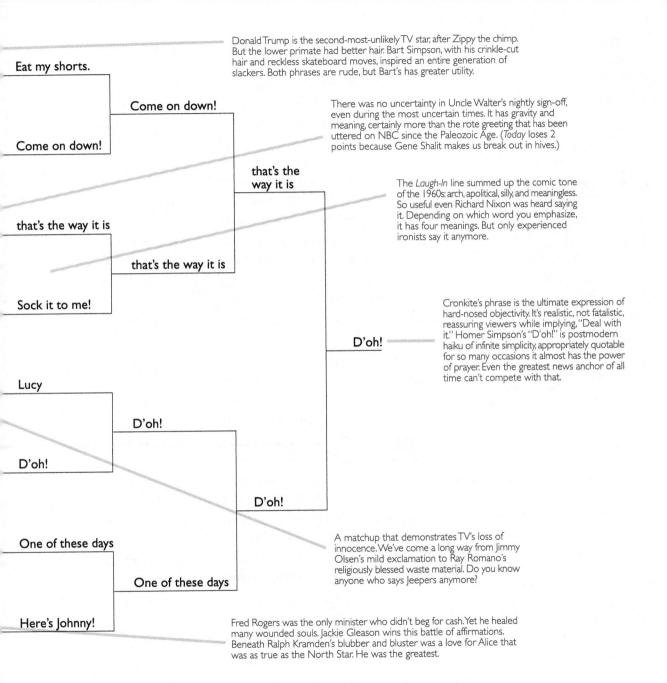

Eat my shorts.

Come on down!

Come on down!

Donald Trump is the second-most-unlikely TV star, after Zippy the chimp. But the lower primate had better hair. Bart Simpson, with his crinkle-cut hair and reckless skateboard moves, inspired an entire generation of slackers. Both phrases are rude, but Bart's has greater utility.

that's the way it is

that's the way it is

that's the way it is

Sock it to me!

There was no uncertainty in Uncle Walter's nightly sign-off, even during the most uncertain times. It has gravity and meaning, certainly more than the rote greeting that has been uttered on NBC since the Paleozoic Age. (*Today* loses 2 points because Gene Shalit makes us break out in hives.)

The *Laugh-In* line summed up the comic tone of the 1960s: arch, apolitical, silly, and meaningless. So useful even Richard Nixon was heard saying it. Depending on which word you emphasize, it has four meanings. But only experienced ironists say it anymore.

D'oh!

Cronkite's phrase is the ultimate expression of hard-nosed objectivity. It's realistic, not fatalistic, reassuring viewers while implying, "Deal with it." Homer Simpson's "D'oh!" is postmodern haiku of infinite simplicity, appropriately quotable for so many occasions it almost has the power of prayer. Even the greatest news anchor of all time can't compete with that.

Lucy

D'oh!

D'oh!

D'oh!

One of these days

One of these days

Here's Johnny!

A matchup that demonstrates TV's loss of innocence. We've come a long way from Jimmy Olsen's mild exclamation to Ray Romano's religiously blessed waste material. Do you know anyone who says Jeepers anymore?

Fred Rogers was the only minister who didn't beg for cash. Yet he healed many wounded souls. Jackie Gleason wins this battle of affirmations. Beneath Ralph Kramden's blubber and bluster was a love for Alice that was as true as the North Star. He was the greatest.

92

Typefaces
by NIGEL HOLMES

Estimates of the existing number of typefaces, or fonts, range from 30,000 to 90,000, so there are plenty to choose from. This leads magazine art director Bob Ciano to wonder why he doesn't see greater font variety in the pages of professionally designed magazines and books; others (myself included) could happily do with no more than about six for the rest of our working lives. But whatever their views on this, most designers advise the producers of newsletters and PowerPoint presentations to keep it simple. In a contest between variety and utility, readability may be a deciding factor.

The starting lineup of typefaces spans five centuries and includes both classics and newcomers (some of which I'll bet will themselves be regarded as classic in the future).

NIGEL HOLMES, the designer of this book, was graphics director of *Time* magazine for 16 years. He specializes in explanations of complex processes and data. He is the author of *Wordless Diagrams* (Bloomsbury, 2005).

Dogma (Zuzana Licko, 1994)
Blockhead (John Hersey, 1995)
— Dogma

Peignot (A.M. Cassandre, 1937)
Remedy (Frank Heine, 1991)
— Peignot

Mistral (Roger Excoffon, 1955)
Snell Roundhand (Matthew Carter, 1965)
— Snell Roundhand

Comic Sans (Vincent Connaire, 1995)
Swing (based on a font by Max Kaufmann, 1936)
— Swing

Triplex (Zuzana Licko, 1989)
Futura (Paul Renner, 1927)
— Futura

Franklin Gothic (Morris Fuller Benton, 1904)
Interstate (Tobias Frere-Jones, 1992)
— Franklin Gothic

Gill Sans (Eric Gill, 1928–30)
Helvetica (Max Miedinger, Edouard Hoffman, 1957)
— Gill Sans

Avant Garde (Ed Benguiat, Herb Lubalin, Tom Carnese, 1970)
Univers (Adrian Frutiger, 1957)
— Avant Garde

Baskerville (John Baskerville, 1757)
Garamond (Claude Garamond, 1532)
— Garamond

Times New Roman (Stanley Morrison, Victor Lardent, 1931-2)
Hoefler Text (Jonathon Hoefler, 1991)
— Hoefler

Rockwell (F.H. Pierpoint, 1934)
Lubalin Graph (Herb Lubalin, 1974)
— Rockwell

American Typewriter (Joel Kaden, Tony Stan, 1974)
STENCIL (GERRY POWELL, 1937)
— American Typewriter

Copperplate (Fredric W. Goudy, 1901)
Old English Text (based on Caslon Black, William Caslon, 1760)
— Copperplate

Kabel (Rudolf Koch, 1926–29)
Cooper Black (Oswald Cooper, 1926)
— Cooper Black

Giddyup (Laurie Szujewska, 1993)
Zapf Chancery (Herman Zapf, 1979)
— Zapf Chancery

Parkinson (Jim Parkinson, 1994)
Bodoni (Giambattista Bodoni, 1790)
— Bodoni

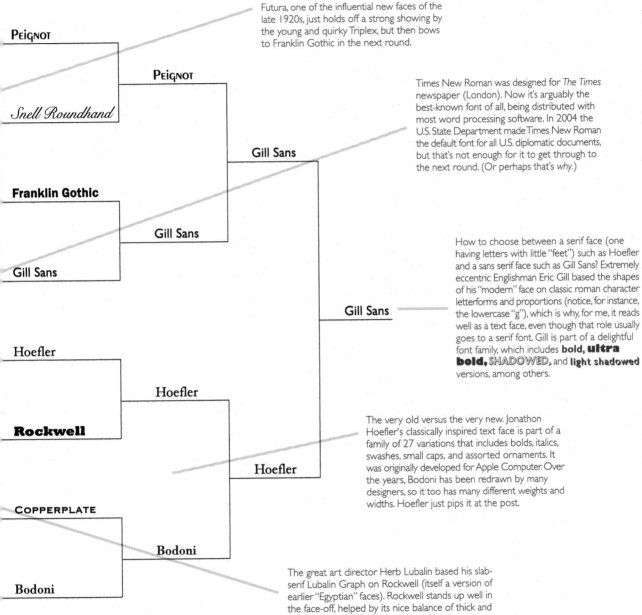

Futura, one of the influential new faces of the late 1920s, just holds off a strong showing by the young and quirky Triplex, but then bows to Franklin Gothic in the next round.

Times New Roman was designed for *The Times* newspaper (London). Now it's arguably the best-known font of all, being distributed with most word processing software. In 2004 the U.S. State Department made Times New Roman the default font for all U.S. diplomatic documents, but that's not enough for it to get through to the next round. (Or perhaps that's *why*.)

How to choose between a serif face (one having letters with little "feet") such as Hoefler and a sans serif face such as Gill Sans? Extremely eccentric Englishman Eric Gill based the shapes of his "modern" face on classic roman character letterforms and proportions (notice, for instance, the lowercase "g"), which is why, for me, it reads well as a text face, even though that role usually goes to a serif font. Gill is part of a delightful font family, which includes **bold, ultra bold,** SHADOWED, and **light shadowed** versions, among others.

The very old versus the very new. Jonathon Hoefler's classically inspired text face is part of a family of 27 variations that includes bolds, italics, swashes, small caps, and assorted ornaments. It was originally developed for Apple Computer. Over the years, Bodoni has been redrawn by many designers, so it too has many different weights and widths. Hoefler just pips it at the post.

The great art director Herb Lubalin based his slab-serif Lubalin Graph on Rockwell (itself a version of earlier "Egyptian" faces). Rockwell stands up well in the face-off, helped by its nice balance of thick and thin strokes (in this weight).

93

Underdogs
by MARK ST. AMANT

The term "underdog" derives from early shipbuilding, when wood planks, called "dogs," were sawn by the senior sawyer, who stood on top of said planks and was called the "overdog." The junior sawyer, who toiled in a pit below, was the "underdog." This *nom de woodwork* eventually became synonymous with the most thrilling moment in sports: the upset victory. Our favorite underdogs not only defy the odds against highly favored opponents, they do so in style—by battling back from injuries, overcoming personal challenges, or getting lucky. Their stories are so unbelievable they could be Jerry Bruckheimer scripts. Since there can be only one underdog in a given match, the question arises: When an underdog meets a more favored underdog, who wins?

MARK ST. AMANT was a breech baby, coming out feetfirst, almost strangled. But nearly four decades later, he used those impetuous feet to become an unlikely placekicker, as detailed in his book *Just Kick It: Tales of an Underdog, Over-Age, Out-of-Place Semi-Pro Football Player*. He writes about fantasy football—the perfect subject for any underdog—in his first book, *Committed: Confessions of a Fantasy Football Junkie*, and for nytimes.com.

Matchup	Winner
Smarty Jones wins 2004 Kentucky Derby & Preakness / Upset hands Man O' War only career loss, 1919	Upset
Red Sox, down 0–3 to Yanks, win 2004 AL pennant / NY Jets beat Baltimore Colts to win Super Bowl III, 1969	Jets
"Cinderella Man" Jim Braddock beats Max Baer, 1935 / Cassius Clay TKOs Sonny Liston for heavyweight title, 1964	Cinderella Man
Jackie Robinson signs with Dodgers, breaks color barrier, 1945 / Villanova tops Georgetown for 1985 NCAA title	Jackie Robinson
Buster Douglas KO's Iron Mike Tyson, 1990 / NC State beats "Phi Slamma Jamma" Houston for 1983 NCAA title	Buster Douglas
Chaminade beats Ralph Sampson's Virginia Cavaliers, 1982 / David over Goliath, Bible, I Samuel 17, 11th Century B.C.	David
Duke beats UNLV for 1991 NCAA title / Rulon Gardner outwrestles Alexander Karelin, 2000	Rulon Gardner
#6 Arthur Ashe beats #1 Jimmy Connors for 1975 Wimbledon title / Rudy Ruettiger suits up for Notre Dame, makes a tackle, 1975	Arthur Ashe
Seabiscuit defeats War Admiral, 1938 / Texas Western beats Kentucky for 1966 NCAA title	Texas Western
Bangladesh stuns world cricket champion Australia, 2005 / S. African Springboks beat New Zealand for 1995 Rugby World Cup	Bangladesh
Greece beats host Portugal twice, wins 2004 Euro Cup / Milan High "Hoosiers" win 1954 Indiana state hoops title	Hoosiers
1994 8-seed Denver Nuggets shock 1-seed Seattle SuperSonics / Jack Fleck beats Ben Hogan in 1955 U.S. Open	Fleck
1969 Miracle Mets / New England Patriots beat Rams in SB XXXVI, 2002	Miracle Mets
11-seed George Mason over 1-seed UConn, makes 2006 Final Four / Billy Mills wins Tokyo Olympics 10k gold, 1964	Billy Mills
1950 U.S. men's soccer beats world power England 1–0 / L.A. Dodgers beat Oakland A's for 1988 World Series title	1950 men's soccer
Soviet men top never-beaten USA for 1972 Olympics hoops gold / 1980 U.S. Men's "Miracle on Ice" hockey team shocks Soviets	Miracle on Ice

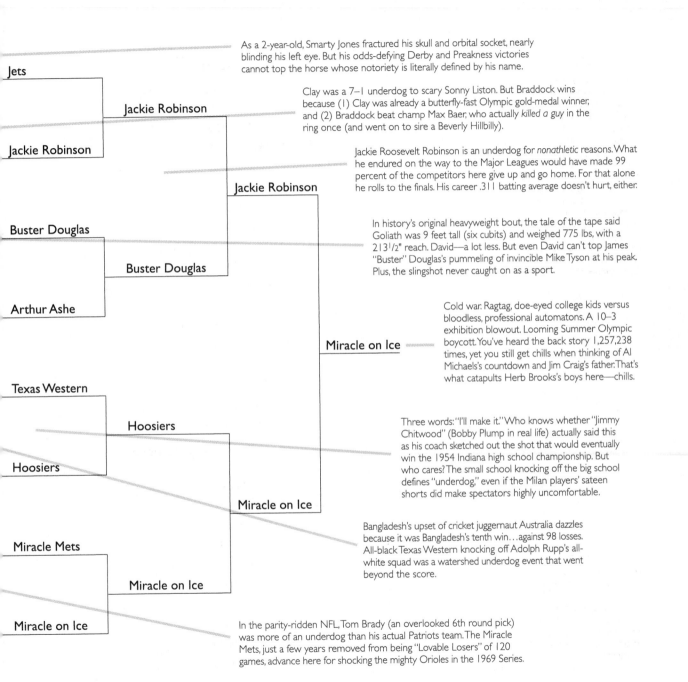

Jets

Jackie Robinson

Jackie Robinson

As a 2-year-old, Smarty Jones fractured his skull and orbital socket, nearly blinding his left eye. But his odds-defying Derby and Preakness victories cannot top the horse whose notoriety is literally defined by his name.

Clay was a 7–1 underdog to scary Sonny Liston. But Braddock wins because (1) Clay was already a butterfly-fast Olympic gold-medal winner, and (2) Braddock beat champ Max Baer, who actually *killed a guy* in the ring once (and went on to sire a Beverly Hillbilly).

Jackie Robinson

Jackie Roosevelt Robinson is an underdog for *nonathletic* reasons. What he endured on the way to the Major Leagues would have made 99 percent of the competitors here give up and go home. For that alone he rolls to the finals. His career .311 batting average doesn't hurt, either.

Buster Douglas

Buster Douglas

In history's original heavyweight bout, the tale of the tape said Goliath was 9 feet tall (six cubits) and weighed 775 lbs, with a 213 1/2" reach. David—a lot less. But even David can't top James "Buster" Douglas's pummeling of invincible Mike Tyson at his peak. Plus, the slingshot never caught on as a sport.

Arthur Ashe

Miracle on Ice

Cold war. Ragtag, doe-eyed college kids versus bloodless, professional automatons. A 10–3 exhibition blowout. Looming Summer Olympic boycott. You've heard the back story 1,257,238 times, yet you still get chills when thinking of Al Michaels's countdown and Jim Craig's father. That's what catapults Herb Brooks's boys here—chills.

Texas Western

Hoosiers

Three words: "I'll make it." Who knows whether "Jimmy Chitwood" (Bobby Plump in real life) actually said this as his coach sketched out the shot that would eventually win the 1954 Indiana high school championship. But who cares? The small school knocking off the big school defines "underdog," even if the Milan players' sateen shorts did make spectators highly uncomfortable.

Hoosiers

Miracle on Ice

Bangladesh's upset of cricket juggernaut Australia dazzles because it was Bangladesh's tenth win…against 98 losses. All-black Texas Western knocking off Adolph Rupp's all-white squad was a watershed underdog event that went beyond the score.

Miracle Mets

Miracle on Ice

Miracle on Ice

In the parity-ridden NFL, Tom Brady (an overlooked 6th round pick) was more of an underdog than his actual Patriots team. The Miracle Mets, just a few years removed from being "Lovable Losers" of 120 games, advance here for shocking the mighty Orioles in the 1969 Series.

94

Video Games
by SETH SCHIESEL

The best video games all ultimately succeed for the same reason: they keep you coming back. Whether simple or complicated, frenetic or measured, the top games provide a playground for the mind. Some do it with memorable characters. Some do it with finely tuned action. All do it with that nagging temptation to come back for just one more turn, just one more game. Many of the competitors here represent entire franchises. A few represent one shining bit of fun.

Since joining the *New York Times* in 1996, SETH SCHIESEL has written about media, technology, and communications. He currently covers video games for the newspaper's culture department and has been an avid gamer since the early 1980s. He plays a human warlock in World of Warcraft.

The Legend of Zelda — Zelda
Soul Calibur

Quake — Quake
Metroid

Pac-Man — Pac-Man
Planescape: Torment

EverQuest — Final Fantasy
Final Fantasy

The Sims — The Sims
Baldur's Gate

Zork — Zork
Doom

Grand Theft Auto — Grand Theft Auto
Fallout

Half-Life — Half-Life
Grim Fandango

Tetris — Tetris
Metal Gear

StarCraft — StarCraft
Gran Turismo

Warcraft — Warcraft
Sonic

Galaga — Galaga
Command & Conquer

Sid Meier's Civilization — Civilization
God of War

Madden NFL — Madden
Ultima

Mario Bros. — Mario Bros.
Diablo

Halo — Halo
SimCity

Zelda

Zelda

Pac-Man

Zelda

The Sims

Grand Theft Auto

Grand Theft Auto

Zelda

Tetris

Tetris

Tetris

Warcraft

Tetris

Civilization

Civilization

Mario Bros.

Who doesn't know Pac-Man? The first global video game smash, Pac-Man is a simple, pure expression of what makes a great game: give players a virtual environment (in this case, a maze) with goals (pellets) and foes (ghosts) and set them free. Two decades after the original Pac-Man, Torment did the same thing on a far different level, with perhaps the most compelling story and some of the most memorable characters ever digitized. But Torment's Nameless One still can't overcome our round yellow friend.

With all of the controversy over sex and violence in Grand Theft Auto, it can be easy to forget how revolutionary its actual game-play really was. GTA was the first to offer players a full living city to explore, with almost no restrictions on where to go or what to do. The Sims actually delivers much the same sort of freedom, just on a more modest (if not less interesting) scale: the suburban family as animated dollhouse. If you have children, you want them playing The Sims. But I'm taking The Sopranos over Leave It to Beaver.

No matter your taste or reflexes, were you stranded on a desert island with our Final Four video games, at least you would never get bored. In variety, character, and scope, the Zelda franchise, Japan's finest digital creation, surpasses GTA. The hypnotic, trancelike power of Tetris nudges past Civilization's cerebral depth. In the end, Tetris is the game that lasts. In 50 years those blocks will still be falling on some screen somewhere.

Galaga may be the perfect arcade game, the seminal blend of color, action, and sound. Every time I walk by a Galaga machine, the quarters in my pocket feel a strange magnetic tug. But the Warcraft franchise is emerging as a worldwide entertainment brand. With more users in China than the United States, World of Warcraft is the Internet's first global game hit.

Back in the Dark Ages (a.k.a. the 1970s) John Madden was known as a football coach. Madden remains one of the most-recognized sports brands in the United States, but to an entire generation of young men he is known mostly as namesake for the top sports game franchise. In the early days of video gaming, the Ultima series was one of the archetypes of Tolkien-style fantasy role-play.

95

Wedding Gifts
by MARCY BLUM

Wedding gifts can be tacky, ugly, useless, trite, or just poorly chosen for the particular newlyweds. Cost is irrelevant if the gift has some thinking behind it—although when guests drop six figures on the adorable couple, it's hard to look that gift horse in the mouth. The best gift is the one with the most utility, the one that induces the bride and groom to gaze lovingly into each other's eyes, think fondly of you forever, pump their fists, and say, "Yes!"

MARCY BLUM is an event and wedding producer based in New York City. She has coordinated hundreds of weddings for the rich and famous as well as for the not so rich and unknown. She encourages all her clients to register for their wedding gifts—largely to avoid having to return 11 crystal decanters.

a piece of original artwork by Warhol — **artwork**
baby grand piano

full china set for 12 — **china**
Frette sheet trousseau

professional knife set — **knife set**
case of champagne

$10,000 honeymoon — **cash**
$10,000 cash

complete luggage set — **luggage**
couples full luxury spa treatment

grandmother's sterling silver flatware for 12 — **flatware**
full set of All-Clad cookware

Tiffany silver candlesticks — **wineglasses**
set of 12 Baccarat wineglasses

season tickets to favorite team — **down payment on mortgage**
down payment on mortgage

personalized Cartier stationery — **espresso**
Illy espresso machine

matching gold Rolex watches — **housekeeping**
housekeeping services 2/week for a year

Dyson vacuum cleaner — **Dyson vacuum**
Loro Piana cashmere throw

Sony flat-screen television — **Napa Valley**
weekend trip to Napa Valley

Cannondale mountain bikes for two — **mountain bikes**
4 private cooking classes at home

Christopher Radko Christmas tree ornament collection — **towels**
complete monogrammed Léron towel set

portrait sitting with Annie Leibovitz — **portrait**
Chevy Tahoe

private ski lessons with accommodations — **Viking range**
Viking six-burner professional range

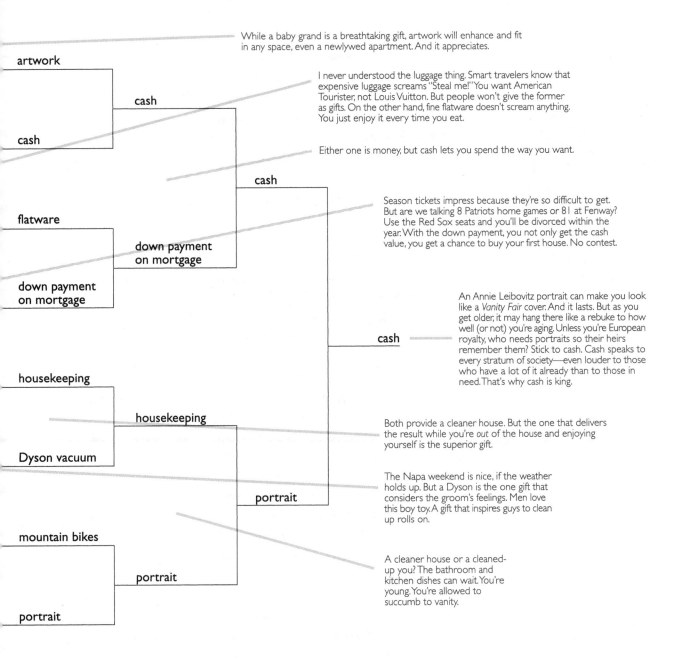

artwork

While a baby grand is a breathtaking gift, artwork will enhance and fit in any space, even a newlywed apartment. And it appreciates.

cash

cash

I never understood the luggage thing. Smart travelers know that expensive luggage screams "Steal me!" You want American Tourister, not Louis Vuitton. But people won't give the former as gifts. On the other hand, fine flatware doesn't scream anything. You just enjoy it every time you eat.

Either one is money, but cash lets you spend the way you want.

cash

flatware

down payment on mortgage

down payment on mortgage

Season tickets impress because they're so difficult to get. But are we talking 8 Patriots home games or 81 at Fenway? Use the Red Sox seats and you'll be divorced within the year. With the down payment, you not only get the cash value, you get a chance to buy your first house. No contest.

cash

An Annie Leibovitz portrait can make you look like a *Vanity Fair* cover. And it lasts. But as you get older, it may hang there like a rebuke to how well (or not) you're aging. Unless you're European royalty, who needs portraits so their heirs remember them? Stick to cash. Cash speaks to every stratum of society—even louder to those who have a lot of it already than to those in need. That's why cash is king.

housekeeping

housekeeping

Dyson vacuum

Both provide a cleaner house. But the one that delivers the result while you're *out* of the house and enjoying yourself is the superior gift.

The Napa weekend is nice, if the weather holds up. But a Dyson is the one gift that considers the groom's feelings. Men love this boy toy. A gift that inspires guys to clean up rolls on.

portrait

mountain bikes

portrait

portrait

A cleaner house or a cleaned-up you? The bathroom and kitchen dishes can wait. You're young. You're allowed to succumb to vanity.

96

Great White Wines

by JOSEPH WARD

France no longer dominates world wine markets the way it did a generation ago. But at the very top it doesn't seem that way. More than two thirds of the greatest whites are French, from Alsace to Bordeaux to the Loire and Rhône. Burgundy, ancestral home of Chardonnay, leads the way in this tournament with seven wines. In terms of grape variety, Chardonnay must share top honors with Riesling, the most versatile and, to my mind, greatest white varietal.

JOSEPH WARD is the wine editor for *Condé Nast Traveler* and the coauthor, with Steven Spurrier, of *How to Buy Fine Wines: Practical Advice for the Investor and Connoisseur.*

Le Montrachet DRC
Leeuwin Estate Chardonnay
— Le Montrachet DRC

Château Climens
Riesling Kellerberg FX Pichler
— Château Climens

Chablis Les Clos Vincent Dauvissat
Maximin Grünhauser Abtsberg von Schubert
— Maximin Grünhauser Abtsberg

Hermitage Chave
Riesling SGN Hugel
— Riesling SGN

Champagne Vintage Krug
Château Rieussec
— Champagne Krug

Riesling Rangen Zind-Humbrecht
Vouvray Cuvée Constance Huet
— Riesling Rangen

Meursault Perrieres Lafon
Ermitage Cuvée de L'Orée Chapoutier
— Meursault Perrieres

Singerriedel Riesling Hirtzberger
Chablis Les Clos Raveneau
— Chablis Les Clos

Condrieu La Doriane Guigal
Château d'Yquem
— Château d'Yquem

Chardonnay Marcassin Vineyard Marcassin
Savennières La Coulée de Serrant Joly
— Chardonnay Marcassin

Wehlener Sonnenuhr J.J. Prum
Château Haut-Brion
— Château Haut-Brion

Champagne Salon
Chardonnay Vine Hill Vineyard Kistler
— Champagne Salon

Chevalier-Montrachet Leflaive
Kiedricher Grafenberg Weil
— Chevalier-Montrachet

Riesling Clos Ste. Hune Trimbach
Château Laville Haut-Brion
— Riesling Clos Ste. Hune

Corton-Charlemagne Coche-Dury
Oberhauser Brucke Donnhoff
— Corton-Charlemagne

Scharzhofberger Egon Müller
Chevalier-Montrachet Les Demoiselles Jadot
— Scharzhofberger

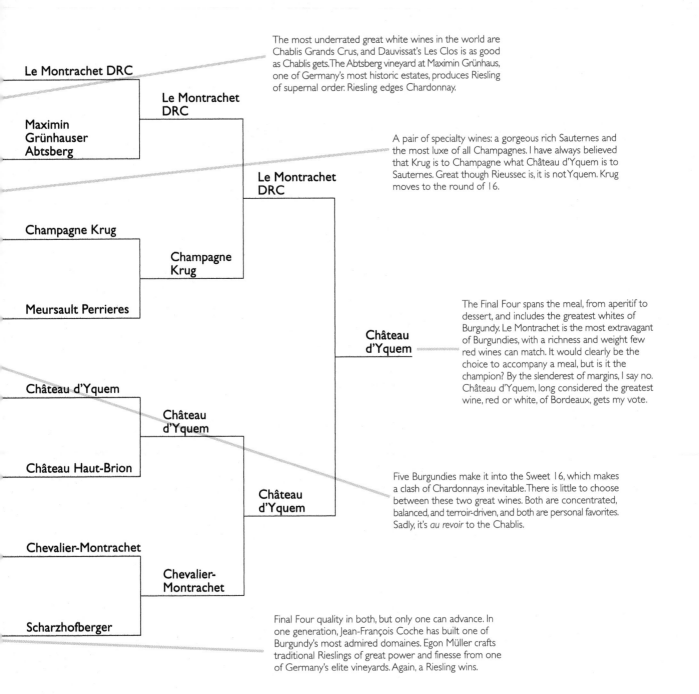

Le Montrachet DRC

Maximin Grünhauser Abtsberg

Le Montrachet DRC

The most underrated great white wines in the world are Chablis Grands Crus, and Dauvissat's Les Clos is as good as Chablis gets. The Abtsberg vineyard at Maximin Grünhaus, one of Germany's most historic estates, produces Riesling of supernal order. Riesling edges Chardonnay.

Champagne Krug

Meursault Perrieres

Champagne Krug

Le Montrachet DRC

A pair of specialty wines: a gorgeous rich Sauternes and the most luxe of all Champagnes. I have always believed that Krug is to Champagne what Château d'Yquem is to Sauternes. Great though Rieussec is, it is not Yquem. Krug moves to the round of 16.

Château d'Yquem

Château Haut-Brion

Château d'Yquem

The Final Four spans the meal, from aperitif to dessert, and includes the greatest whites of Burgundy. Le Montrachet is the most extravagant of Burgundies, with a richness and weight few red wines can match. It would clearly be the choice to accompany a meal, but is it the champion? By the slenderest of margins, I say no. Château d'Yquem, long considered the greatest wine, red or white, of Bordeaux, gets my vote.

Chevalier-Montrachet

Scharzhofberger

Chevalier-Montrachet

Château d'Yquem

Château d'Yquem

Five Burgundies make it into the Sweet 16, which makes a clash of Chardonnays inevitable. There is little to choose between these two great wines. Both are concentrated, balanced, and terroir-driven, and both are personal favorites. Sadly, it's *au revoir* to the Chablis.

Final Four quality in both, but only one can advance. In one generation, Jean-François Coche has built one of Burgundy's most admired domaines. Egon Müller crafts traditional Rieslings of great power and finesse from one of Germany's elite vineyards. Again, a Riesling wins.

97

Women's Magazine Sex Clichés

by STEPHANIE DOLGOFF

To men, sex is like pizza: even when it's bad it's pretty good. Not so for women. Fortunately, there are women's magazines, which provide euphemistic how-tos for the easily embarrassed and explicit road maps for the insatiably curious. As long as you're going for better sex, how about amazing, seismic, glass-shattering, chandelier-swinging, earthmoving, life-altering, exponentially orgasmic sex? Women's magazines are unrivaled when it comes to new ways to say the same thing (i.e., buy this magazine, and you, too, will experience the stove-hot passion known only to bodice-ripped heroines), and that includes titles from *Cosmo* to *Ladies' Home Journal*. The result, despite the cumulative efforts of sharp Ivy League minds, is phrasemaking worthy of the Cliché Hall of Fame. The promise has to be real and the language surreal for winners to keep advancing.

STEPHANIE DOLGOFF, the health director of *Self* magazine, has observed, employed, and even tested a few of the promises on this page at home during the course of nearly two decades writing and editing for *Glamour*, *Cosmopolitan*, and *Seventeen*, among many others.

20 Ways to Spice Up Your Sex Life
Recharge Your Relationship in One Weekend
→ Recharge Weekend

Six Secrets of Highly Orgasmic Women
Sex Secrets of Really Happy Couples
→ Six Secrets

Banish Boredom in Bed
Are You Sex Smart?
→ Banish Boredom in Bed

Seven Secrets of Sexually Satisfied Women
Realize Your Full Passion Potential
→ Seven Secrets

Are You Sabotaging Your Sex Life?
12 Secrets of Sensational Solo Sex
→ Sabotaging?

10 Hot New Sex Positions to Try Tonight
Supersize Your Sex Life—Tonight!
→ Supersize Tonight!

The Good Girls' Guide to Talking Dirty
Are You Sexually in Sync?
→ Talking Dirty

The Good Girls' Guide to Bad-Girl Sex
Love: What Makes It Last
→ Bad-Girl Sex

Get in Touch with Your Inner Sex Goddess
What Your Mother Never Told You About Sex
→ Inner Goddess

What Does He Really Want in Bed? Find Out—Now!
Unleash Your Inner Sex Kitten
→ Inner Kitten

Your Burning Sex Questions—Answered!
Are You Boring in Bed? How to Tell
→ Burning Questions

The Ultimate Guide to Bedroom Bliss—Revealed!
What Really Makes Men Cheat
→ Bedroom Bliss

Thrill Every Inch of Him—Tonight!
How to Blow His Mind in Bed
→ Thrill Every Inch

Go from Oh to OOOOOO!
Great Sexpectations! Make Long-Term Sex Sizzle
→ Oh to OOOOOO!

Is He Cheating? How to Tell
25 Ways to Rev Up Your Romance
→ Is He Cheating?

30 Sizzling Ideas for Mind-Blowing Sex
7 Ways to Make Him Ache for You
→ Make Him Ache

Who has time to try 20 ways of doing anything? Sounds like a lot more work than plugging your relationship into a wall socket for one weekend.

Six Secrets

Which would you rather do: 8-Minute Abs or 7-Minute Abs? Six secrets are so much easier to remember in the sack—and you get to be "highly orgasmic" instead of "really happy." A no-brainer.

Six Secrets

Seven Secrets

A good girl playing bad girl is fun once in a while, like wearing a naughty nurse outfit when he's laid up with the flu. Six Secrets of Highly Orgasmic Women, however, is a sex pantry staple to be used whenever, wherever, and with whomever.

Six Secrets

While solo sex is often the best there is, even if you have a partner, you wouldn't buy a magazine to learn about it. It's like adopting 13 cats or taking up batik: you've given up.

Supersize Tonight!

Alhtough we're not sure what "supersize" sex looks like, it sounds like we're getting bigger portions of everything. Hmmm, better sex or learning why it's our fault that we're bored in bed? Not a tough choice. Supersize me.

Bad-Girl Sex

Bad-Girl Sex

You don't need six secrets if one works, and judging from the sound effects, this one does. A cliché that employs onomatopoeia is a winning cliché.

Oh to OOOOOO!

It's a given that you're a "good girl." But having bad-girl sex wins by a whisker over talking dirty, because the former, by definition, includes a smutty script.

Inner Kitten

Bedroom Bliss

Sex goddess suggests flowing tunics and New Age crystals and pastoral workshops to appreciate your menses. Sex kitten sounds more playful.

Bedroom Bliss

Oh to OOOOOO!

A tough matchup because bedroom bliss has, er, sex appeal. But why only in the bedroom? OOOOOO is venue-agnostic: good on the sofa, in the backyard tent, or behind the bleachers at your son's Little League game. As long as you time your vocalizing to when the crowd goes wild.

Oh to OOOOOO!

Oh to OOOOOO!

The words "mother" and "sex" should never appear in the same sentence.

Is He Cheating?

If he's cheating, you'll eventually find out, with or without this article—and dump him. What you learn from OOOOOO ensures your own happy ending, with or without him.

98

Women's Undies
by SPANKY VAN AKEN

Ladies' lingerie dates at least to Roman days, but this collection of scanties and unmentionables will avoid loincloths and wrapped leather breastcloths, as well as less-ancient chastity belts, farthingales, bustles, and hoop skirts. And don't get me started on those giant rubber Playtex girdles my grandmother wore in the 1950s. Corsets and camisoles predated Victoria divulging her first Secret, but they're here, along with 30 others competing on the basis of sex appeal, popularity, practicality—and sometimes comfort.

The erotic hausfrau known as SPANKY VAN AKEN has been an active participant in ladies' lingerie since she was 10. Her passion for things silky, lacy, and sexually explicit made her a much sought-after date from junior high school on. Today, Ms. Van Aken—a dazzling 34D (DD if she ups her caffeine intake)—is no dilettante when seeking out comfort and style for her "girls." In addition, her spectacular glutes are well acquainted with every cut of panty known to humankind.

While sensuality and sluttiness are important components of lingerie, the bizarre aesthetic of these senior citizen essentials cannot be ignored, much as we'd like. OLP's gained serious street cred when Renée Zellweger sported a pair in *Bridget Jones's Diary*. Knee-high stockings, on the other hand, are clearly mutants.

soft-cup bra	underwire bra
underwire bra	
full slip	chemise
chemise	
bikini briefs	bikini briefs
boy-cut briefs	
teddy	camisole
camisole	
strapless/bandeau bra	strapless bra
spandex top/Sassybax	
body stocking	garter belt & stockings
garter belt & stockings	
push-up bra/Wonderbra	push-up bra/Wonderbra
corset/waist cincher	
girdle	spandex shorts
spandex shorts	
half slip	half slip
pettipants	
thigh-high stockings	panty hose
panty hose	
crotchless panties	high-cut briefs
high-cut briefs	
bustier	bustier
pasties	
old lady panties	olps
knee-high stockings	
thong	thong
G-string	
panty girdle	sports bra
sports bra	
fishnet stockings	body shaper
body shaper	

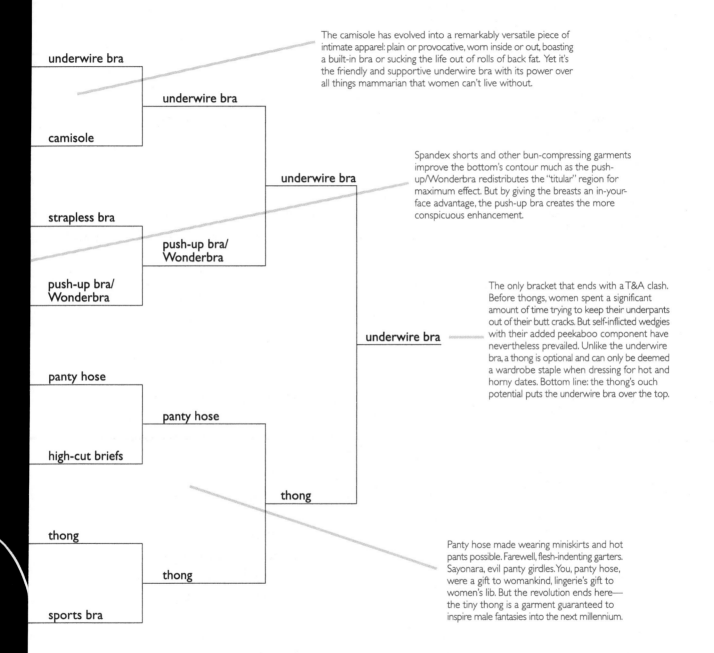

underwire bra

underwire bra

camisole

The camisole has evolved into a remarkably versatile piece of intimate apparel: plain or provocative, worn inside or out, boasting a built-in bra or sucking the life out of rolls of back fat. Yet it's the friendly and supportive underwire bra with its power over all things mammarian that women can't live without.

strapless bra

underwire bra

push-up bra/
Wonderbra

push-up bra/
Wonderbra

Spandex shorts and other bun-compressing garments improve the bottom's contour much as the push-up/Wonderbra redistributes the "titular" region for maximum effect. But by giving the breasts an in-your-face advantage, the push-up bra creates the more conspicuous enhancement.

panty hose

panty hose

high-cut briefs

underwire bra

The only bracket that ends with a T&A clash. Before thongs, women spent a significant amount of time trying to keep their underpants out of their butt cracks. But self-inflicted wedgies with their added peekaboo component have nevertheless prevailed. Unlike the underwire bra, a thong is optional and can only be deemed a wardrobe staple when dressing for hot and horny dates. Bottom line: the thong's ouch potential puts the underwire bra over the top.

thong

thong

thong

sports bra

Panty hose made wearing miniskirts and hot pants possible. Farewell, flesh-indenting garters. Sayonara, evil panty girdles. You, panty hose, were a gift to womankind, lingerie's gift to women's lib. But the revolution ends here—the tiny thong is a garment guaranteed to inspire male fantasies into the next millennium.

99

Your Boss's Annoying Habits

by MARSHALL GOLDSMITH

Everyone has a boss. Even the president of the United States reports to the electorate (or, in some cases, to the vice president). That explains why people love to complain about bosses. Bosses do annoying things habitually. Even when we admire our bosses, they are guilty of workplace behavior that proves they are far short of perfect. Sometimes we let it slide; other times it upsets us. But it becomes serious when bosses fail to see how counterproductive their often well-meaning behavior actually is. For an annoying habit to advance here there has to be a disconnect between how annoying it is to people and how much the boss is aware of it. The bigger the disconnect, the further it goes.

MARSHALL GOLDSMITH is one of the world's top executive coaches. He is the author of *What Got You Here Won't Get You There: How Successful People Can Become Even More Successful* (Hyperion, 2007).

playing favorites	adding too much value
adding too much value	
not recognizing others' achievements	hogging the credit
taking credit for others' achievements	
micromanaging	speaking when angry
speaking when angry	
not listening	not listening
making cynical or sarcastic comments	
sucking up (or playing politics)	sucking up
clinging to the past	
encouraging territoriality (silo management)	making destructive comments
making destructive comments	
overcommitting	negativity
negativity	
refusing to apologize or admit a mistake	won't apologize
disrespecting direct subordinate's time	
failing to communicate vision	not communicating vision
giving responsibility without authority	
passing judgment	passing judgment
saying "We've always done it this way"	
sending nasty e-mails	not providing feedback
not providing performance feedback	
needing to win too much	needing to win too much
withholding information	
making excuses	making excuses
dominating team meetings	
failing to "coach" the team	failing to coach
talking too much	
phoniness	shooting from hip
shooting from the hip	
needing to prove how smart he/she is	proving how smart
overanalyzing	

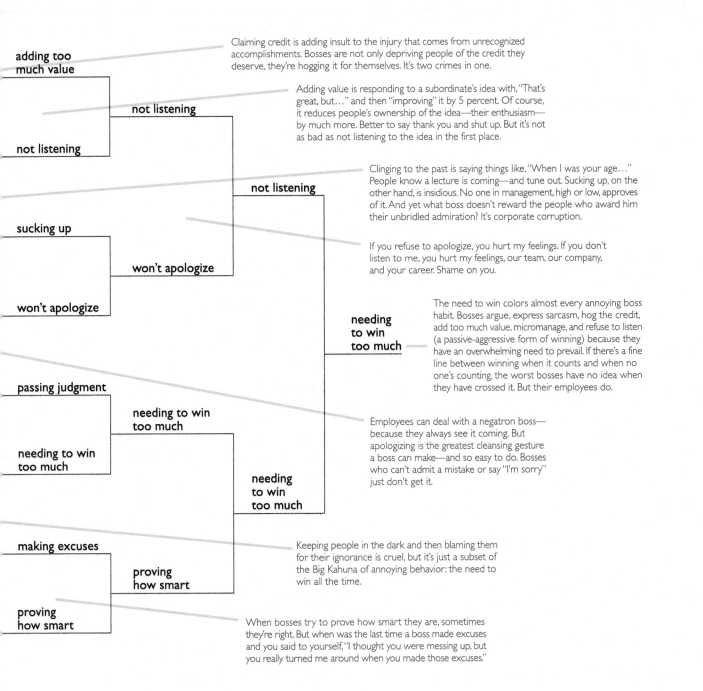

adding too
much value

not listening

not listening

Claiming credit is adding insult to the injury that comes from unrecognized accomplishments. Bosses are not only depriving people of the credit they deserve, they're hogging it for themselves. It's two crimes in one.

Adding value is responding to a subordinate's idea with, "That's great, but…" and then "improving" it by 5 percent. Of course, it reduces people's ownership of the idea—their enthusiasm— by much more. Better to say thank you and shut up. But it's not as bad as not listening to the idea in the first place.

sucking up

won't apologize

not listening

Clinging to the past is saying things like, "When I was your age…" People know a lecture is coming—and tune out. Sucking up, on the other hand, is insidious. No one in management, high or low, approves of it. And yet what boss doesn't reward the people who award him their unbridled admiration? It's corporate corruption.

If you refuse to apologize, you hurt my feelings. If you don't listen to me, you hurt my feelings, our team, our company, and your career. Shame on you.

won't apologize

needing
to win
too much

The need to win colors almost every annoying boss habit. Bosses argue, express sarcasm, hog the credit, add too much value, micromanage, and refuse to listen (a passive-aggressive form of winning) because they have an overwhelming need to prevail. If there's a fine line between winning when it counts and when no one's counting, the worst bosses have no idea when they have crossed it. But their employees do.

passing judgment

needing to win
too much

needing to win
too much

needing
to win
too much

Employees can deal with a negatron boss— because they always see it coming. But apologizing is the greatest cleansing gesture a boss can make—and so easy to do. Bosses who can't admit a mistake or say "I'm sorry" just don't get it.

making excuses

proving
how smart

Keeping people in the dark and then blaming them for their ignorance is cruel, but it's just a subset of the Big Kahuna of annoying behavior: the need to win all the time.

proving
how smart

When bosses try to prove how smart they are, sometimes they're right. But when was the last time a boss made excuses and you said to yourself, "I thought you were messing up, but you really turned me around when you made those excuses."

100

Yiddish Phrases
by MICHAEL WEX

If even people who speak nothing but Yiddish sometimes sit around discussing their favorite words and arguing about which ones are the most deeply Yiddish, who are we not to do likewise? Given the fact that Yiddish speakers would rather vent their feelings than share them, the language is full of colorful locutions that are meant to be remembered forever. Words that made the cut did so on the basis of euphony, utility, and frequency of use. They're all typically Yiddish; the ones that wouldn't come up in a Yiddish-language discussion of the same topic would be overlooked only because they'd be driving the conversation.

MICHAEL WEX was once paid to translate *The Threepenny Opera* from German to Yiddish so that someone else could be paid to do surtitles in English. He is the author of *Born to Kvetch* and the forthcoming *Wex's Shmooze Essentials*.

kvetchn [to complain]
shlepn [to drag, pull, trudge]
kvetchn

orelteh [non-Jewish woman]
farshnoshket [tipsy, whiffled, evenly toasted]
orelteh

vey [as in "Oy…"]
khrakn [to clear throat loudly and wetly; to hawk]
khrakn

nivetch [gone to waste]
balehbusteh [proprietress, housekeeper, landlady]
nivetch

shvants [tail, penis, idiot, shmuck]
shmontses [nonsense, pointless time-wasting]
shmontses

epes [something, somewhat]
kileh [hernia, rupture]
epes

tukhes [hindquarters]
khmalyeh [wallop, brain-addling blow]
tukhes

nakhes [pride and pleasure rolled into one]
mekhayeh [delight, pleasure]
nakhes

lapnmitsl [hat with earflaps]
geshrey [scream, cry]
lapnmitsl

kveln [to beam with nakhes or delight]
nu [so, well, then, come on, of course]
nu

khutspeh [chutzpah]
phnyeh [nothing special, not too good, not up to much]
phnyeh

oy
mitsveh [positive commandment, good deed]
oy

orkhe-porkhe [hoboes, bindlestiffs]
shmooze [chat, talk, conversation]
shmooze

shoyn [already, right away, really, that's all]
shpilkeh [pin]
shoyn

bupkehs [goat droppings, bugger-all]
koshmar [nightmare]
bupkehs

kenehoreh [no evil eye]
paskudnyak [s.o.b.]
kenehoreh

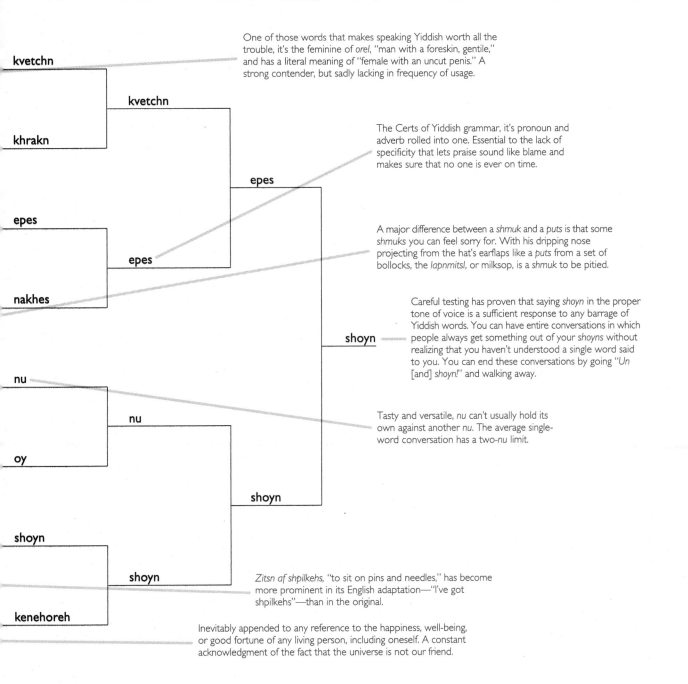

kvetchn

kvetchn

khrakn

One of those words that makes speaking Yiddish worth all the trouble, it's the feminine of *orel*, "man with a foreskin, gentile," and has a literal meaning of "female with an uncut penis." A strong contender, but sadly lacking in frequency of usage.

epes

epes

epes

nakhes

The Certs of Yiddish grammar, it's pronoun and adverb rolled into one. Essential to the lack of specificity that lets praise sound like blame and makes sure that no one is ever on time.

A major difference between a *shmuk* and a *puts* is that some *shmuks* you can feel sorry for. With his dripping nose projecting from the hat's earflaps like a *puts* from a set of bollocks, the *lapnmitsl*, or milksop, is a *shmuk* to be pitied.

shoyn

Careful testing has proven that saying *shoyn* in the proper tone of voice is a sufficient response to any barrage of Yiddish words. You can have entire conversations in which people always get something out of your *shoyns* without realizing that you haven't understood a single word said to you. You can end these conversations by going "*Un* [and] *shoyn!*" and walking away.

nu

nu

oy

Tasty and versatile, *nu* can't usually hold its own against another *nu*. The average single-word conversation has a two-*nu* limit.

shoyn

shoyn

shoyn

kenehoreh

Zitsn af shpilkehs, "to sit on pins and needles," has become more prominent in its English adaptation—"I've got shpilkehs"—than in the original.

Inevitably appended to any reference to the happiness, well-being, or good fortune of any living person, including oneself. A constant acknowledgment of the fact that the universe is not our friend.

101

Shakespeare Insults

by LAWRENCE GOODMAN

Yes, the writer who brought us such great lines as "To be or not to be" and "Parting is such sweet sorrow" also came up with some of the greatest potty-humor put-downs and bawdy insults in the history of English literature. Whether he was remarking on the size of someone's genitals, making fun of their inexperience in the sack, or just coming up with a fancy new way to call them an idiot, Will knew how to sling the mud. Choosing the best Bard barbs is as tough as fathoming Iago's motivations or why Hamlet procrastinates. But in head-to-head face-off, it all came down to which packed the most zing per beat of iambic pentameter, which I could actually understand, and which I would most want to say to an ex-girlfriend.

LAWRENCE GOODMAN is a journalist and playwright living in Providence, RI. His plays have been produced in New York and Philadelphia, and he is a founding member of NeoShtick Theater ("What Derrida would have said if he'd ever played the Catskills").

There's no more faith in thee than in a stewed prune.
Thou art the Mars of malcontents.
— There's no more faith

They have marvelous foul linen.
Live and love thy misery.
— Live and love

Why should she live to fill the world with words?
He appears as I would wish mine enemy.
— Why should she live

I'll pray a thousand prayers for thy death.
You whoreson cullionly barbermonger!
— You whoreson

Thou art as loathsome as a toad.
If I hope well, I'll never see thee more.
— loathsome as a toad

Rump-fed ronyon!
Thou wouldst eat thy dead vomit up, And howl'st to find it.
— eat thy dead vomit

Hang! Beg! Starve! Die in the streets!
Let vultures gripe thy guts.
— Hang! Beg! Starve!

What folly I commit, I dedicate to you.
Thou cam'st on earth to make the earth my hell.
— make the earth my hell

He has not so much brain as earwax.
Pernicious bloodsucker of sleeping men!
— brain as earwax

Lean raw-boned rascal.
Thou art a boil, a plague-sore, or embossed carbuncle in my corrupted blood.
— Thou art a boil

Thou clay-brained guts, thou knotty-pated fool, thou whoreson obscene greasy tallow-catch.
Thou wert best set thy lower part where thy nose stands.
— Thou clay-brained guts

I'll beat thee, but I should infect my hands.
You breathe in vain.
— You breathe in vain

You are not worth the dust which the rude wind blows in your face.
You blocks, you stones, you worse than senseless things.
— not worth the dust

A vengeance on your crafty wither'd hide!
She's the kitchen wench, and all grease, and I know not what use to put her to but to make a lamp of her, and run from her by her own light.
— She's the kitchen wench

Irksome brawling scold.
Most excellent, accomplished lady, the heavens rain odors on you!
— Irksome brawling scold

Thou crusty botch of nature!
His brain is as dry as the remainder biscuit after a voyage.
— Thou crusty botch of nature!

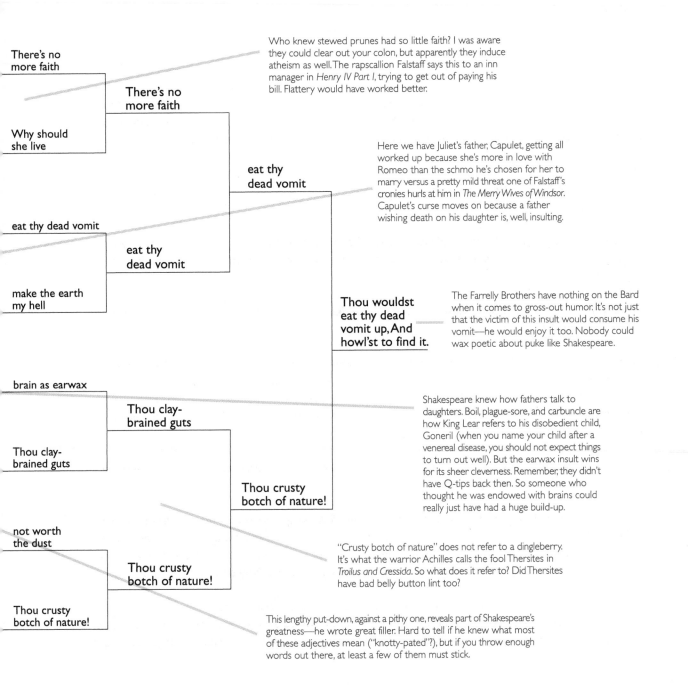

There's no
more faith

Why should
she live

There's no
more faith

Who knew stewed prunes had so little faith? I was aware
they could clear out your colon, but apparently they induce
atheism as well. The rapscallion Falstaff says this to an inn
manager in *Henry IV Part I*, trying to get out of paying his
bill. Flattery would have worked better.

eat thy
dead vomit

Here we have Juliet's father, Capulet, getting all
worked up because she's more in love with
Romeo than the schmo he's chosen for her to
marry versus a pretty mild threat one of Falstaff's
cronies hurls at him in *The Merry Wives of Windsor*.
Capulet's curse moves on because a father
wishing death on his daughter is, well, insulting.

eat thy dead vomit

make the earth
my hell

eat thy
dead vomit

Thou wouldst
eat thy dead
vomit up, And
howl'st to find it.

The Farrelly Brothers have nothing on the Bard
when it comes to gross-out humor. It's not just
that the victim of this insult would consume his
vomit—he would enjoy it too. Nobody could
wax poetic about puke like Shakespeare.

brain as earwax

Thou clay-
brained guts

Shakespeare knew how fathers talk to
daughters. Boil, plague-sore, and carbuncle are
how King Lear refers to his disobedient child,
Goneril (when you name your child after a
venereal disease, you should not expect things
to turn out well). But the earwax insult wins
for its sheer cleverness. Remember, they didn't
have Q-tips back then. So someone who
thought he was endowed with brains could
really just have had a huge build-up.

Thou clay-
brained guts

Thou crusty
botch of nature!

not worth
the dust

Thou crusty
botch of nature!

"Crusty botch of nature" does not refer to a dingleberry.
It's what the warrior Achilles calls the fool Thersites in
Troilus and Cressida. So what does it refer to? Did Thersites
have bad belly button lint too?

Thou crusty
botch of nature!

This lengthy put-down, against a pithy one, reveals part of Shakespeare's
greatness—he wrote great filler. Hard to tell if he knew what most
of these adjectives mean ("knotty-pated"?), but if you throw enough
words out there, at least a few of them must stick.

CODA
By Richard Sandomir

For decades, Bracketology has been a crude activity: a committee meets in secret one weekend each March to create a bracket of 64 men's (and women's) basketball teams that will induce fans to guess, and wager on, which colleges will advance in the annual NCAA tournament known as March Madness.

Despite its passivity and utter reliance on outside forces, this form of Bracketology enraptures the sports world each year. But it made us wonder: what if Bracketology were employed in a truly dynamic way to promote personal choice?

Instead of confronting a scribbled list of Do's and Don'ts or She Loves Me/She Loves Me Nots, why not draw up a bracket of one-on-one options that gives structure to the many choices clouding each decision in your life?

Then, why not pit these options against each other in a series of matchups that boils down all your either/or choices into one "winner"?

That's the hidden virtue of Bracketology. It provides an elegant solution to one of the deep-rooted paradoxes of everyday life. The more choices we have, the less happy we are with our decision. If our only menu choice is between a hot dog and a burger, we don't whine that we really wanted a ham sandwich. But if the menu offers too many choices, our decision-making process slows and the likelihood of our being satisfied with our choice decreases.

After compiling these many brackets—and watching our brave contributors bracketize—we have some advice for future bracketologists.

Don't seed. In March Madness, the committee selecting the field weighs various factors to determine who will face whom in the first round. So the first seed faces the no. 16 seed, the no. 2 seed faces the no. 15, and so on. Forget that folly. It's time consuming and nearly impossible when you're bracketizing anything that can't be quantified. Basketball teams have win-loss records, but what you bracketize will not.

Not seeding promotes bracketological freedom and can create meaningful or strange or simply ironic matchups that reveal less-than-apparent parallels. In Henry Petroski's Simple Things, is it serendipity that pits two stalwarts of oral hygiene, toothpick and dental floss, against each other in round 3? In James Boice's

Sports Innovations, the fourth-round matchup of Free Agency against Integration reminds us that not every advance in sports happens during play. And what about Richard Hoffer's Sucker Bets? What are the odds that Powerball would resemble the AOL Time Warner merger in wagering futility?

Play God, just a little. As you bracketize your life's decisions, you will sometimes discover that some choices truly are stronger than others, so you now know which two should meet in the final, or which quartet should be in the Final Four. Place them there, then work backward, making sure that they cannot meet and knock each other out in an early round. It's a bit of an intellectual end run, but no one is going to arrest you for bracket-fixing.

Regionalize if possible. If your 16 or 32 teams can be divided into two, four, or eight distinct groups, then consider regionalizing. It will give greater clarity to your decision-making. The Bald Guys bracket was divided into the fringe-haired and shaved-headed regionals, which ensured that Michael Jordan and Winston Churchill would move along parallel tracks. Talk Show Hosts was split into Late Night, Morning, Daytime, and Hard News regionals, which yielded a weighty, intellectually gratifying Final Four that probably wouldn't have come up in a random selection: Johnny Carson, Oprah Winfrey, Katie Couric, and Ted Koppel.

Bracketology can accelerate and illuminate serious or frivolous decisions that require analyzing a slew of options.

Deciding on a vacation spot? Bracketize.

Looking to buy a hi-def TV and can't decide between DLP and plasma, Panasonic and Samsung, 42 inches and 56? Bracketize.

Seeking the perfect anniversary gift? Bracketize.

Trying to determine the best Dickens character? Bracketize.

Need to name your unborn child? Bracketize. Sure, it's one of the more fraught, emotionally charged decisions parents make. And yet, Bracketology can ease the agonizing. At least that's what a friend of ours discovered. Stephen Garvey and his wife, Donna, were expecting their first child. If it was a girl they'd name her Harper. But there were too many good boy names, so they decided to let Bracketology do the heavy lifting. Here's one final bracket to show how it turned out. On November 1, 2006, they had a girl.

After Steve's bracket you'll find a blank template. Go forth and let your brackets multiply.

Baby Boy Names

by STEPHEN GARVEY

When my wife, Donna, and I discovered we were expecting our first child, we decided not to find out if it was a boy or a girl. There are so few surprises left in life and we wanted this to be one of them. While we instantly agreed that a girl would be named Harper, naming our son was more challenging. We pored over name books, researched our family trees, and reached back to the historical figures and fictional characters that touched our lives. We spent a month amassing names, each candidate having to pass three tests: the name had to mean something to us, it had to go well with Garvey, and it had to be unique without making our child wonder "What were they thinking?" We trimmed the list of names down to a lean and mean 32, poured a couple glasses of wine (I was drinking for two), and got to work.

STEPHEN GARVEY wrote the short film *Boy-Next-Door*, which features the character names Calvin, Tim, Ivan, and Fido, none of which were invited to this bracket.

It was mandated that I consider passing my name onto my firstborn. But I wasn't sure I wanted to extend the tradition of being asked about "the real Steve Garvey." Xavier's the name of Donna's sweet grandfather and wins in a walk.

Two fictional heroes go at it, one courtesy of Salinger; the other, Sturges. Both are more flawed than Atticus Finch, but they are high-minded, well-meaning characters in their own right. Fear that Sullivan would be shortened to the unfortunate "Sully Garvey" gives Holden the edge.

Atticus Finch: the moral backbone of an American classic. A warm, wise man of strongly held convictions. Who doesn't want an Atticus in their life? Unfortunately, Donna couldn't get past the (accurate, I'm certain) visions of a young Atticus being pummeled in the schoolyard because of his unusual name. Samuel moves on to the next round.

Carter — Carter
Addison

Stephen — Xavier
Xavier

Eli — Eli
James

Cooper — Cooper
Francis

Russell — Truman
Truman

Carson — Carson
Felix

Dustin — Benjamin
Benjamin

Campbell — Isaac
Isaac

Kyle — Kyle
Anderson

Blake — Max
Max

Nathan — Nathan
Benson

Holden — Holden
Sullivan

Samuel — Samuel
Atticus

Daniel — Daniel
Frasier

Harrison — Sawyer
Sawyer

Everett — Oscar
Oscar

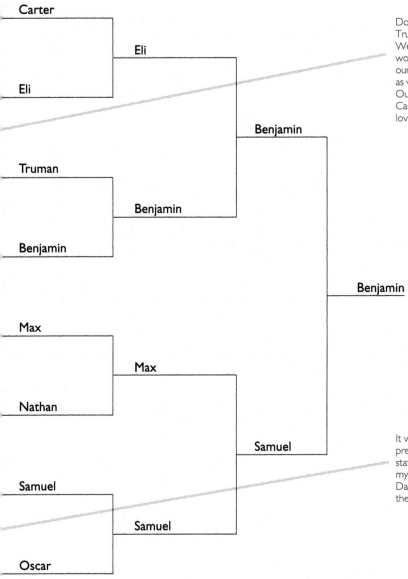

Carter

Eli

Eli

Eli

Benjamin

Truman

Benjamin

Benjamin

Benjamin

Max

Max

Nathan

Benjamin

Max

Samuel

Samuel

Samuel

Samuel

Oscar

Donna and I met this awesome kid named Truman while honeymooning in Bermuda. We dug the name and wanted to extend the wonderful memories of that vacation onto our son. Donna and I loved the name Carson, as we grew up watching Johnny on late night. Our son, conversely, will grow up watching Carson Daly on late night. I want my son to love me. Truman prevails.

Benjamin Franklin is the Big Man on Campus in elementary schools (where Donna teaches). Inventor. Politician. Drinker. Writer. Playboy. What's not to love about this guy? We love Samuel too, as in Samuel Clemens, who gave us Huck Finn. Plus, if we went with Sam Garvey, I could pass down all my monogrammed stuff to him. Sam looked like a lock, but as Franklin said, nothing is certain except death and taxes. We suddenly remembered that Ben Folds's "The Luckiest" was our wedding song. And just like that, Ben took the crown!

It was Oscar night when we discovered Donna was pregnant. We joked about naming our boy after the statuette, and how I could finally have an Oscar to call my own (though hopefully less gold…and with genitals). Days passed, and the name stuck, easily beating out the Twain-inspired Sawyer.

1 ....

2 ....

3 ....

4 ....

5 ....

6 ....

7 ....

8 ....

9 ....

10 ....

11 ....

12 ....

13 ....

14 ....

15 ....

16 ....

17 ....

18 ....

19 ....

20 ....

21 ....

22 ....

23 ....

24 ....

25 ....

26 ....

27 ....

28 ....

29 ....

30 ....

31 ....

32 ....

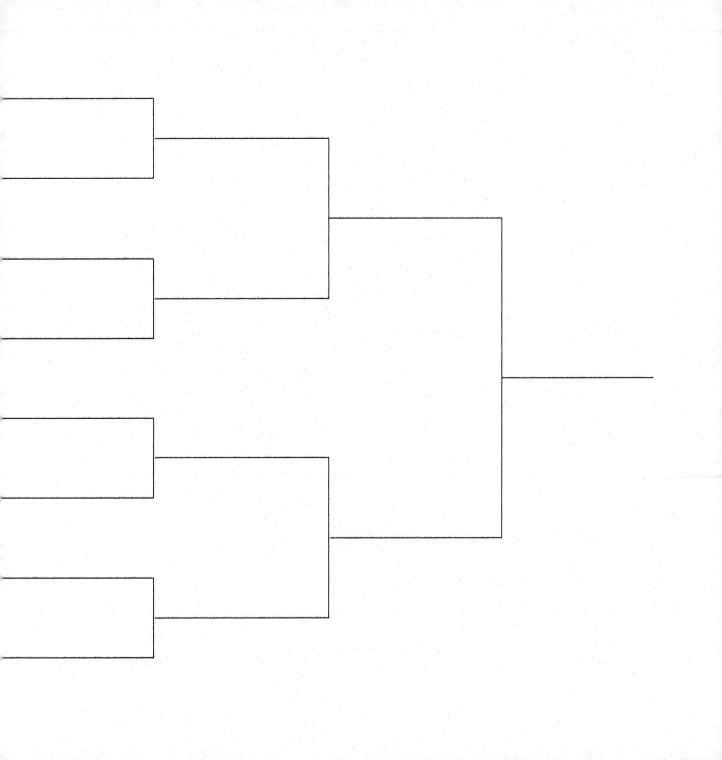

ACKNOWLEDGMENTS

To our contributors, who got the idea and jumped in without asking questions. (That's why we've printed each of their names at least three times in the book.)

To our editor, Annik LaFarge, who got the idea, sent a check, and *then* started asking questions. This book is as much hers as anyone else's. Plus, she found Nigel Holmes.

To our designer, Nigel Holmes, who provided this modest brain exercise with an elegant look that brought everything into focus.

To Greg Villepique, for keeping the trains running on time.

To Ben Adams, for punching the passengers' tickets (and creating the template that saved unimaginable hours of labor and misunderstanding).

To Laura Keefe, for getting the word out (and for singing the Mondegreens to publisher Karen Rinaldi).

To Emily Sklar, for logistical discipline.

To Candy Lee, David (the Grand Rebbe) Hirshey, Brant Rumble, Ben Loehnen, Charlie Conrad, Will Schwalbe, Robert Pearlstein, Judith Newman, Maria Wilhelm, David Carden, Rebecca Riley, Zareen Jaffery, Michael Davis, Peter Kaminsky, Bill Paterson, Valerie Frankel, Jennifer Weis, Sean Kelly, Simon Trewin, Caroline Dawnay, Steve Eubanks, Zoe Pagnamenta, Anne Jump, Lisa Queen, Vince Emilio, David McCormick, Roger Director, Peter Edidin, Will Reiter, Marie Rama, Nick Reiter, Vince Wladika, Jonathan Schwartz, Jim Bouton, William Safire, Chris Widmaier, Eric Handler, Bob Combs, David Remnick, Alex Riethmiller, Chris LaPlaca, Al Siegal, Will Shortz, Kathy Connors, John Branch, and Wally Matthews for their ideas, connective tissue, and support.

A NOTE ON THE AUTHORS

Richard Sandomir is the award-winning sports television columnist for the *New York Times*. His previous books include *Bald Like Me: The Hair-Raising Adventures of Baldman* and, with Rick Wolff, *Life for Real Dummies* and *Don't Worry, Stop Sweating…Use Deodorant.*

Mark Reiter is a literary agent and writer who has collaborated on books with Twyla Tharp, Phil Dusenberry, Mark McCormack, and Marshall Goldsmith.